CALIFORNIA'S LUMBER SHORTLINE RAILROADS

CALIFORNIA'S LUMBER SHORTLINE RAILROADS

JEFF MOORE

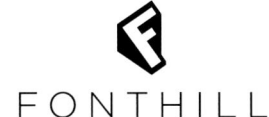
FONTHILL

Front cover: Feather River Railway #3. *C.G. Heimerdinger Jr.*
McCloud River Railroad #39. *Lee F. Hower*

Back cover: Sierra Nos. 44 and 42 in June 1981. *Dave Stanley*

Fonthill Media Inc.
www.fonthillmedia.com
office@fonthillmedia.com

First published 2016

Copyright © Jeff Moore 2016

ISBN 978-1-63499-007-3

All rights reserved. No part of this publication may be reproduced, stored in a retrieval system or transmitted in any form or by any means, electronic, mechanical, photocopying, recording or otherwise, without prior permission in writing from Fonthill Media Inc.

Typeset in Minion Pro 10pt on 13pt
Printed and bound in England

CONTENTS

Acknowledgements — 6

Introduction — 7

  1 Almanor Railroad — 15

  2 Amador Central — 24

  3 Arcata & Mad River — 37

  4 California Western — 51

  5 Camino, Placerville & Lake Tahoe — 68

  6 Eureka Southern/North Coast/California Northern/Northwestern Pacific — 78

  7 Feather River Railway — 92

  8 Great Western/Lake County/Modoc Northern/Lake Railway — 103

  9 McCloud River — 113

10 Quincy — 128

11 Sierra — 140

12 Yreka Western — 154

13 Other Roads — 166

Principle References — 173

ACKNOWLEDGEMENTS

First off, I want to thank all of the people who contributed photographs and other information for this book, including Travis Berryman, Jim Bryant, E. O. Gibson, Don Hansen, Martin E. Hansen, C. G. Heimerdinger Jr., Jim Heringer, Lee Hower, Drew Jacksich, Wayne Monger, Tom Moungovan, Dave Stanley, John Taubeneck, Roger Titus, and Sean Zwagerman. This book would not have been possible without their contributions. I wish I could have used everything these people provided to me.

Second, I wish to acknowledge all of the early railfan historians, especially Stanley Borden, David Myrick, and Jack Wagner, together with the early publications—especially *The Western Railroader*—that gave these and other authors a place to publish early accounts on obscure roads, thereby preserving a lot of history that otherwise might have been lost. This work is built upon many of these early efforts, both in substance and spirit.

Finally, thank you to my family for your love and support through all of these projects.

INTRODUCTION

On January 24, 1848, James W. Marshall discovered gold nuggets on the banks of the American River in the foothills of the Sierra Nevada mountains. Nine days later, the United States and Mexico signed the Treaty of Guadalupe Hidalgo, officially ending the Mexican-American War and expanding the U.S. boundaries to the Pacific Coast, furthering the "Manifest Destiny" sentiment to span the continent then gripping much of the nation. These two events rapidly changed the arc of the American story, as news of Marshall's discovery launched one of the biggest migrations in recorded human history. Prospectors by the hundreds of thousands poured into the gold country, prompting the United States to admit California as its thirty-first state on September 9, 1850.

Not to be overlooked in all this was that, at the time of his discovery, Marshall was in the process of building a sawmill.

BEGINNINGS

Three hundred million years ago, California did not exist. The nearest substantial dry land at the time lay hundreds of miles to the east, roughly near today's Salt Lake City, Utah. Two hundred million years ago, the North and South American continents detached from the European and African continents and started moving westward, opening the Atlantic Ocean behind them. As the North American continent moved west it overran and incorporated into the landmass three major and at least five minor island chain arcs. The gold Marshall discovered arrived with the Smartville Block, the last of the three major island chains, which docked against the continent's western edge approximately 165 million years ago. Another smaller island chain later overran by the advancing continent added another gold bearing rock body in what is today the Klamath Mountains, covering much of northwest California and southwest Oregon. These island chains, plus new land mass built by volcanic activity and ocean floor sediments accumulating against the leading edge of the advancing continent, added California, Oregon, Washington, Nevada, parts of Idaho and Utah, and much of western Canada.

Cone bearing trees started appearing across the Northern Hemisphere roughly two hundred million years ago. Most of the modern tree species were in evidence by roughly thirty million years ago, when they started advancing from the Arctic south to California. The individual tree species had firmly settled into their modern ranges by the time the first humans arrived in

California. The native cultures utilized the forests mostly plant materials such as seeds and bark, and for the wildlife habitat the forests provided. Europeans brought a different perspective on the forest uses, but it would take many decades for a timber industry to develop within the state.

ORIGINS OF THE CALIFORNIA LUMBER INDUSTRY

In order to become established, any industry requires at least four components—a source for materials, a method (if necessary) for converting the materials into a useable product, a demand for the products, and a way of delivering the products to markets. In California's vast forests, Europeans discovered the raw materials required to support a full-fledged timber industry; along the coast lay the coastal redwood, producing high quality, rot resistant lumber, along with tan oak, who's bark leached out an acid ideally suited for tanning cow hides; up north, in the Cascades and along the Sierra crest, lay vast stands of Ponderosa, Jeffrey, Sugar, and Lodgepole pines, ideal for construction lumber, wooden boxes, patterns, paneling, and a myriad of other uses; scattered amongst the pines lay great stands of Douglas fir, prized for its lumber, and incense cedar, especially well-suited to producing pencils, fence posts, roofing shingles, and other products.

Despite the abundant wealth found in the standing crop of "green gold", exploitation of these forests had to wait. Given late 1700s and early 1800s technologies, adobe bricks could be made at far less cost than cutting trees and bringing them out of the mountains, and they remained the standard California building material for well over a century. Limited sawmilling started in the 1830s and 1840s, but even then the available capital did not exist to build a substantial industry. Almost all of these early sawmills depended on water for moving logs to the mill, powering the mill itself, and then to move lumber to market; however, most streams—especially in the Sierras—lacked sufficiently consistent water flows to be of much use to the early lumbermen.

The gold rush changed everything. San Francisco and Sacramento, the gateway cities to the new mining areas, rapidly transitioned into booming cities, and up in the foothills new mining camps appeared in almost every drainage, creating a crushing demand for lumber. Merchants initially imported almost all lumber on ships sailing from the east coast; however, some foresaw vast fortunes could be made building sawmills in California. Labor problems often plagued the first ones built, as more often than not the only workers to be had were gold-crazed prospectors who had exhausted their resources and were just trying to get enough of a stake put back together to get back into the diggings. Despite the obstacles, a lumber industry started to emerge, much of it concentrated in the redwood stands along the coast. In 1852, two enterprising men ran a side wheeled steamer aground on the shores of Humboldt Bay in what is now Old Town in Eureka, removed one of the side wheels, and retrofitted the power shaft to operate a saw blade. Boilers stripped from other idled ships or manufactured in San Francisco's new foundries replaced water wheels to power other mills built along the coast or in the stands of pine trees in the foothills. Up in the Sierras, pioneering lumbermen developed flumes to facilitate overland transport. Before long lumber was being loaded onto ships at the many treacherous "doghole" ports developed along the coastline or could be found snaking down out of the Sierras on flumes. The boom was on.

EVOLUTION OF THE CALIFORNIA LUMBER INDUSTRY

The California lumber industry started as a local business. The earliest mills were very small affairs, built with often scant locally available capital to fulfill local lumber needs. Large facilities would require enormous capital expenditures, and up until 1849 the potential for returns on any such investments did not exist.

The Gold Rush produced many newly minted millionaires in Sacramento and especially in San Francisco. Capitalists from San Francisco became instrumental in launching new timber ventures, especially in the redwoods along the coast. The builders of the Central and Southern Pacific railroads played their own role in starting timber companies, especially along the lines the companies built eastward over the Sierras and northward into Oregon.

Lumber operations of the era followed a typical pattern. One or more often a group of investors would capitalize a company, and then either purchase or lease harvesting rights to a tract of timber. The size of the sawmill was determined in large part by how much timber was available, what kind of market existed, obtainable sawmill equipment, and other factors. Once started, the operating life of a sawmill was dependent upon how long timber supplies lasted and the ability of the company to sell lumber at a consistent price; this last factor proved difficult, as an extremely volatile lumber market resulted in wild price fluctuations from the 1870s through the middle 1890s. Many promising lumber companies started operations during this time period, only to fail during one of the many crashes in the market.

The situation started to change in the last part of the 1890s. California experienced a sustained population boom, prompting increased housing and other structure construction. Additional uses for lumber came into prominence, especially wood boxes used to transport California produce eastward as the railroad and agricultural industries perfected refrigerator cars. Some of the agricultural interests—especially in the citrus industry—entered the California timber industry directly so as to protect their box supplies. Finally, in the years immediately after 1900 many experienced timber capitalists from the upper Midwest, having exhausted forests in those states, started investing in the west coast lumber industry. These capitalists brought with them substantial financial resources and lots of expertise to invest in new operations and properties, and most also had already existing and extensive sales and distribution networks in the population centers in the Midwest and along the east coast. New products, new markets, and increased demand produced prosperous times for California's lumber producers.

The combination of the flush of capital, the access to markets railroads provided, and stable prices resulted in progressively larger sawmills, often located in newly built company towns in which the lumber company owned and controlled all aspects of life. These sawmills had to shortly deal with the problem of transporting logs increasing distances from the woods to the sawmill, which they mostly solved by building private logging railroads to bring logs to the mills. Financial institutions considered lumber concerns, especially in the pine regions, to be good financial investments and freely made loans to the industry. However, as the 1920s progressed lumber demand did not keep up with increasing production, very shortly resulting in a glutted market. No internal or external controls existed to regulate the industry, and as such it did not detect growing problems that quickly resulted in a crash in lumber prices. Unforgiving bond holders and financial institutions made the problem much worse as they insisted on increased production, with the hope that volume could make up for the lower prices. However, this only exacerbated the oversupply problems, further depressing prices. Then the Depression hit, and almost all lumber markets dried up. Many sawmills closed, and those that remained open suffered mightily.

The California timber industry experienced boom times again as the Second World War progressed, followed by equally prosperous times in the post-war housing boom. Truck logging started replacing private railroads, resulting in a resurgence in smaller sawmills that could either buy logs on the open market or otherwise did not have to rely upon the high capital costs associated with a logging railroad system.

The post-war era also saw a movement towards corporate conglomeration and consolidation. Most of California's larger independent lumber companies vanished, purchased by larger corporations. Industry giants such as U.S. Plywood, Fibreboard, Georgia Pacific, Louisiana Pacific, Simpson, and others entered the California industry in force. These mergers generally saddled the larger companies with substantial debt loads, especially if the new owners added new facilities such as plywood or particleboard plants. In many cases, the new owners boosted timber harvests to often unsustainable levels to generate income to service debts. Woodchips and other sawmill waste material became merchantable products and increasingly were shipped by rail to newly built paper mills, particleboard facilities, and power plants burning wood biomass to produce electricity. Fibreboard played an outsized role in this market, building a huge paper plant at Antioch, California, and the company went so far as to purchase several sawmills in order to protect its woodchip supply.

The California lumber industry faced changing times at the end of the 1970s. Rapidly escalating operating costs and declining lumber markets, compounded by mounting log shortages created by a combination of the excessive logging levels in previous decades and increasingly stringent environmental regulations, hurt the industry. Sawmill closures started in mass at the end of the decade and accelerated in the early 1980s. The large timber companies started leaving California in droves, resulting in California's homegrown company—Sierra Pacific Industries—playing an increasingly dominant role in the state. SPI had roots in California dating to the 1920s, and as the big corporations left SPI embarked on an acquisition binge, buying sawmills and timberlands to complement its already vast holdings. Many of these sales resulted in more sawmill closures, especially if acquired sawmills duplicated existing SPI sawmills. SPI also continually reviewed its own operations, resulting in the closure of some of its own facilities that became duplicate in light of declining harvests and ever increasing modernizations of its remaining mills.

Though California remains a major lumber market, the state's sawmill industry is only a shadow of what is used to be. Those sawmills still operating now mostly buy logs on the open market, mostly harvested from private land, and it is not uncommon for logs to pass through the custody of several different companies and travel long distances before reaching a sawmill. The social impacts on the sawmill communities have been enormous—the industry relied upon a mostly transient workforce in the early years, becoming more stable as the decades progressed. This industry grew largely on the backs of its employees; in exchange for their labor in what are still today some of the most dangerous occupations around, the lumber industry provided good wages and secure employment in areas with little other substantial economic activity. A typical way of life in many of these communities was to graduate from high school Friday afternoon and go to work setting chokers, pulling green chain, or replacing crossties Monday morning. By the late 1970s it was not uncommon to find two and sometimes three generations of the same family working on one logging, sawmill, or railroad crew. The turbulence of the industry in recent decades has been hard on the workforce. Several once thriving timber towns have vanished completely, while others are now communities of retirees and weekend homes for city dwellers. A few are doing what they can to attract tourists or other industries, but most struggle to find a new niche amongst ever changing realities and economies, and wages for available work don't come close to comparing to what timber jobs paid.

RAILROAD DEVELOPMENT

The eventual cooling of the gold mining boom did not significantly slow lumber demand. Many of those who came to California looking for gold and others who followed seeking new opportunities stayed on to work on the state's other major industries, principally agriculture. However, transportation would continue to be a major hurdle in furthering California's nascent timber industry, and as the 1850s progressed railroads started providing the answer. The Union Wharf and Plank Walk Company is generally credited as operating the first railroad inside California by January 1855, on a wharf extending out into Humboldt Bay. Several months later the Sacramento Valley Railroad broke ground on their line, eventually connecting Sacramento to Folsom. Other railroad plans followed.

In many ways, California's railroad and timber industries matured together. The timber industry required railroads to expand beyond the fringes of the forests; the railroads, in turn, created a substantial initial market for the timber industry, as the construction and operation of the railroads consumed vast quantities of forest products, and then once built the railroads would depend on freight revenues generated by moving lumber to distant markets for survival. In the end, five mainline railroads—Central Pacific (Southern Pacific); Atchison, Topeka & Santa Fe; Union Pacific; Western Pacific; and Great Northern would build lines within California, providing the main framework for the state's rail system. A series of mergers consolidated these mainline railroads—in 1970, the Great Northern merged with several other roads to form Burlington Northern. Then, in 1982, Union Pacific purchased the Western Pacific. The final two major mergers saw Burlington Northern and the Atchison, Topeka & Santa Fe merge to form Burlington Northern Santa Fe (later shortened to BNSF) in 1996, and Union Pacific completed purchasing the Southern Pacific in 1997.

CALIFORNIA'S LUMBER SHORTLINE RAILROADS

As California's timber industry grew, especially in the period after 1900, sawmill location became one of the most important considerations a lumber company faced. These sawmills would be in one place for decades, and as such the timber stands upon which the mill would depend had to be reasonably accessible. Fortunate companies were able to build directly on mainlines or otherwise already established railroads; however, many others did not have this luxury and ended up having to build their mill closer to the timber, often forcing them to construct their own railroad to the nearest mainline carrier connection. If the company did end up building a railroad, it was usually advantageous to make the line a common carrier shortline rather than a private railroad; as a common carrier, the railroad gained the ability to condemn needed right-of-ways and, more importantly, share in a division of the freight revenues for traffic interchanged to the connecting carrier, but this came at the price of increased regulatory scrutiny, stringent equipment standards and inspections, and high reporting requirement to the Interstate Commerce Commission (I.C.C.) and state Public Utility Commissions for all aspects of the railroad business.

There is no single universally accepted definition as to what constitutes a shortline railroad. It is often and correctly said that all railroads started as shortlines; some grew into the major mainline carriers, while others remained small, "*the unballasted pikes of forty-pound rails and a single steam locomotive, of vice-presidents who are also roadmaster and legal department, the railroads of lonely outlands and bread-and-cheese destinies implicit in stub switches, hand firing and a mixed train daily*", as Lucius Beebe wrote in 1947 in his classic *Mixed Train Daily*. Generally, railroads today are considered shortlines if they operate less than 350 miles of track and fall into the Surface Transportation Board's Class III revenue category, defined as a carrier earning less than $20 million per year in 1991 dollars, adjusted annually for inflation ($37.4 million as of this writing).

Beebe wrote at length in *Mixed Train Daily* about what made shortlines special in his world of 1947.

> The essential flavor of a little railroad is so elusive, for all that its rails and rolling stock may be the quintessence of factual reality, that it must be seen and experienced—almost touched—in order to apprehend and faithfully evaluate it. To photograph a short line is not enough; it should be ridden, if possible both head-end and in its coaches or caboose, and the truly perceptive reporter will drink whiskey with its crew member and talk crops, if such colloquy is within his gift. For the short line is so delicately integrated to the region it serves or traverses, touches so closely the lives of its countryside, that it ranks in importance of function with those of the banker, the leading merchant and the parish man of the cloth.

While shortlines—like almost all railroads—have become increasingly insulated from the communities they serve in the intervening decades, the spirit of Beebe's words remains applicable today. Beebe further wrote about the shortline railroad's place in the world:

> And above all other matters in which the authors of this book were schooled and instructed, is the transcendent fact that the entire being and economy of the United States is not located along the sides of U.S. 40 or even Texas 1, any more than it is conveniently arranged outside the windows of the Union Pacific's City of San Francisco. The little railroads were built to go where the main lines and highways do not and they have their being in a remote and older world of river fords and silos and shady four-corners communities which the untarrying traveler along the Harrisburg Superhighway never knows.

Shortline railroads played an important role for many California sawmills, but there is no one storyline covering all of them. Some were built by the timber industry, while others originally served other trades. A few railroads were built for no better reason than to connect a town to the mainline railroad that bypassed it. Some railroads were owned by lumber companies their entire lives, others remained independent, and yet others floated into and out of lumber industry ownership. A few fortunate timber companies built railroads prosperous enough to be sold to a connecting carrier, but most remained independent. Many of the roads earned substantial revenues serving other shippers or industries, including some special movements such as hydroelectric projects and motion picture industry work, while others remained completely dependent upon a single sawmill. Passenger and express traffic played heavily into the history of many of these shortlines, as until the advent of automobiles and paved roads the railroads often provided the only dependable transportation into and out of isolated sawmill camps, and often served a much larger area tributary to the railroad.

The fortunes of these shortlines matched those of the sawmills. Lumber dominated their traffic base, supplemented by woodchips and other commodities. The 1960s saw a resurgent interest in rail travel, and tourist railroads started popping up all across the country. Several of California's lumber shortlines purchased passenger equipment, restored or purchased steam locomotives, and launched into this business with varying levels of success and longevity.

Several California lumber shortlines capitalized on an industry trend in the 1970s. When one railroad uses a railcar belonging to another road, the using carrier pays a *per diem* charge to the owning carrier for the amount of time the car is in use on its railroad. By the late 1960s, *per diem* rates fell well below actual car ownership costs, and despite efforts to correct the problem railroads invested capital dollars in more specialized equipment providing higher return rates. The nation's boxcar fleet especially suffered, declining from 546,000 to 372,000 cars between 1963 and 1970. Boxcar shortages started becoming a serious issue in the industry, and to correct the situation the I.C.C. implemented in the fall of 1970 additional *per diem* payments for new or rebuilt boxcars, and a simultaneous change in the U.S. tax code also provided investment tax credits for such boxcars. Alert venture capitalists and investment bankers quickly moved to cash in on this newly created boxcar market, creating companies like Itel (SSI) and Brae. Under a typical arrangement, these firms would buy new boxcars and then lease them to a shortline, who agreed to pay a base lease rate for each car, plus a portion of the *per diem* payments the cars earned should fleet utilization average a certain amount (typically around 90 percent). The leasing companies focused the majority of their marketing efforts on western lumber shortlines, as they typically generated substantial lumber carloads destined for eastern markets, and chances were good cars ending up on the east coast would be kept busy there, resulting in enormous potential *per diem* payments to the lessors and the shortlines. Railroads that had seldom owned more than maybe a caboose and a couple maintenance cars suddenly found their name, colors, and herald splashed on hundreds of new boxcars. These cars also allowed the lumber roads to supply their shippers with modern boxcars for which the shortline paid no *per diem* charges. However, by the middle 1980s the program faced an intensive backlash, as more often than not the big railroads found it cost them more to handle an incentive *per diem* boxcar than what the railroad received in revenues for moving the car. Southern Pacific placed a $500 surcharge against loaded incentive *per diem* boxcars received from connecting shortline railroads not owned by its major shippers; while this protected those California roads owned by lumber companies, the move had an immediate chilling effect on the independent roads. Shortly thereafter, both incentive *per diem* payments and the tax shelters these cars provided vanished. The boxcars became an albatross around the necks of everyone involved, and shortline railroads in droves turned their cars back to the lessors.

The 1960s and 1970s also saw development of a few car types specialized for lumber transport service. Chief amongst these was the all-door boxcar, an otherwise standard boxcar featuring fixed floors, roof, and ends, but with the car sides composed of four large sliding doors that could pass over each other. These cars gave lumber shippers the combination of the loading ease of a flatcar coupled with the load protection characteristics of a boxcar. Several manufacturers built variations on these cars, including Thrall's "Thrall Door" and Evan's "Side-Slider" models. A couple of the timber companies purchased these cars and leased them to subsidiary shortline railroads, and several more California timber companies acquired fleets of these cars directly. Several shortline railroads also leased fleets of bulkhead flatcars and, in later years, centerbeam flatcars for lumber service.

The late 1970s were not kind of California's lumber shortlines. Changes in lumber markets increasingly diverted finished lumber shipments onto trucks, often leaving the railroads with only low value woodchip loads to haul. In 1980, Congress passed the Staggers Act deregulating the railroad industry; one of the provisions eased requirements major railroads faced to sell off marginal branch lines, rapidly creating a wave of newly established shortline railroads. While popular in many parts of the country, it would take several years to catch on in California, and only a few examples in the Golden state resulted in new railroads serving the timber industry.

Even the continued operation of a sawmill did not mean security for a railroad. Railroading is one of the most capital intensive industries, requiring constant re-investment in road and equipment in order to remain viable. A short line railroad could find itself vulnerable in many ways. The connecting carrier, or another main line railroad in the area, could offer a truck-to-rail reload site for lumber at a cheaper cost than continuing to ship by rail directly from the plant over the short line railroad. Also, if the railroad itself dated from the era when railcars had a 40-ton weight capacity, it just might not be economical to upgrade the railroad so as to handle 100—or 120—ton capacity freight cars. Both scenarios have been responsible for the demise of more than one lumber dependent shortline in California.

Of the railroads detailed in this book, seven exist today. Only three of those still derive substantial revenues hauling forest products, two more are presently moribund and face questionable futures, and one may be on the cusp of again generating substantial lumber loads.

ORGANIZATION OF THE BOOK

This book is restricted to those railroad operations in California that (1) were or are common carrier shortline railroads, and (2) derived much to all of their livelihood originating lumber traffic. These factors exclude common carriers handling only raw logs (such as Minarettes & Western), private railroads carrying either logs or lumber traffic, and carriers earning revenues either as bridge lines—those roads who handle lumber traffic as an intermediate carrier—or roads generating income as a terminating road, such as those handling lumber loads to a lumber yard. These are somewhat artificial, but are needed to keep the scope of the work within reasonable bounds. Those railroads with substantial lifespans and/or interest are given extended treatments, while other roads either having little impact or significance to the timber industry, are historical lines, or did not have lengthy service lives, are lumped together in one chapter.

Let us look mostly backwards at the railroads associated with a way of life that has now mostly vanished and is not likely to be seen again.

1

ALMANOR RAILROAD

BACKGROUND

T. D. Collins launched his family's lumber business in Pennsylvania in 1855. The Collins Company prospered, allowing the family to start expanding their horizons. Collins entered California in 1902 when the company, as part of the partnership of Curtis, Collins & Holbrook, purchased its first timberlands in Plumas and Tehama Counties. The company's ownership expanded over the first half of the 1900s, mostly through acquiring cut over timberlands from other owners and then allowing the forests to re-establish. Collins' California landownership base eventually totaled 94,000 acres.

Collins let their forests grow through the tumultuous economies of the 1920s and 1930s. The onset of the Second World War finally presented the opportune time for the family to start developing their holdings. On June 6, 1941, the Collins family incorporated the Collins Pine Company and announced plans to build a new sawmill in the small town of Chester, California.

Chester lay on the line of the The Red River Lumber Company's private logging railroad. Thomas Barlow Walker established Red River in the 1880s in Minnesota. Walker started purchasing timberlands in northeastern California in 1899, eventually accumulating over 750,000 acres. In 1914, Red River placed one of the largest pine mills in the world in operation at its new company town of Westwood, California. Red River built an extensive logging railroad network radiating into its holdings. The sixteen miles connecting Westwood to Chester quickly developed into a main line, and in 1927, Red River took advantage of free electricity the company received as partial compensation for various hydroelectric projects constructed on its lands to electrify this line. For the next decade and a half, conventional steam and a few early diesel locomotives brought endless trainloads of logs down into Chester, where Red River's pair of Baldwin-Westinghouse electric motors took over for the balance of the run into Westwood.

At the time Collins announced their mill plans, Red River was nearing the end of the timber supply tributary to their Chester mainline. By this point Red River had sold the first three miles of the mainline south from Westwood to the Western Pacific, who incorporated the line into their "Northern California Extension", stretching north from Keddie, California, to a connection with the line the Great Northern built south from Klamath Falls, Oregon; the completed mainline then became known as the "Inside Gateway". Collins decided it wanted rail service to its new mill, and to that end Theodore Walker and Truman Collins, representing their respective families, met to work out a deal on the remaining thirteen miles of Red River's

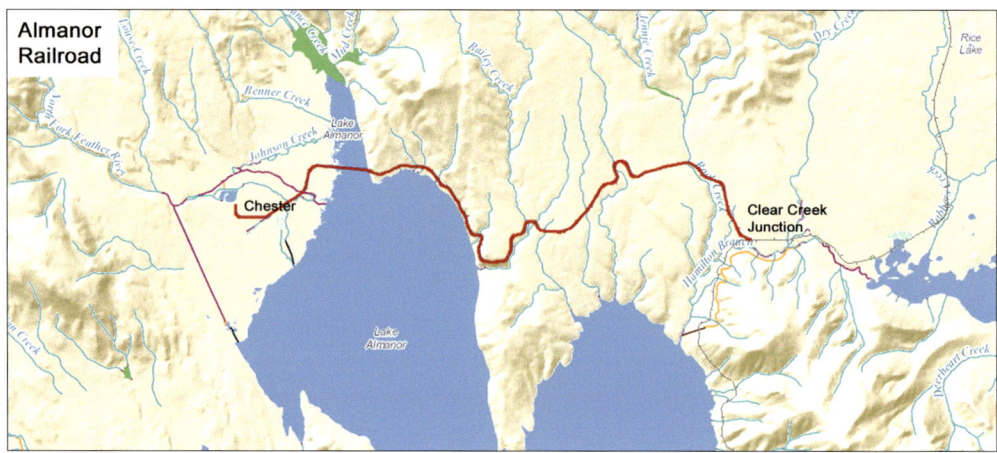

mainline. The two figured the scrap value of the line to Red River, added to that the cost of rebuilding the line without electrification, then divided that total in half to reach the final sale price. On September 15, 1941, Collins incorporated the Almanor Railroad Company as a wholly owned subsidiary of Collins Pine Company. The Almanor established an interchange with the WP at Clear Creek Junction and commenced common carrier operations in May 1942.

OPERATIONS

The Almanor Railroad lived a simple life. Collins Pine trucked logs from the woods to the mill, and as such the railroad existed only to move outbound lumber loads from the Collins Pine mill to the WP interchange. The railroad's profile included a stiff adverse grade against the loads on most of the outbound trip towards Clear Creek Junction. The railroad never did offer passenger service, but did handle a few railfan excursion trips in the early 1950s.

At startup, Collins transferred to Almanor a two-truck Heisler type geared locomotive from their Big Creek & Telocaset Railroad at Pondosa, Oregon. The locomotive, equipped with an auxiliary tender, provided all the motive power Almanor required through the first several years. In 1947, Almanor purchased a new 44-ton diesel electric switcher from General Electric; the diesel served the railroad well, but its small size and limited tractive effort proved increasingly unable to cope with the stiff adverse grades. In 1955, Collins shipped the original diesel off to the Big Creek & Telocaset, replacing it with a new General Electric 70-ton diesel-electric.

A typical workday on the Almanor through the next several decades started around 5:30 in the morning when the two-person crew reported to work at the mill. They would fire up the diesel, gather the day's outbound loads, and head for Clear Creek Junction. Outbound trips with the loads typically consumed an hour and a half, with the return trip taking about half that time. The railroad also employed a small section gang to inspect and maintain the tracks, using self-propelled speeders to move themselves and their tools and equipment. When not running trains, the employees would perform routine maintenance on the diesel and complete the never ending paperwork associated with common carrier railroad operations.

The railroad's connecting carrier changed in 1982 when Union Pacific purchased the WP. The merger had little direct impact on the Almanor; however, the importance of the Inside Gateway as a through route had been severely diminished since the Great Northern merged into the Burlington Northern in 1970. By the early 1990s, the future of the Inside Gateway looked tenuous at best, and indeed, in November 1990, a tunnel fire just north of Keddie put the line out of service for an extended period of time and almost killed the line as a through route. During the closure UP maintained the Almanor interchange using locomotives leased from the BN, with all loads the shortline generated hauled north to the BN at Nubieber.

Collins' careful stewardship of its forests allowed the company to survive and prosper. The company practiced sustained yield and uneven age stand management decades before most of the rest of the lumber industry, resulting in the company's timberlands actually increasing the volume of timber growing upon them from one year to the next. In 2002, Collins completely rebuilt and modernized the Chester mill, giving the company a state of the art facility.

The Almanor continued to handle around 300 lumber loads a year, and in the late 1990s and early 2000s the railroad entertained serious but ultimately unproductive discussions about starting passenger excursion operations in association with the nearby Portola Railroad Museum (now the Western Pacific Railroad Museum). In 1997, the BNSF—successor road to the Burlington Northern—acquired the Nubieber-Keddie line from Union Pacific as part of the reconfiguration of the western railroad map after the UP–SP merger. BNSF immediately rebuilt the entire line and started routing over the Inside Gateway higher traffic levels than the line had ever historically handled.

ABANDONMENT

The continued prosperity and stability of the Chester mill and the revitalization of the connecting line did not spell security for the Almanor Railroad. The diesel received a new paint job around 2000; however, by this point the venerable locomotive started showing its age, and by 2003 it could only handle one loaded car at a time over the road. The Almanor turned to the used locomotive market, picking up a second GE 70-ton diesel in late 2003. The railroad's

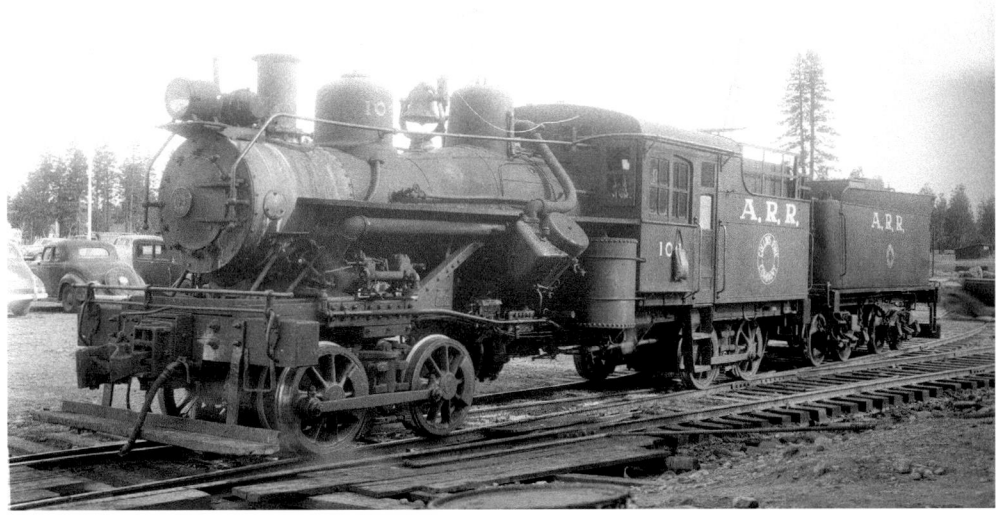

No. 104 in Chester. *Martin E. Hansen collection*

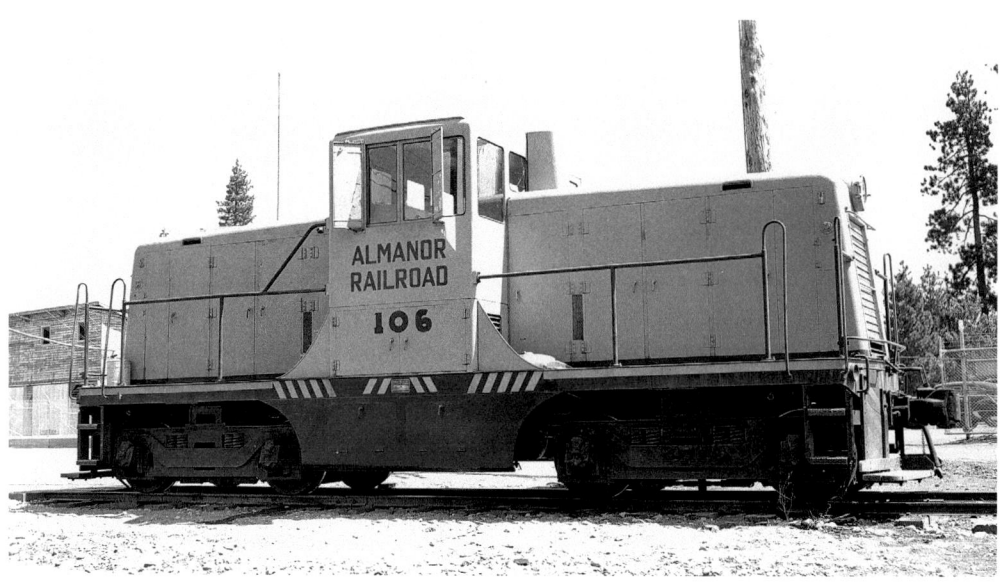

No. 106 in Chester on 8/21/1950. *Martin E. Hansen collection*

track maintenance program had kept the physical plant in good condition, but the light weight rail on much of the line limited the railroad to handling 225,000 pound cars. The beginning of the end arrived in early 2003, when Collins imported some logs from southern California by rail; however, instead of bringing the logs into Chester, Collins built a railcar to truck transload at Clear Creek Junction, and trucks made the final delivery to the mill. The existence of the reload suddenly made the railroad vulnerable, and BNSF offered Collins a new deal on loading lumber cars at the reload at a cheaper rate than what it cost to continue operations of the Almanor Railroad. Almanor ran its last train to Clear Creek Junction on Friday, October 8, 2004, and the following week trucks started transporting lumber from the mill to the reload.

The Almanor Railroad entered a state of suspended animation after the last train operated. Collins placed the two locomotives in storage in one of the mill buildings. By the end of the 2000s Collins decided to abandon the line. The company quickly obtained authority from I.C.C. successor Surface Transportation Board to effect the abandonment, but in the process agreed to a proposal advanced by local groups to preserve the right-of-way as a recreational trail under the "railbanking" provisions of Federal railroad abandonment regulations. Scrapping the railroad commenced in early January 2010, and the process of converting the grade into a trail has been slowly progressing since. Collins subsequently placed the original 70-tonner and a speeder on display in a logging museum built next to the Chester mill and returned the second locomotive to the party from which they purchased it. Thus ended the story of the Almanor Railroad.

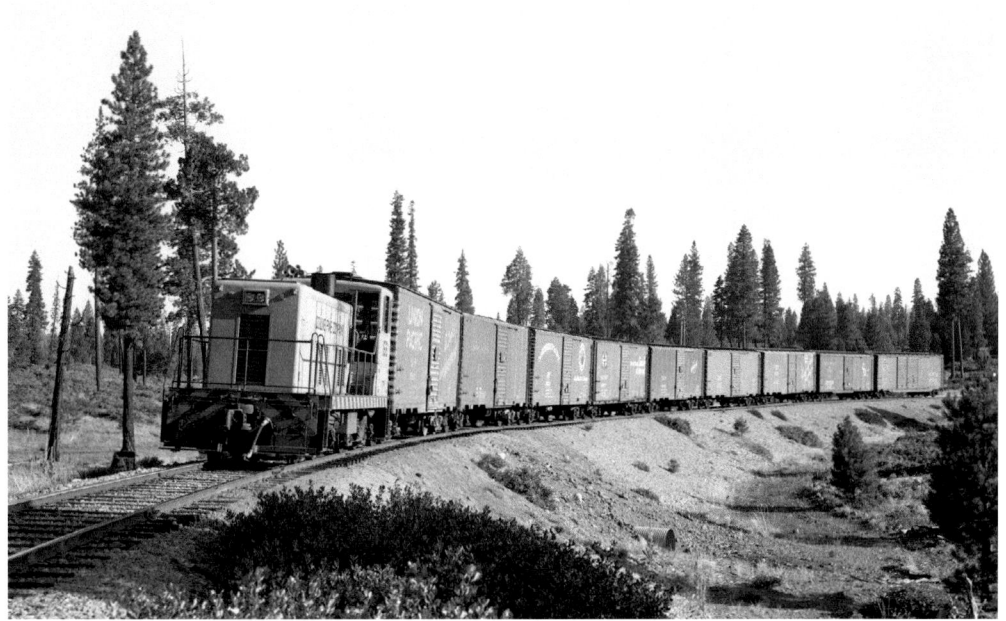

No. 166 returning to Chester with a string of empty boxcars on 8/10/1964. *Don Hansen*

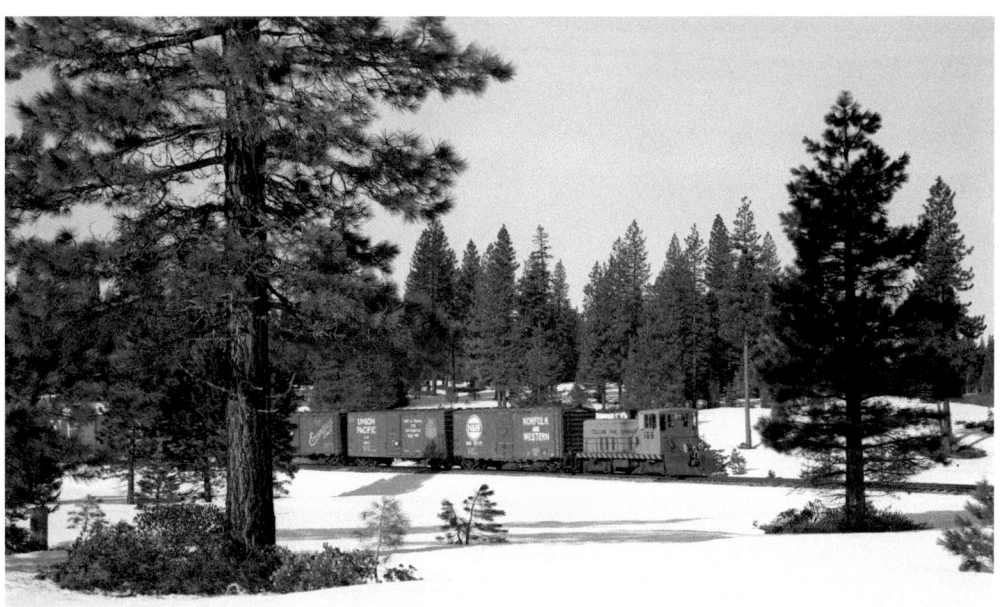

No. 166 in snow on 3/29/1971. *Don Hansen*

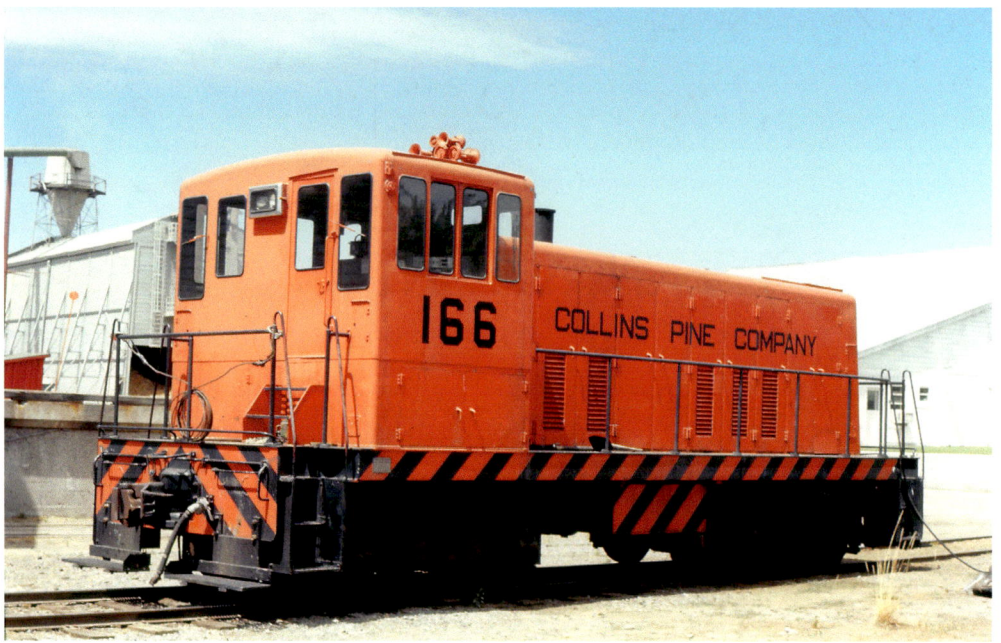

No. 166 between runs in Chester in 1971. *Lee F. Hower*

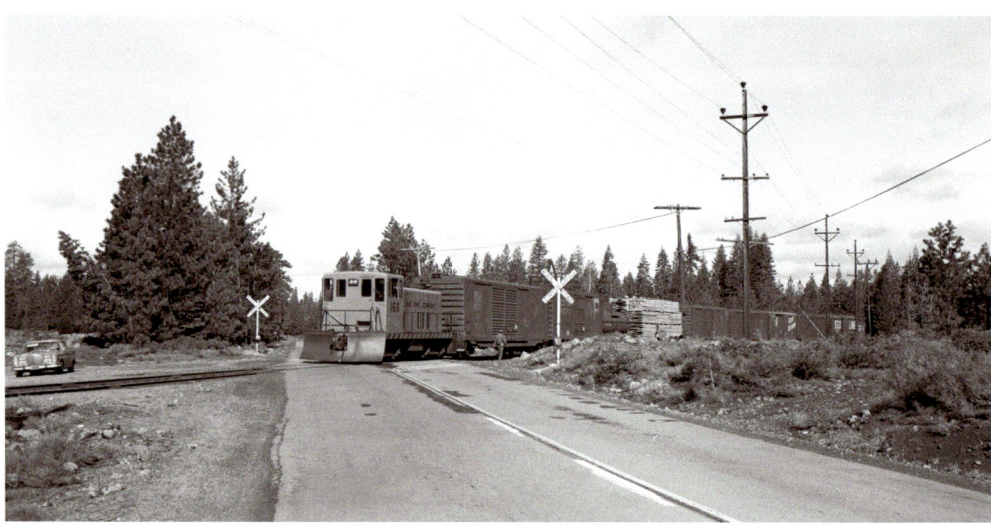

No. 166 switching Clear Creek Junction on 5/26/1971. *Don Hansen*

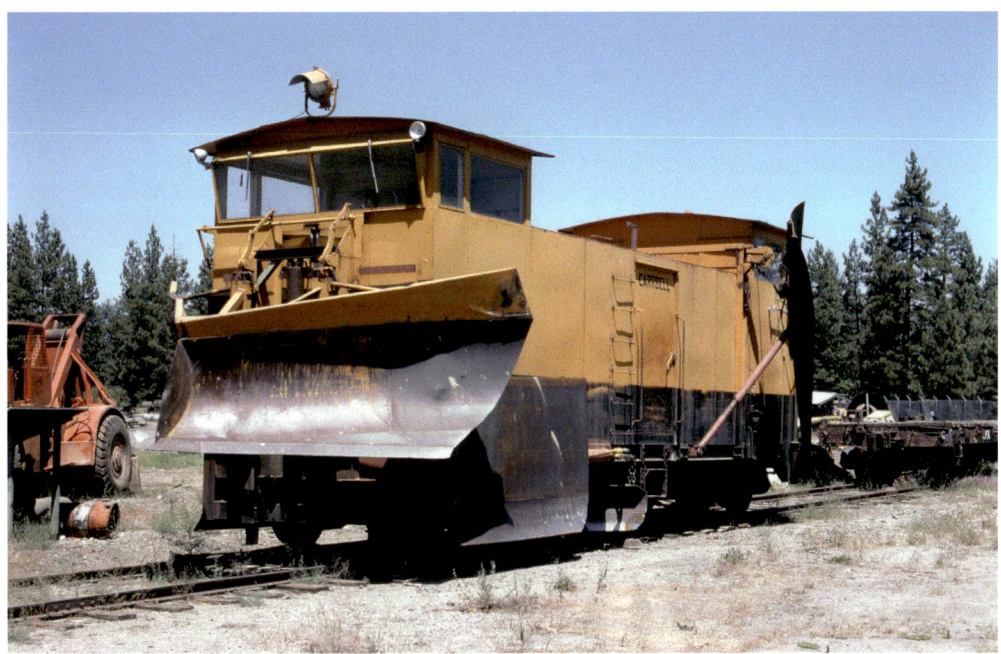

Above: Almanor's snowplow waiting for the next winter. *Lee F. Hower*

Right: No. 166 starting the climb up from Lake Almanor. *Sean Zwagerman*

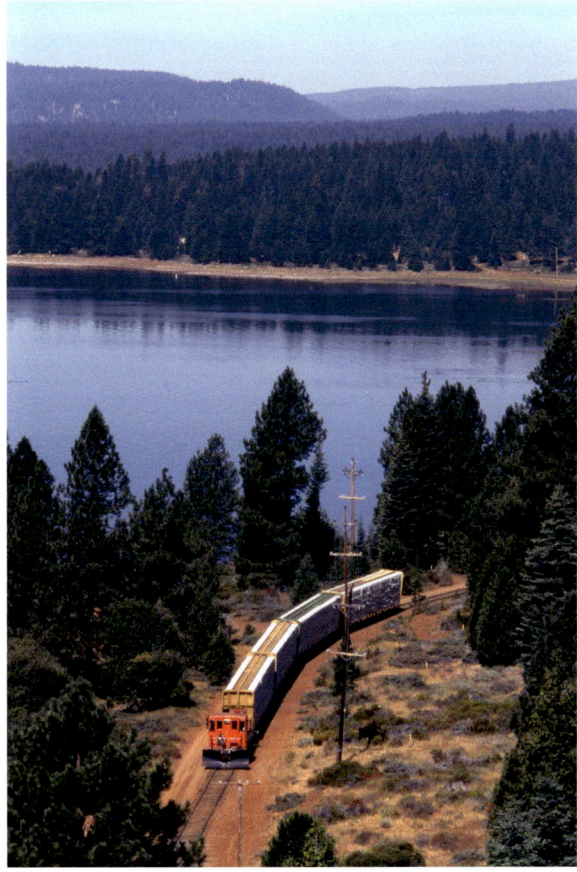

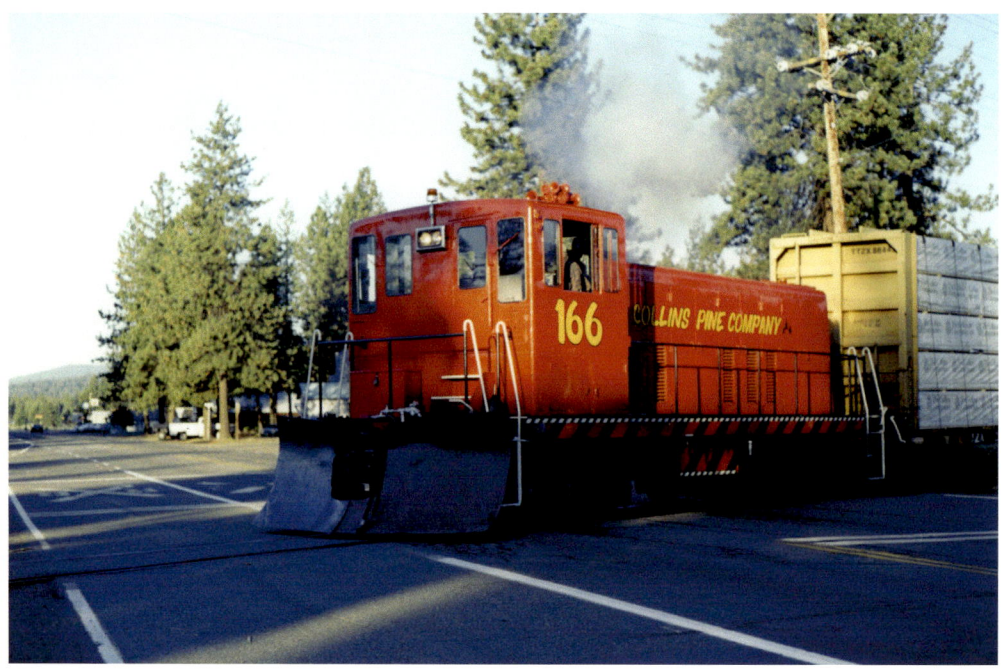

Freshly painted No. 166 crossing Highway 36 in downtown Chester. *Jim Bryant*

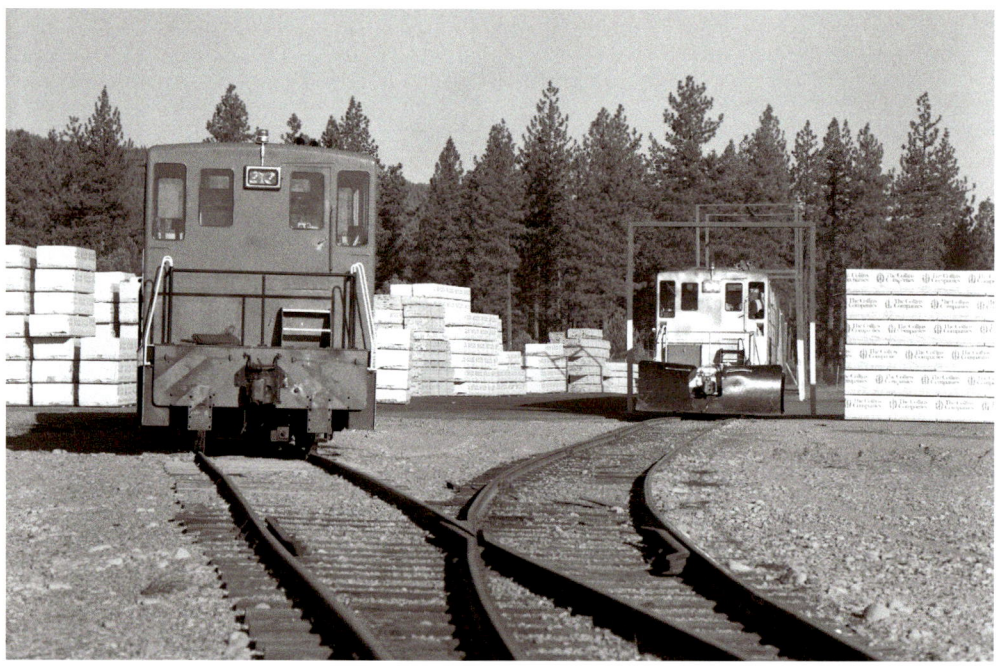

No. 165 preparing to depart the Chester mill while the idled No. 166 looks on. *Dave Stanley*

LOCOMOTIVE ROSTER

104—2-truck Heisler, c/n 1496, Built 1924. Originally Grande Ronde Lumber Company #104, Perry, Oregon, then Pondosa, Oregon; to Stoddard Lumber Company #104 1930; to Grande Ronde Pine Company #104 1931; to Almanor Railroad #104 1941; to Whitney Company, Tacoma, Washington, *circa* 1947. Scrapped.

106—General Electric 44-ton, c/n 28340, Built 1946. Purchased new; to Big Creek & Telocaset Railroad, Pondosa, Oregon, 1955, but never relettered from Almanor; to Valsetz Lumber Company #1, Valsetz, Oregon, 1959; to Boise-Cascade #1, Valsetz, Oregon; to Valley & Siletz Railroad #8, Independence, Oregon; to Stimson Lumber Company, Gaston, Oregon, 1985; to Oregon Coast Scenic Railroad, Garibaldi, Oregon, 2009. Stored in Tillamook, Oregon.

165—General Electric 70-ton, c/n 32679, Built 1956. Originally Lehigh Portland Cement #1, then Lafarge Cement Corporation #109 1990, both Metaline Falls, Washington; to North Pend Oreille Valley Lions Club #109, Metaline Falls, Washington, 1990; to Pend Orielle Valley Railroad #103, Usk, Washington, 2001; to Almanor Railroad #165 2003. Never repainted from solid silver or lettered while on the Almanor. To Oregon Shortline LLC #70. Presently leased to Oregon Rail Connect, Port of Morrow, Orego

166—General Electric 70-ton, c/n 32296, Built 1955. Purchased new. Always lettered for Collins Pine Company. Retired at closure and placed on display in Collin's logging museum adjacent to their Chester, California mill.

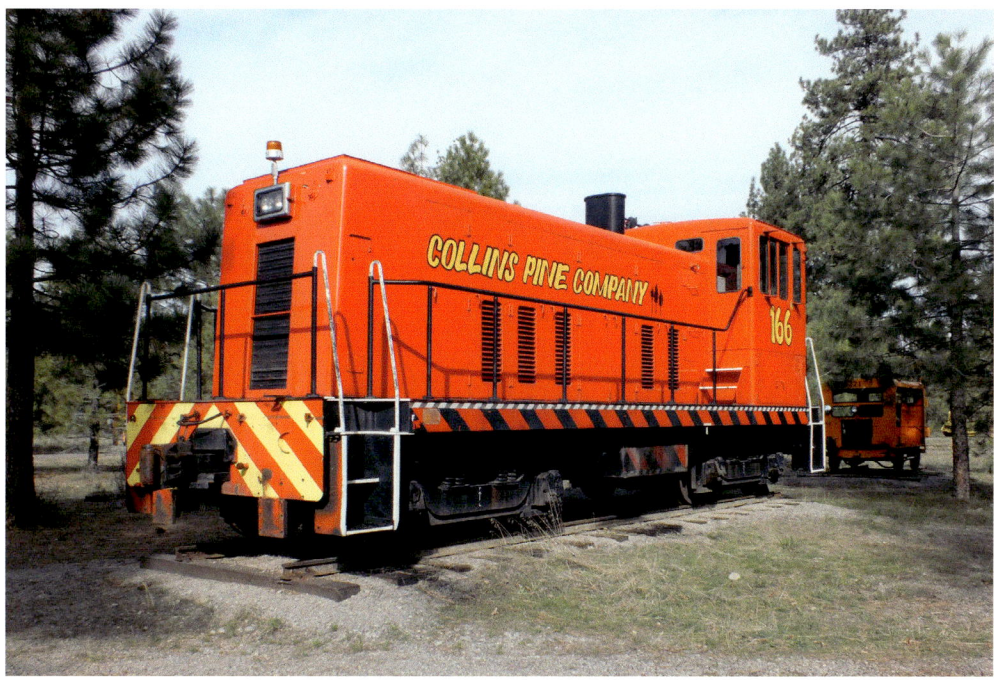

No. 166 and motorcar 121 on display in Collin's logging museum. *Jeff Moore*

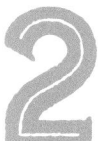

AMADOR CENTRAL

BACKGROUND

Amador County prospered on the backs of its gold mines from its inception in 1854. The county's location on top of the Smartville Block attracted prospectors by the thousands; however, the hilly topography along the Sierra foothills discouraged railroad construction. It would take the discovery of coal beds and the development of a thriving industry converting the clay soils prevalent along the base of the foothills into firebrick to finally attract a railroad. On July 3, 1875, the Central Pacific interests incorporated the Amador Branch Railroad, which built a line from the CP/SP mainline at Galt eastward towards the foothills. The line, operated as a branch line of the SP, opened to Bed Bug—quickly renamed Ione, after a character in Bulwer-Lytton's *The Last Day of Pompeii*—on December 3, 1876. The railroad became the primary route for commerce into and out of Amador County, and in addition to the traffic to and from the mining camps in the foothills the railroad also handled carloads of bricks and coal.

Ione as the area's railhead prospered, as did all towns with the only rail access in that era. The mining activity farther up the foothills kept other towns like Sutter Creek, Martell, Amador City, and the county seat of Jackson thriving, but those communities faced significant transportation challenges due to the slow and often impassible in winter wagon roads connecting them to the railhead at Ione. The area needed an extension of the railroad, and eventually the residents concluded they had to do it themselves.

THE RAILROAD IS BORN

On April 12, 1904, a group of Amador County citizens incorporated the Ione & Eastern Railroad. The company hired San Francisco based contractor Erickson and Peterson to build the line, starting at Ione and heading east. The railroad completed the first six miles by the end of the year, with the balance of the line to Martell completed in 1905. Over the course of twelve miles, the railroad climbed 1,244 feet on grades of up to 3.8 percent, crossed twelve trestles, and negotiated sixty-nine curves. By 1908, the Ione & Eastern was insolvent, and on September 24, 1908, Erickson and Peterson incorporated a new company, the Amador Central Railroad, who took over operations from the Ione & Eastern on January 1, 1909.

The Amador Central settled down to a quiet existence. Outbound traffic consisted primarily of

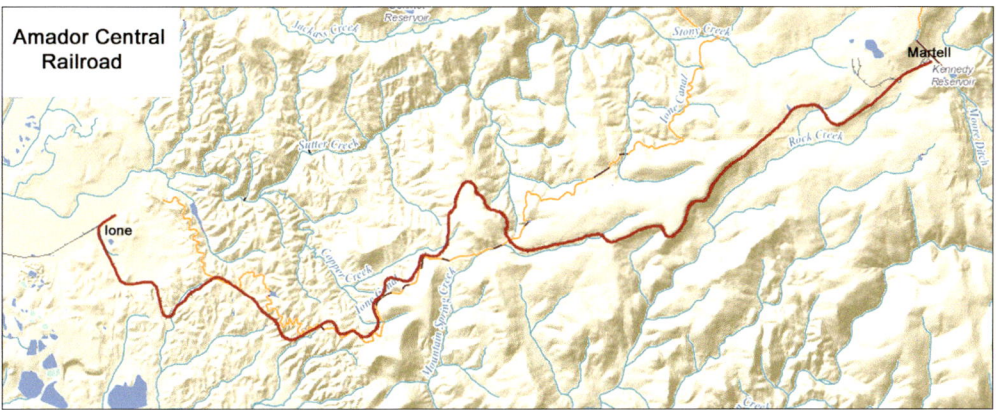

firebrick from the quarries just above Ione and roughly twenty carloads of gold ore concentrates per month, mostly from the Argonaut and Kennedy mines in Jackson bound for the large smelter at Selby, California, on the shores of San Pablo Bay twenty miles north of Oakland. Inbound traffic consisted of a mix of animal feed, fuel oil for the steam engines powering the mines, and general merchandise. Passenger traffic moved in both directions.

Improved highways, private automobiles, competing trucking companies, and Great Depression cut into the railroad's revenues as the 1920s rolled into the 1930s. Passenger operations ceased in 1932, mostly because SP ended its passenger operations on its Galt-Ione line. As the end of the decade approached the railroad gained the reputation as having the worst roadbed in California, and the owners concluded the line had no viable future. On November 5, 1938, the California Railroad Commission granted an application to abandon the railroad, and the company had a similar petition pending before the I.C.C; however, this action galvanized local businessmen and the few remaining shippers still depending on the railroad, including an Ione firebrick plant and Jackson mining concerns, and together they raised sufficient cash to purchase the company .

"WORKING STEAM IN THE BRET HARTE HILLS"

The new ownership group pumped money into the property after acquiring it, including upgrading the motive power fleet and starting some track upgrades; however, the railroad suffered a rash of devastating fires in 1939, including a mysterious one inflicting $5,000 worth of damage to the Martell roundhouse and the loss of two trestles valued at $18,000. The railroad obtained a bulldozer and power shovel to build new grades around the burned trestles. The overall economy of the line failed to improve, and this coupled with the fire damage forced the railroad into another reorganization in 1939. Fate intervened at this point in the form of the Amador Lumber Company, who acquired some timberlands up in the Sierras and built a substantial sawmill at Martell. The flow of lumber traffic the mill generated starting in 1940 brought the railroad back from the brink of oblivion; without it, the line would have almost assuredly faced abandonment at the start of the Second World War, when the U.S. Government deemed gold mining non-essential to the war effort and ordered all mines closed. In the mid 1940s the Winton Lumber Company acquired both the Amador Lumber Company and the Amador Central Railroad, securing the future of the entire operation. The mines reopened

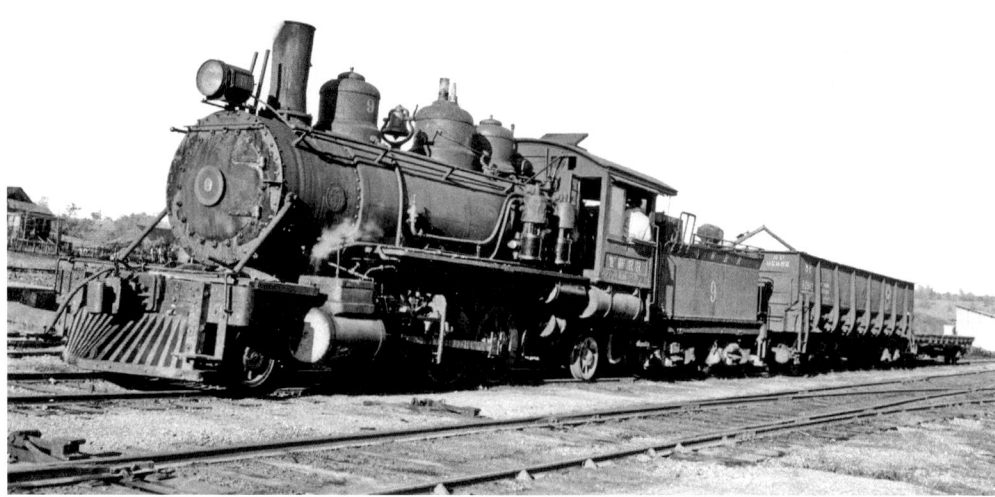

First No. 9—still lettered for the Yreka Western—switching the Martell yards on 2/19/1945. *Pennington photo, Tom Moungovan collection*

on a sporadic basis after the war ended, but only shipped ore concentrates at a rate of three to four cars per month.

It was at this point that the railroad and western history writing and photographic duo of Lucius Beebe and Charles Clegg spent a night of gambling and strong drink at the El Encanto Casino and other such gambling houses then operating in Jackson:

> despite crusades by San Francisco and Sacramento papers, humorless feuilletons having their origin in subdued and docile communities obviously obsessed with jealousy of Jackson's easy ways and candid wealth.

In the morning the pair emerged:

> … in J. P. Morgan mood and stimulated with winnings and champagne, to go up the hill and take some pictures of the Amador Central Railroad at Martell.

The pair spent a day following and photographing the railroad's #7 as it went about its chores as "*The sole remaining steam locomotive … in the Bret Harte hill country of California*", a nod to the famous author's works set in the California gold rush mining camps. The #7 was operating on borrowed time by this point, as Beebe noted the railroad had recently purchased, but had yet to accept delivery of, a new $50,000 General Electric 44-ton diesel electric locomotive. Beebe later immortalized the road by describing his visit in the classic *Mixed Train Daily*.

The new diesel Beebe mentioned arrived not too long after their visit and soon relegated the #7 to a display stand in Ione. The diesel proved its worth, reducing the railroad's operating ratio from 203 percent in 1945 to 42 percent in 1946; however, the locomotive's small size and limited power increasingly became an issue as the years progressed and as car size and weight steadily increased. The railroad upped the horsepower, from 380 to 400, but even that was not enough; the unit consumed four full hours on each round trip and could only drag five empty cars up to Martell, and by the early 1960s the railroad was running at least two round trips a day six and sometimes seven days a week to keep up with the shipping needs of the sawmill.

In 1964, American Forest Products acquired Winton Lumber and the railroad. By this point the motive power situation had become acute, with the diesel suffering from a cracked frame and failing traction motors. The new owner allowed the railroad to go shopping for motive power more appropriate to the railroad's needs, resulting in the purchase of a 120-ton, 1,200-horsepower Baldwin switcher in 1965; however, it proved too heavy for the physical plant, forcing the 44-ton back into operation until the tracks could be rebuilt so as to support the larger power. These upgrades eliminated the last of the trestles in 1968 and shortly thereafter allowed the Baldwin to operate full time.

"A RAILROAD LOST IN TIME"

By the early 1970s the Martell mill provided the only traffic keeping the Amador Central alive. A major expansion of the Martell mill included a new particleboard plant, increasing traffic over the railroad and forcing the purchase of a second Baldwin switcher. Woodchip traffic also appeared on the line, outbound loads destined for Fibreboard's Antioch paper mill plus a few inbound loads for the particleboard plant. The railroad also jumped into the incentive *per diem* boxcar market, leasing a fleet of powder blue boxcars and a few Evans "Side-Slider" all-door boxcars.

The railroad remained healthy into the middle 1970s, operating six days a week and handing an average of 400–500 cars per month. Sixteen employees drew pay checks from the front

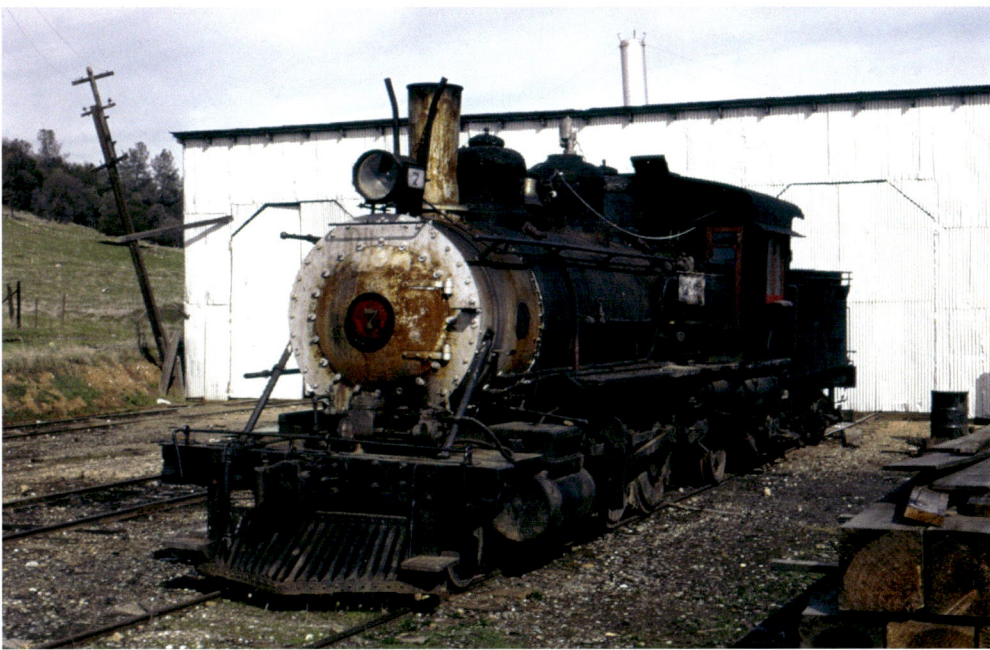

No. 7, the railroad's mainstay locomotive in the early years of the lumber hauling era, at rest in Martell shortly before being placed on display in Ione. *C. G. Heimerdinger Jr.*

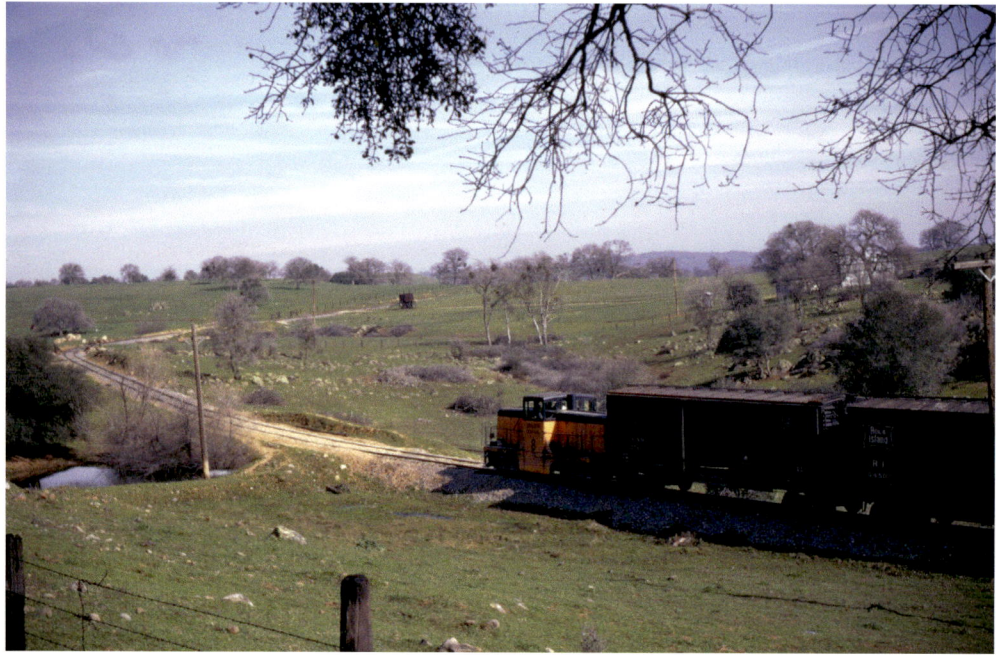

No. 8 navigates AMC's undulating profile in March 1969. *Henry Brueckman photo, Tom Moungovan collection.*

office, two on the train crew and fourteen maintaining track. However, the pulse of the railroad slowed in the 1980s, and by the middle of that decade the railroad handled but 60–70 carloads each month, evenly split between lumber and particleboard loads, and employed three or four people. Two to four days each week one of the Baldwins would be fired up at Martell to gather the outbound loads from the sawmill and head for Ione, pausing halfway down the grade for a half hour to allow the brakes to cool. Downhill trips still consumed two hours, but the Baldwins completed the uphill run to Martell in an hour.

The Amador Central was increasingly an anachronism by the dawn of the 1990s. It was possible to stand in the yards at Ione and watch Amador's 40-year old Baldwins swap cars with equally aged SP power and wonder just what year it actually was. A new owner entered the picture in 1988 when timber industry giant Georgia Pacific purchased American Forest Products. The ownership change had essentially no immediate impact on the railroad, and it continued on as before. However, things began to change in the early 1990s; Georgia Pacific closed a sawmill in nearby Forest Hill and expanded Martell operations. The railroad handled an even 600 loads in 1992; by 1993 traffic shot up to 999 loads, and then further increased to 1,273 cars in 1994; 1,096 loads in 1995; and 1,229 loads in 1996. Some of the carloadings in 1991–1994 were gold tailings from the Argonaut mine, purchased by a Nevada mining company and shipped east for processing. The increased traffic also resulted in the Amador Central clearing a larger profit than Georgia Pacific in at least one year. The cost of Baldwin spare parts increasingly became an issue, and in 1995 and 1996 Georgia Pacific transferred two EMD switchers to the Amador Central. SP also placed its Galt to Ione branch on the sale block as part of its line sales program initiated in 1993, and the Amador Central nearly closed a deal to purchase the line several times, but in the end the sales fell apart.

It was too good to last. Georgia Pacific decided to get out of California in 1997, placing its Amador County operations up for sale. California lumber giant Sierra Pacific Industries purchased the Martell mill and the Amador Central; however, SPI already had enough sawmills in the area and closed the sale principally for the 127,000 acres of timberlands packaged in the deal. On Friday, March 28, 1997, Amador Central #11—complete with special signs marking the event—led six cars of finished lumber and one boxcar of particleboard to Ione and returned light to Martell. The Amador Central was finished.

Or so it seemed.

AMADOR FOOTHILLS RAILROAD

Sierra Pacific Industries immediately closed the Martell mill after completing the purchase. SPI removed the two EMD switchers from the property, transferring both north to their Quincy Railroad operation (Chapter 10). However, after some deliberation SPI decided to retain the particleboard plant under the Ampine Division of SierraPine name. SPI concluded Ampine would benefit from rail service, and shopped the railroad around to other parties in hope someone would buy it and restart operations. At one point announcements were made the company had been sold to the owners of the Sierra Railroad (Chapter 11) for $1.5 million; however, the deal fell apart before it could be consummated.

SPI finally concluded the company would have to restart operations on its own if it wanted rail service. The company incorporated the Amador Foothills Railroad, and work on resurrecting the railroad began. The two Baldwins remained on the property, neither one having operated much if at all since 1995. The two men hired to run the Amador Foothills returned one to

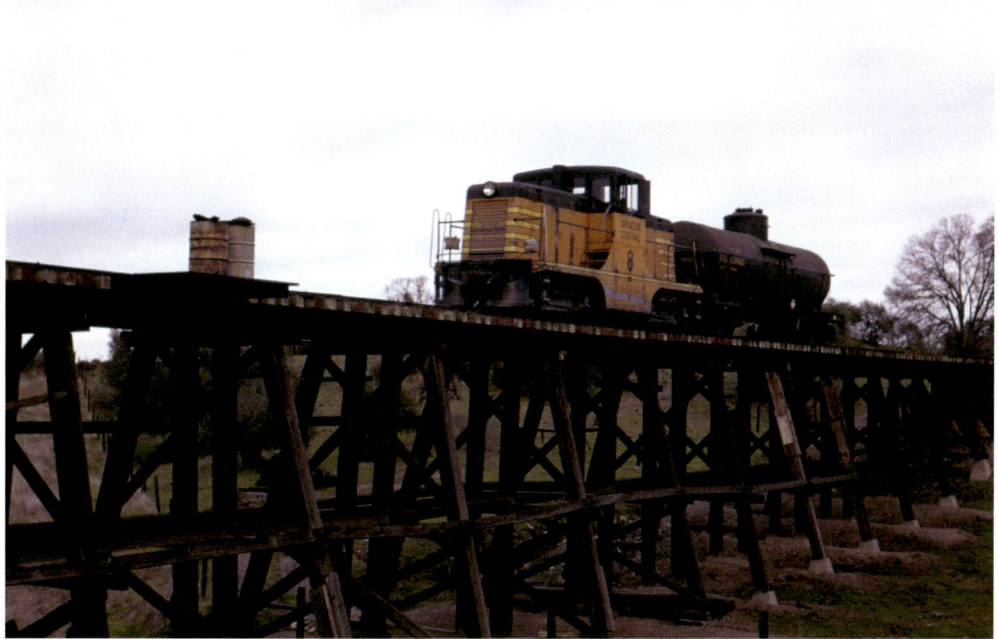

No 8 crosses a trestle with a single tank car bound for Martell. *C. G. Heimerdinger Jr.*

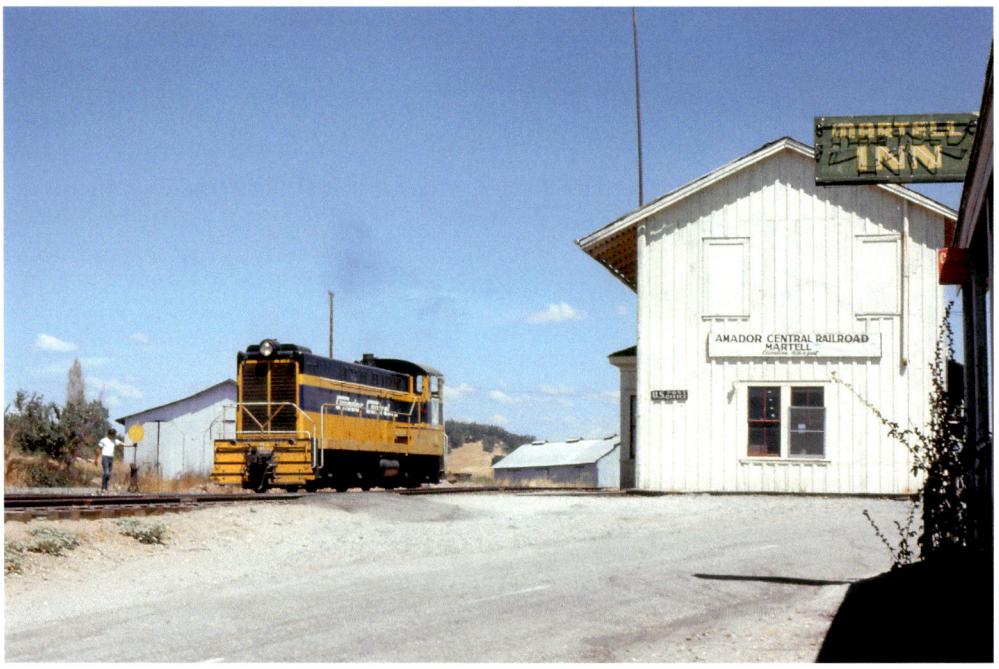

No. 9 in its original paint switching next to AMC's Martell depot on 8/15/1972. *Lee F. Hower*

service. On March 1, 1999, the Amador Foothills commenced operations, hauling outbound particleboard loads and occasional inbound veneer loads. Traffic held up well, averaging 550–600 loads a year.

As late as early 2004 the future still looked at least secure for the railroad; however, concerns had been growing within SPI over the costs, safety, and liability issues surrounding the railroad, compounded by increasingly poor track conditions. Baldwin parts had not become any more available or cheaper either, and the diesel would need substantial work in the near future to remain operational. In the end the Ampine plant simply did not generate sufficient traffic to keep the railroad alive, nor was Ampine's continued survival dependent upon having rail service to the plant, and despite talks of establishing industrial parks in Martell and Ione extending over several decades there were no other immediate prospects of attracting other rail users to locate on the line. On June 7, 2004, the Baldwin took four particleboard loads to Ione and returned light to Martell, and once again the railroad fell silent.

A RECREATIONAL RAILROAD

On November 12, 2004, Amador Foothills sought permission from the Surface Transportation Board to abandon operations. Over the objections of the California Department of Transportation, the Amador County Transportation Commission, the county Board of Supervisors, and the Martell Industrial Center, LLC, the STB granted the abandonment application in February 2005, finding that:

These exemptions will foster sound economic conditions and encourage efficient management by relieving SierraPine from the costs of operating and SPI from the costs of owning and rehabilitating the line.

However, the story of the railroad once again was not quite over. When railroads in general started moving away from self-propelled motorcars for track inspection and maintenance chores, they found a ready market for the motorcars in the form of railroad enthusiasts. Motor car owners eventually formed several clubs to arrange for organized speeder trips over various railroads. In 2006, a local organization named the Recreational Railroad Coalition reached a deal to lease the Amador Foothills from SPI for the purpose of establishing a railroad devoted exclusively to hosting motorcar runs. The initial lease lasted through March 2010, when SPI terminated the agreement and announced plans to start removing trackage, causing significant angst amongst the motorcar groups and others hoping to keep the railroad intact. In September SPI started removing the first two miles of the railroad west from Martell, finishing the job within several weeks. At this point SPI relented, and in late October 2010 the company announced it would sell for $1 the remaining ten miles of the line to the Recreational Railroad Coalition and the Amador County Historical Society.

The sawmill that kept the Amador Central alive for a half century is now gone, with much of the site now occupied by a shopping center. The adjacent SierraPine plant continues operations, but trucks all of its products out to market. Amador Central's depot and office building in Martell survived until August 2012, when workers tore it down on account of the structure's badly deteriorated condition. An auto shop now occupies the Martell engine house. On the intact parts of the railroad, speeder groups are periodically seen touring the line, and each Memorial Day weekend sees the Ione Rail Fair, complete with motor car rides offered to the public. The groups who own the remnants of the Amador Central are also contemplating establishment of a tourist railroad operation, with at least some plans laid to remove the #7 from its display stand and return it to operation.

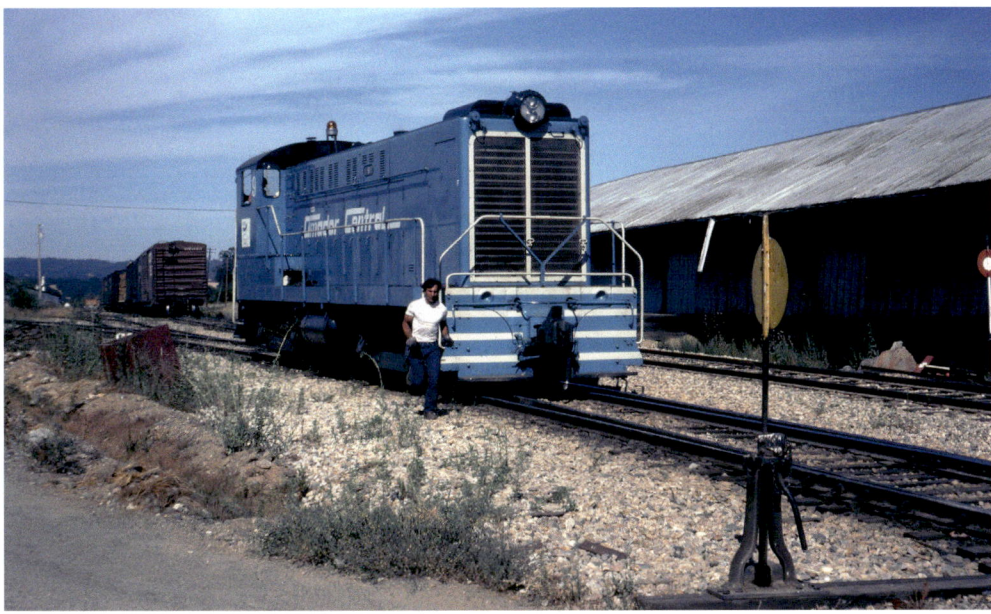

A brakeman sprints to line a switch for No. 9's passage in the Martell yards. *Wayne I. Monger*

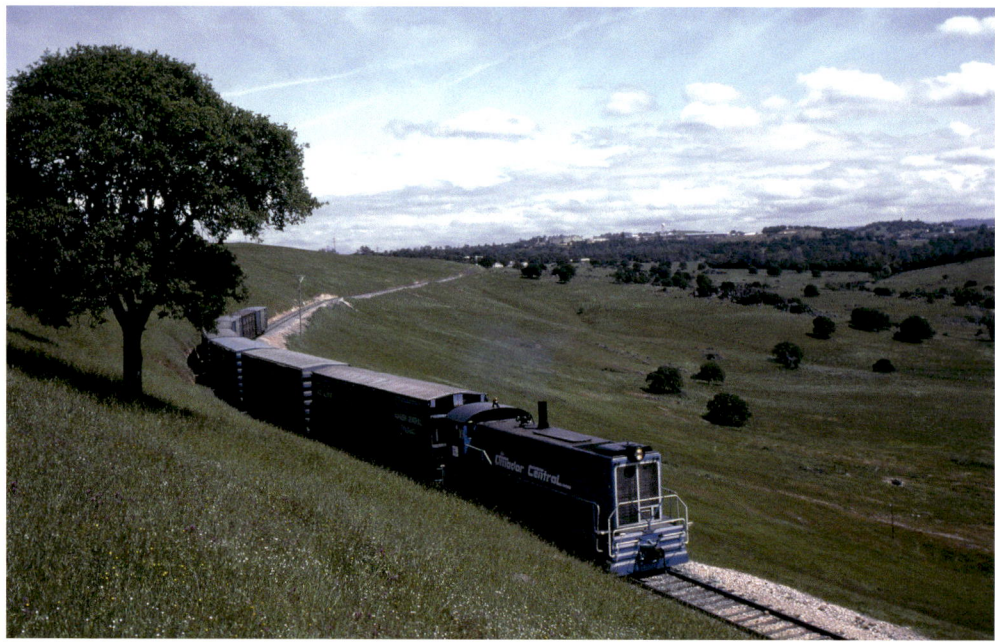

No. 10, with a mixture of AMC's "Slide Slider" and incentive *per diem* boxcars, not far out of Martell on 4/19/1985. *Dave Stanley*

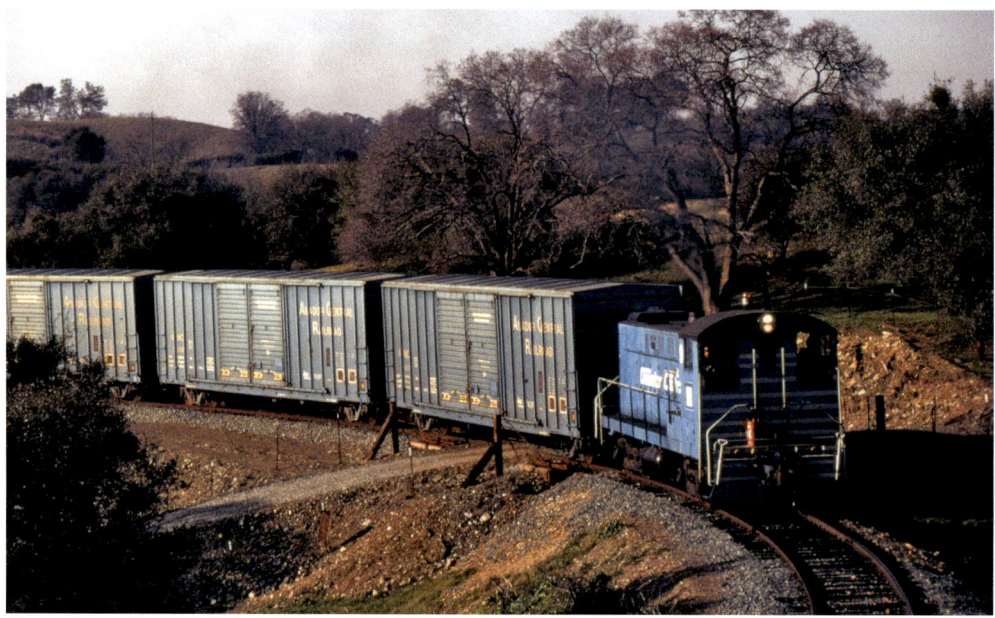

AMC incentive *per diem* boxcars trail the No. 9. *Wayne I. Monger*

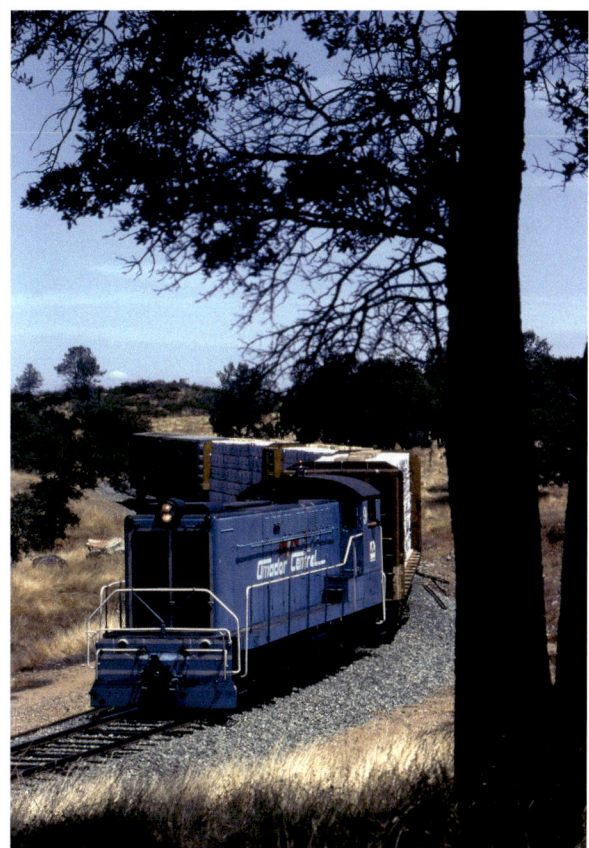

Right: No. 9 leading a train towards Ione. *Dave Stanley*

Below: AMC and SP train crews exchange greetings while switching the Ione yards. *Sean Zwagerman*

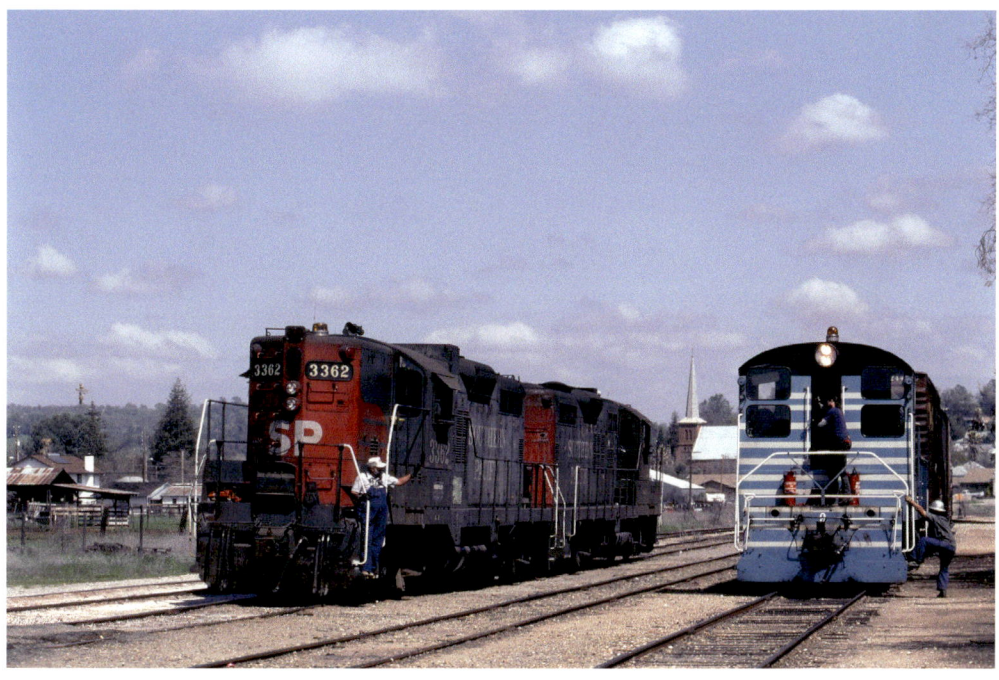

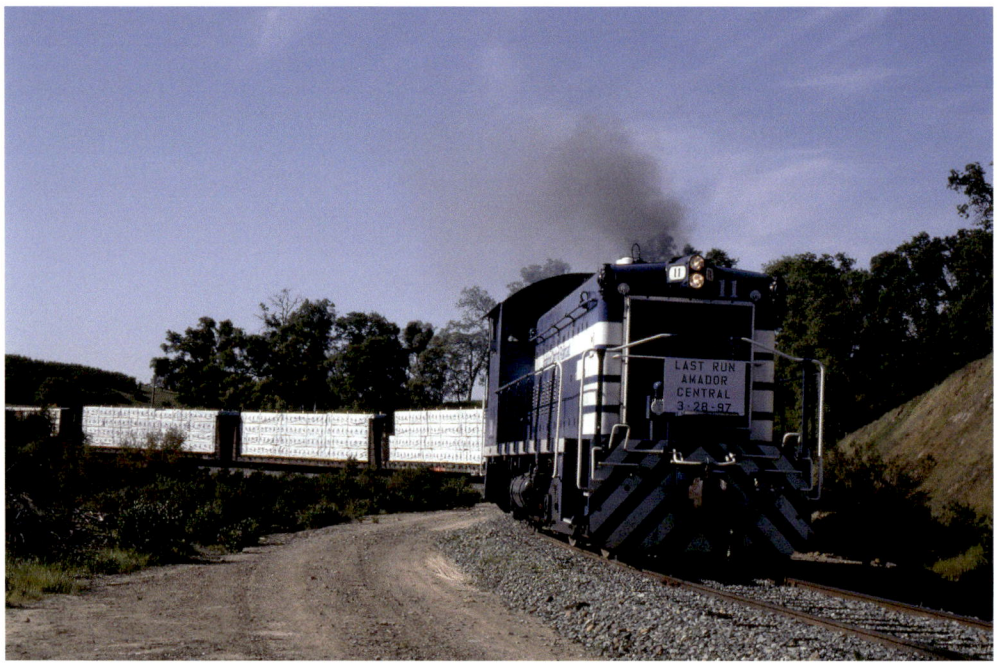

The last Amador Central train rolling downhill towards Ione. *Sean Zwagerman*

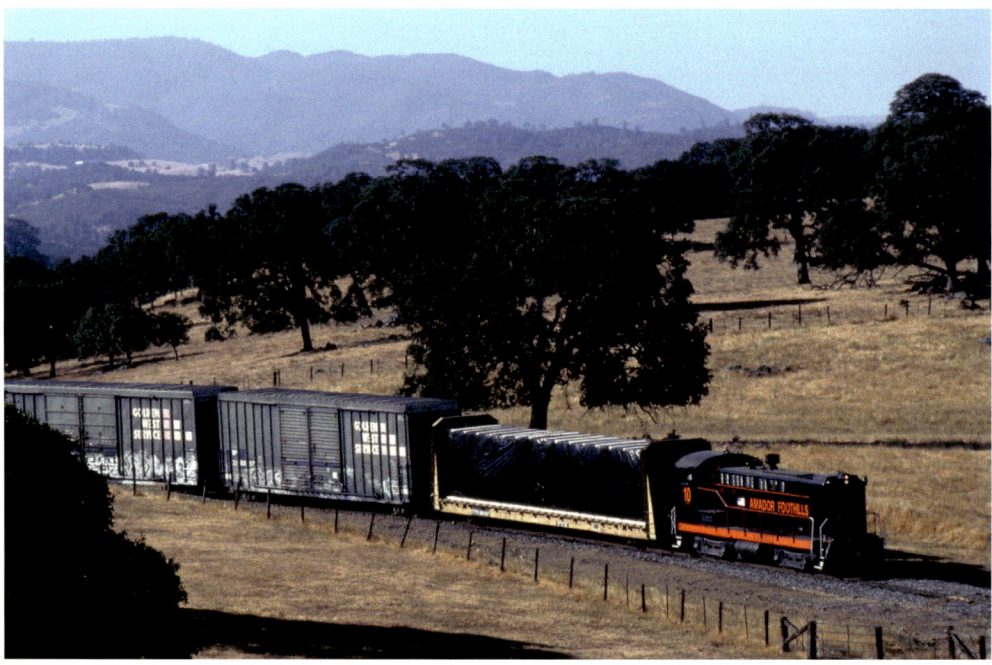

Amador Foothills No. 10 with outbound loads on 5/14/2004. *Dave Stanley*

AMADOR CENTRAL

LOCOMOTIVE ROSTER

1—Portland 4-4-0, c/n 382, Built 1881. Originally Northern Pacific #205, then #855; to California Northeastern #1; to Ione & Eastern #1. Retired 1910 and sold to Southern Pacific. Scrapped.

2—Lima 3-truck Shay, c/n 867, Built 1904. Displayed at St. Louis Exposition in 1904, then sold to Charles Erickson; to Ione & Eastern #2; to Amador Central #2; to Metropolitan Redwood Lumber Company #2 1912. Scrapped.

3—Lima 2-truck Shay, c/n 976, Built 1905. Originally Charles Erickson #3; to Ione & Eastern #3; to Amador Central #3; to Great Western Power Company #3 1920; Scrapped. Remains may be buried under California Highway 70 near Bucks Creek Powerhouse.

4—McKay & Aldus 0-6-0, Built 1866 as a 4-6-0. Originally Central Pacific #21, named *Tamaroo*; to Southern Pacific #1524, then #1055 and rebuilt to 0-6-0 configuration; to Erickson & Peterson (Amador Central) 1909; to Stone & Webster #10 1917; to Modesto & Empire Traction #2; Scrapped.

5—Schenectady 4-6-0, c/n 981, Built 1875. Originally Central Pacific #189, then #1584; to Southern Pacific #2023; to Amador Central 1910. Re-boilered *circa* 1920. Scrapped 1945.

6—Baldwin 2-6-2, c/n 27686, Built 1906. Originally Klamath Lake Railroad #1, Thrall, California; to Amador Central *circa* 1912. Scrapped 1945.

7—Baldwin 2-6-2, c/n 18595, Built 1901. Originally McCloud River #8; to Amador Central #7 1939. Retired 1945 and placed on display in Ione as "Iron Ivan".

8—General Electric 44-ton, c/n 27980, Built 1945. Purchased new; to Colorado Fuel & Iron #32 1974.

9:1—Baldwin 2-6-2, c/n 18596, Built 1901. Originally McCloud River #9; to Yreka Western #9 1939; to Amador Central #9:1 1942; to Nezperce & Idaho Railroad #9 1945; to private party 1967; moved to Mid-Continental Railroad Museum, North Freedom, Wisconsin, for restoration, then to Kettle Moraine Scenic Railroad, North Lake, Wisconsin, 1972. Operated on Kettle Moraine until it closed in 2002. To Age of Steam Roundhouse, Sugarcreek, Ohio, 2015.

9:2—Baldwin S-12, c/n 75032, Built 1951. Originally Sharon Steel #1; to Amador Central #9 9/1965; to Amador Foothills #9 1999. Scrapped 4/2007.

10—Baldwin S-12, c/n 75613, Built 1952. Originally Texas & New Orleans #105; to Southern Pacific #2121; to Amador Central 7/1972; to Amador Foothills 1999. Locomotive moved from Martell to Ione 6/2008, where it remains in the yard pending resolution of litigation surrounding competing ownership claims.

11—EMD SW-1200, c/n 28344, Built 1963. Originally Ashley, Drew & Northern #178, then #1208; to Amador Central 1995; to Quincy Railroad #5, Quincy, CA, 1997.

12—EMD SW-7, c/n 15636, Built 1952. Originally Arkansas & Louisiana Missouri #11; to Chattahoochee Industrial #11; to Amador Central 1996; to Quincy Railroad #12, Susanville, CA, 1997, then Quincy, CA.

331, **334**, **335**—Alco 0-4-0T locomotives, c/n 44250, 43292, and 44390, all built 1907 for Nevada Consolidated Copper Corporation, Ely, Nevada. Purchased *circa* 1938 as rebuild projects for the Martell shop and intended for resale; however, #334 used to switch the fire-brick plant and other shippers at Ione while the railroad rebuilt a burned trestle. #331 to Pacific States Steel #331, to Judson Pacific #331; #334 to Pacific States Steel #334; #335 sold to AD Schader #335, to Granite Rock #335.

In addition, the railroad was reported to have an ex-SP 4-4-0, though this was not supported by available SP records. This locomotive was reportedly later used by a contractor near Placerville.

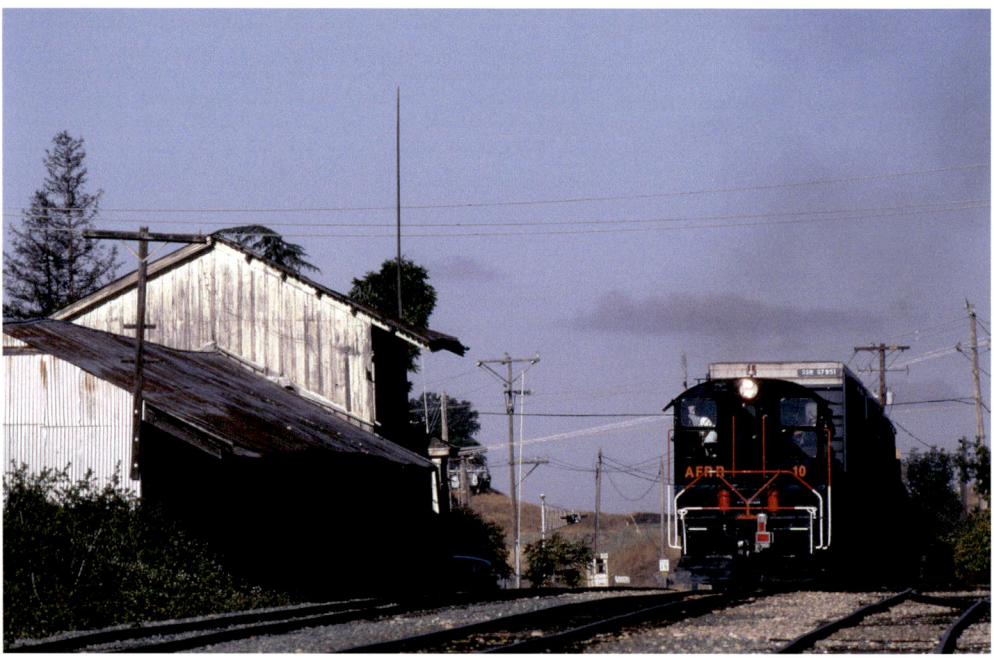

Amador Foothills #10 switching in Martell. *Dave Stanley*

3

ARCATA & MAD RIVER

BACKGROUND

The flood of prospectors pouring into California following James Marshall's gold discovery rapidly spread out to other parts of the territory. In the spring of 1849, some of them struck gold in the hills off the west side of the north end of the Sacramento Valley, prompting a rush to the region. A new town named Shasta quickly rose around the new strike. More discoveries followed in rapid succession as the prospectors foraged on to the north and west, resulting in the establishment of many new mining camps, such as Weaverville in 1850 and what would become Yreka in 1852.

Transportation into the suddenly booming region became a major obstacle to the further development of the mines and growing communities. Sacramento initially became the jumping off points for the new strikes; pack trains routinely departed there headed 188 miles north to Shasta, and then to the mining camps beyond. It is said over one hundred mules trains would be gathered into Shasta on some nights. In 1849, a group of explorers departed the gold discoveries that would shortly become Weaverville and headed west in search of a shortcut to the Pacific Ocean, reaching Humboldt Bay near the end of the year. The party then walked south along the coastline until they reached San Francisco.

Humboldt is the only deep water bay on the Pacific Coast between Coos Bay to the north and San Francisco Bay to the south; however, a sand bar usually blocked its mouth, making detecting the opening from the ocean difficult at best. The party from Weaverville allowed navigators to get a fix on the bay's mouth, and in March 1850 the first two ships from San Francisco finally crossed the sand bar and entered the bay. Despite this, ship traffic remained slow for the first several years; however, by 1853 traffic into and out of the bay started becoming common, as navigators learned how to safely cross the bar at least most of the time, helped immeasurably by the first markers placed at the harbor entrance that year.

Humboldt Bay becoming increasingly hospitable to ship traffic immediately allowed for the development of new freight routes into the mining camps. Ships would depart San Francisco heavily laden with supplies and passengers bound for the gold mines. Once across the bar the ships would head for the newly established town of Union located at the north end of the bay, where the cargo would go ashore to begin the ascent into the Trinity and Klamath mountains to the east. However, the bay tended to be very shallow near Union, with only one slough providing any real docking space, and even then ships ran the risk of finding themselves resting on the mudflats when the tide went out.

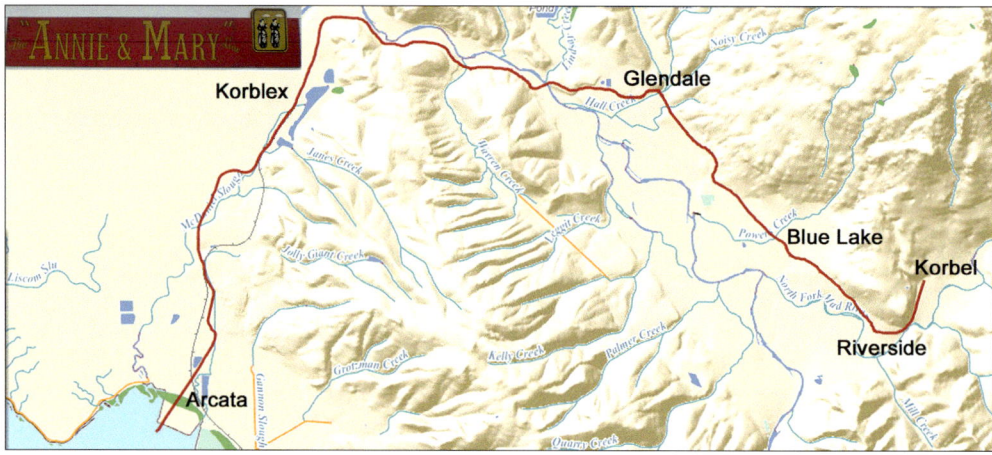

RAILROAD ON THE WHARF

As the volume of shipping grew, the wharf situation at Union became a critical issue requiring immediate attention. In 1854, the California state legislature authorized construction of a wharf from Union out into Humboldt Bay to ease the loading and unloading of freight. On December 15, 1854, a group of local investors incorporated the Union Wharf and Plank Walk Company, who immediately commenced constructing the wharf. By February 22, 1855, the *Humboldt Times* reported the wharf had been completed a mile out into the bay and was in regular use. Further construction completed by May extended the wharf to a full two miles long.

The company constructed a railroad along the length of the wharf to facilitate transporting freight and passengers between downtown Union and docked ships, allowing the company to lay claim to having been the first operating railroad in California. Rails for this operation initially consisted of 6" × 6" redwood timbers topped with 2" × 4" pepperwood. The rails lay 45¼ inches apart, the gauge reportedly set by the first set of wheels the builders could find. The rolling stock consisted entirely of one or more four wheel carts, and horses provided all the motive power the railroad required. One horse in particular, an aging white horse named Spanking Fury, received special mention in local press.

California's first operating railroad lived out its first twenty years in a period of relative stability. Union changed its name to Arcata in 1860, a move that otherwise had no impact on the railroad. The operating company lived in a boom and bust cycle, alternating between periods of relative prosperity and dark economic times when the company fell deep into debt; these latter instances occasionally resulted in ownership changes, usually effected by creditors receiving ownership of the company to satisfy debts.

FROM GOLD TO LUMBER

Opening Humboldt Bay to ship traffic had far reaching effects beyond expediting transportation routes into the gold camps. The tall stands of redwood trees blanketing the hills around Humboldt Bay attracted the immediate attention of lumbermen, who built the first sawmill on the shores of the bay in 1850. By the time the Union Wharf and Plank Walk Company started building the wharf, the area could boast of nine sawmills cutting 200,000 feet of lumber and 80,000 feet of lath per day. By the middle part of the 1870s, the Union company found itself hauling an increasing amount of lumber traffic out onto the wharf for trans-loading onto specially designed shallow-drafted schooners in the Humboldt to San Francisco lumber trade.

After two decades of a relatively static existence, the year 1875 saw many changes happen on the road. For starters, in June 1875 a new company, the Union Plank Walk and Railroad Company, assumed operations of the property. The railroad placed into service a small four wheeled steam locomotive, consisting of an upright boiler providing steam to a pair of oscillating cylinders powering the machine through a system of gears. The locomotive, named *Black Diamond*, could pull six lumber cars loaded with 2,500 board feet of lumber each on level track. After a few years of service, the railroad retrofitted the locomotive with a horizontal boiler. The locomotive and heavier lumber traffic took its toll on the track, forcing the railroad to add an iron strap to the top of the wooden timbers.

The year 1875 also saw the railroad start expanding its horizons. Two local lumbermen, Noah Falk and Isaac Minor, formed a partnership to lease and harvest redwood from 490 acres lying immediately northeast of Arcata. Minor and Falk set out to build two sawmills to saw this timber, the Jolly Giant mill located on the creek of the same name and the Dolly Varden mill another mile to the north. In 1875, the railroad commenced laying track, reaching the first mile to the Jolly Giant mill by the end of the year and the Dolly Varden mill the following year.

RAILS UP THE MAD RIVER

On June 15, 1878, local interests incorporated the Arcata Transportation Company to acquire and operate the Union Plank Walk and Railroad. Two years later, Isaac Minor built another sawmill on Warren Creek, and the Arcata Transportation Company dutifully extended its railroad three and a half miles up the south bank of the Mad River to reach the new sawmill. The railroad celebrated completion of the new extension with a special picnic and party held on the river near the new mill site, and the company operated special trains transporting people to and from the event. The ride back proved to be a memorable experience, as passenger rode on loose seats placed on the decks of the lumber flats, with no railings or other containment devices; the train also lacked brakes of any kind, resulting in a sometimes wild ride back down into Arcata.

The Arcata Transportation Company was destined to last but three years. Two local businessmen, Richard Fernald and G. W. Yocum, acquired all the company's stock in 1881, and on July 22nd, the men incorporated the Arcata & Mad River Railroad, with stated plans to operate the narrow gauge steam powered railroad line extending from the north shore of Humboldt Bay up the North Fork of the Mad River. The new owners invested money into the property; capital expenditures in the A & MR's first year included a new locomotive purchased from Porter to replace the *Black Diamond*, a new sternwheel steamship providing service from the Arcata wharf to Eureka and other points around Humboldt Bay, and replacing the wooden rails with 35-pound "T" rails.

 The A & MR had barely started its existence when Anton, Francis, and Joseph Korbel entered the picture with plans that would forever change the face of the company. The Korbel brothers emigrated from Bohemia to California in the 1860s, and quickly established their premier wineries in the vineyards of Sonoma County. The Korbel brother's search for lumber suitable to make wine vats ended in the vast redwood forests up the Mad River; in April 1883 the brothers incorporated the Humboldt Lumber Mill Company, which shortly commenced constructing a large mill at North Fork, a new town established on the river. At around the same time the brothers purchased the Arcata & Mad River Railroad and immediately continued or commenced work on extending the railroad five miles up the river to North Fork. This extension included three substantial wooden trestles, the largest of which crossed Warren Creek, plus a large multi-span bridge crossing the Mad River. The A & MR placed its road into service on January 18, 1884. Railroad construction did not stop, as the Humboldt Lumber Mill Company started building private logging railroads up both the North and South Forks of the Mad River. To keep up with the expanded operations, the Korbels purchased additional locomotives and invested heavily in improvements to the wharf and other parts of the physical plant.

The A & MR entered a period of relative prosperity that would last through the rest of the century. In 1885, the railroad handled 21 million board feet of lumber, 38 million shingles, 22 thousand fence posts, and sold around 24,000 passenger tickets. The railroad became popularly known as the "Annie and Mary", reportedly after Annie Carroll and Mary Buckley, bookkeepers at the North Fork and Arcata depots. Short branches built at Glendale in 1885 and Riverside in 1886 established rail service to other sawmills, and by 1893 the railroad hauled the combined output of five sawmills. The lumber company rechristened North Fork to Korbel in 1891, in honor of the family that by this time had become a dominant force in the region's economy. The worst wreck the railroad ever experienced occurred on September 13, 1896, when stringers on the Mad River bridge gave way under the weight of a passenger train bound for Korbel, sending one locomotive, a boxcar, and two passenger coaches crashing forty feet into the riverbed. Of the thirty three people on the train, seven died and twenty-three suffered various injuries.

THE NEW CENTURY

By the start of 1903 the Korbel brothers decided to retire from the lumber industry to focus on their winery. In February 1903, the owners of the Riverside Lumber Company and the Charles Nelson Steamship Company incorporated the Northern Redwood Lumber Company, which acquired both the Humboldt Lumber Mill Company and A & MR. Operations continued on largely as they had before the ownership change, though the new owner did invest in additional locomotives and equipment, including several Heisler-type gear driven steam locomotives for use primarily on the logging railroads.

The A & MR no longer had Arcata to itself by the time of the ownership change. In 1874, lumberman John Vance built his Humboldt and Mad River Railroad along the north bank of the Mad River, parallel to the A & MR's line on the south bank for several miles. By 1896, Vance's nephew John M. Vance controlled the various entities the elder Vance started, and in that year he incorporated the Eureka & Klamath River Railroad; this company constructed a new road from Samoa north up the peninsula, then across the Arcata Bottoms to and through Arcata before turning northeast to a crossing of the Mad River to a connection with the Humboldt & Mad River. This railroad crossed the A & MR twice at grade, once in Arcata and the second at Korblex, just downstream from E & KR's Mad River bridge. On October 30, 1901, the California & Northern Railroad completed its line from Eureka along the eastern shore of Humboldt Bay to Arcata, terminating at A & MR's Arcata depot; however, before it could begin operations the company lapsed into litigation with the competing Eureka & Klamath River, and it fell to a third company, the Eel River & Eureka, to lease the C & N line and commence operations. Finally, in

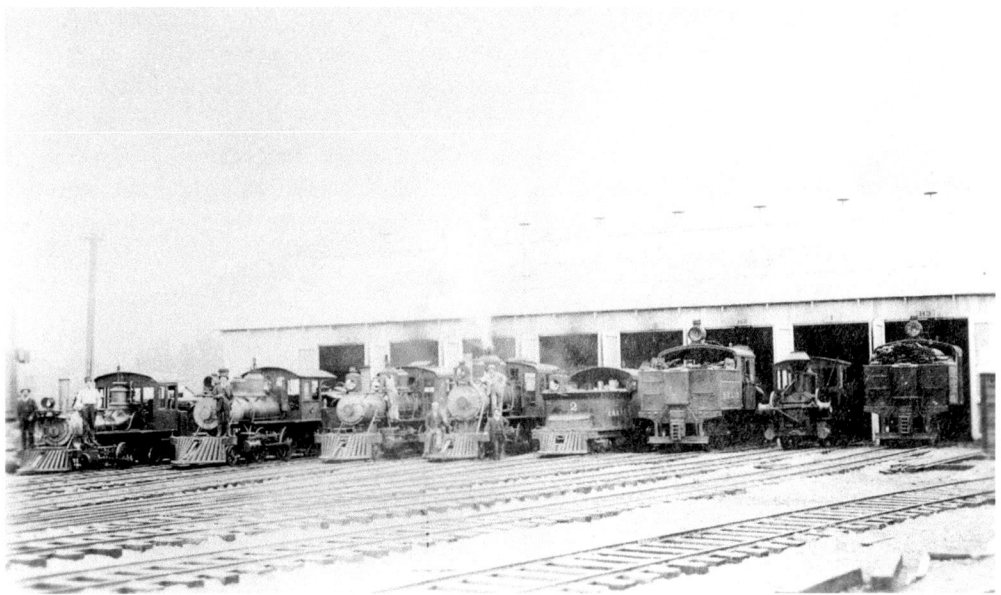

A&MR's Arcata engine house in 1914. From left to right are A & MR Nos. 3, 4, 5, 6, and 2, then Northern Redwood Lumber Heisler No. H2, "Gypsy" No. 1, and Heisler No. H3. Note each locomotive has its own designated stall. *Jeff Moore collection*

1904–1905 the Dolbeer & Carson Lumber Company built their Humboldt Northern Railroad north from the Samoa Peninsula, including a branch line built into Arcata from the west.

As the century progressed, the railroad world around the A & MR changed. Two giant railroads, the Atchison, Topeka & Santa Fe and Southern Pacific, each started purchasing railroads in their battle over which one would control California's north coast. By 1903, SP interests purchased the Eureka & Klamath River and leased it to the Oregon & Eureka. Then, in 1906, the AT & SF and SP jointly incorporated the Northwestern Pacific to consolidate their efforts, and by 1911 the new company owned the Eureka & Klamath River and California & Northern railroads. In 1914, the NWP completed its through line connecting the Humboldt Bay area with the rest of the nation's railroad network; however, despite the multiple times the A & MR crossed the NWP in Arcata, the small road chose not to establish an interchange with the connecting road, as the steamship line controlling the company preferred to continue delivering freight the A & MR handled to its ships docking on the wharf.

The A & MR's self-imposed isolation lasted for eleven years before the company finally gave into reality. In 1925, the A & MR rebuilt its line with heavier rail, and in the process added a third rail to the line from a new interchange established with the NWP at Korblex to Korbel so that standard gauge cars could be handled to and from the sawmills located along the railroad. Northern Redwood converted their logging railroads and rebuilt their four Heislers to standard gauge at the same time. In 1927, the California Barrel Company built a logging railroad off Northern Redwood's lines up the North Fork of the Mad River, shipping their logs over a NRL-A & MR-NWP routing to their sawmill in Arcata. Most of the lumber traffic the A & MR handled shifted to all-rail routings, resulting in a steep decline in the use of the wharf. Then the Great Depression hit; passenger service ended on June 6, 1931, and in 1933

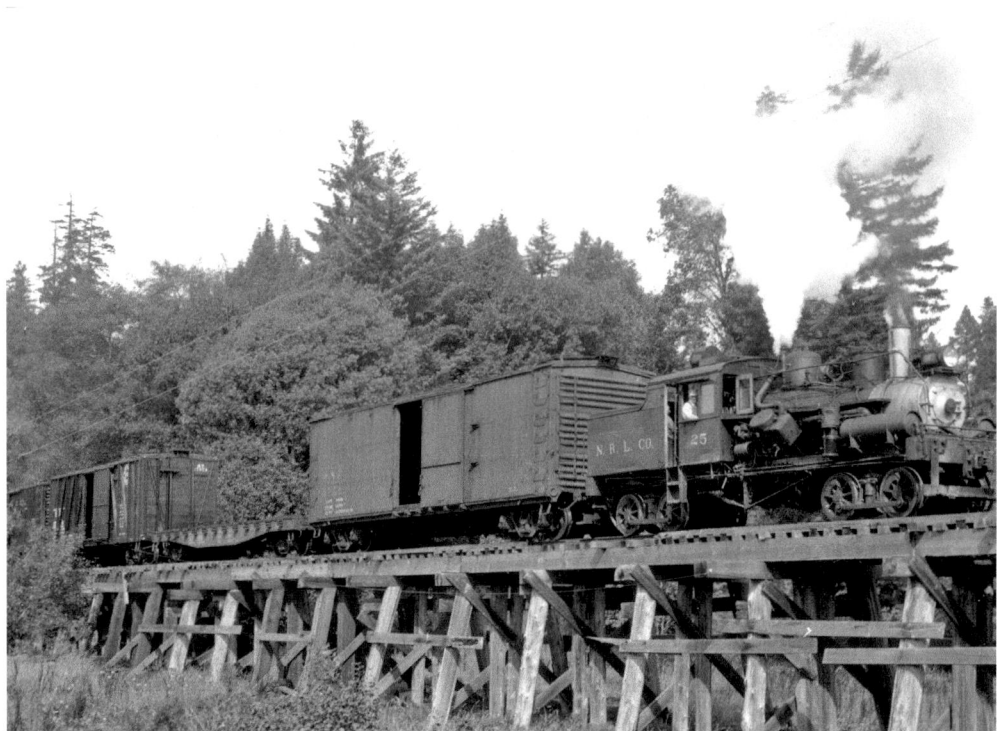

Northern Redwood No. 25 on a trestle near Glendale on 10/12/1948. *Pennington photograph, Tom Moungovan collection.*

the poor economic conditions caused Northern Redwood to close the Korbel mill. The A & MR suspended operations as the mill closed.

POST WAR PROSPERITY

The Korbel mill and the railroad remained shuttered for eight years. During that time period the lumber company kept a small number of employees active maintaining and servicing mill equipment, and one of the Heislers was kept hot so as to provide steam for the fire pumps. Once a month one of the other Heislers would make a run to Korblex to take out a single empty oil car and bring a loaded car back. In 1941, the Northern Redwood Lumber Company reorganized and applied for Reconstruction Finance Corporation loans. The first loan, received in 1942, enabled the company to rehabilitate the sawmill and railroad; however, when work began on the A & MR, part of it included removing all 12.9 miles of the narrow gauge. The remaining narrow gauge locomotives were scrapped and most of the rolling stock burned. The A & MR retreated to the form it would hold for the rest of its days, stretching 7.5 miles from Korblex to Korbel.

The revitalized mill and railroad prospered through the war years, then even more so as the post-war era dawned. The entire region experienced a sawmill building boom starting in the 1940s, and by the early 1950s the A & MR served fifteen sawmills. Traffic increased with each new spur the railroad built, and the railroad reached its high water traffic mark in 1953, when it hauled record amounts of carloads—6,917 lumber, 171 logs, and 153 woodchips. The single busiest day the railroad ever had came one day in December 1953 when the A & MR interchanged fifty lumber loads to the NWP at Korblex. In 1950, both the A & MR and Northern Redwood railroads tried out Baldwin's DS-4-4-750 and General Electric's 70-ton diesel electric demonstrators, but the first threat to steam power would not come until 1953, when the A & MR acquired the first of several General Electric 44-ton switchers purchased off the used market.

In April 1956, the Simpson Redwood Company purchased the Northern Redwood and A & MR companies. Simpson got its start in the woods around Shelton, Washington, and first entered the Redwood region in 1948, when it purchased a sawmill and 23,000 acres of associated timberlands at Klamath, California. Simpson shortly closed and scrapped out the logging railroads above Korbel. The end of the logging railroad, coupled with a second GE 44-ton and a Whitcomb 65-ton switcher purchased off the used market, finally ended the use of steam locomotives. The railroad continued to prosper, and by the middle 1960s the volume of business the company handled made it one of the highest paying railroad properties per mile in the United States. The company also handled a few special excursions, including one in 1954 to mark the 100th anniversary of the road and a another one for a railfan group in 1956.

THE FINAL DECADES

The A & MR remained a busy railroad throughout the 1960s and 1970s. The railroad weathered the multiple shutdowns of the NWP, including the recovery from the 1955 floods, the three-month rebuild of the 1964 floods, and other periodic service interruptions such as an engineer's strike that closed the NWP for twenty-five days in 1954. During these shutdowns, the A & MR generally kept its employees busy on the incessant maintenance and strengthening work the large trestles required.

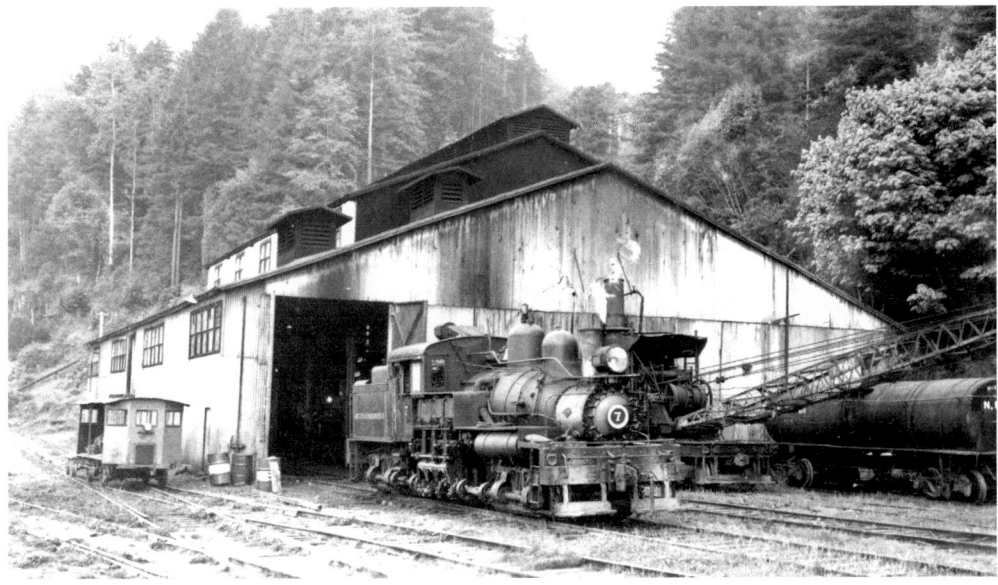

No. 7 shares track space at Korbel with a speeder, crane, and tank car. *John A. Taubeneck*

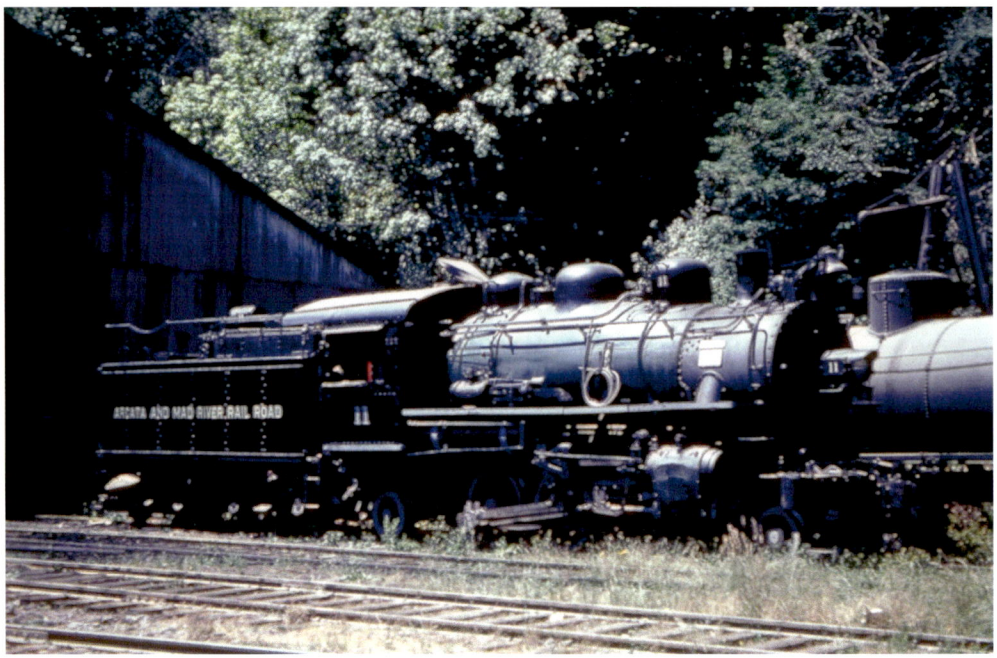

No. 11 outside the Korbel engine house. *Tom Moungovan collection*

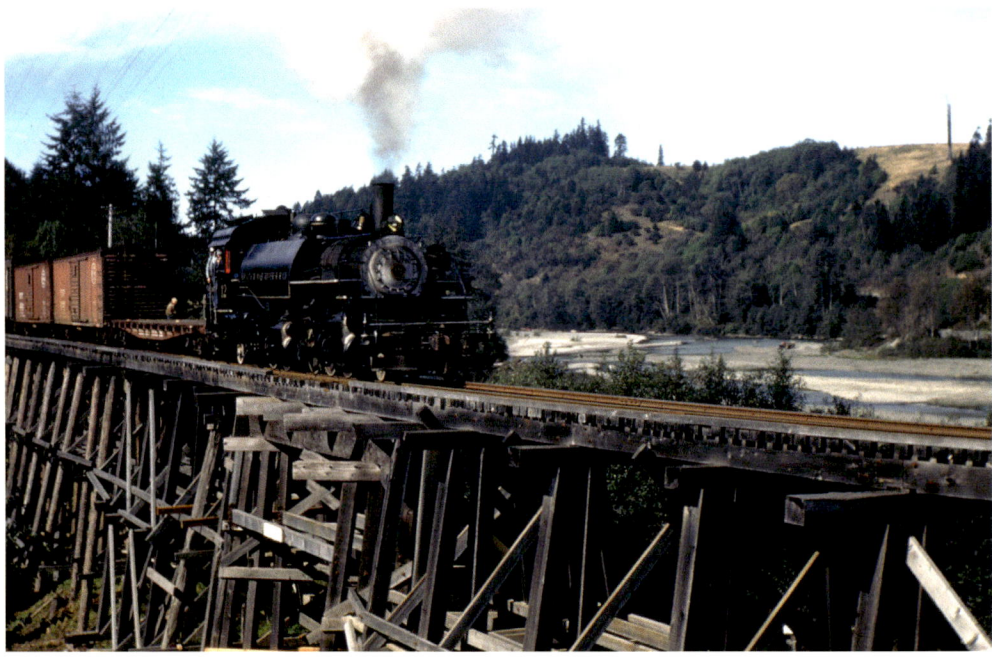

No. 12 crossing the Warren Creek trestle with empties bound for Korbel. *Bob Hanft photograph, Tom Moungovan collection*

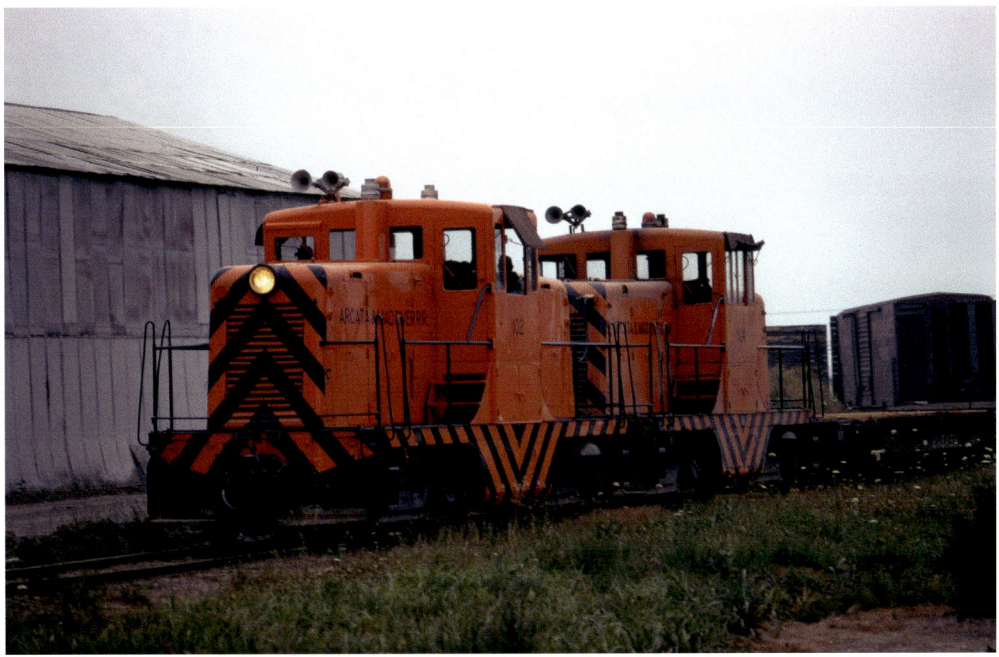

Nos. 102 and 104 lead a string of empty cars bound for Korbel on 8/1/1973. *Mel Lawrence photo, Dave Stanley collection*

In 1968, the railroad negotiated with the City of Arcata for the return to the road of its Shay locomotive #7, which the company had donated to the city in 1956. The company also purchased four 60-foot "Harriman" style passenger coaches from the Southern Pacific. The Korbel shops restored the #7 to operation, naming it the *Spanking Fury* in the process, and applied a bright red paint scheme to the four coaches. In May 1969, the railroad launched an excursion train based out of the Blue Lake depot traversing almost the entire length of the railroad. The revived passenger operations lasted for three seasons before low ridership caused the railroad to end the program. The railroad sold the four coaches to the Heber Valley Railroad in Utah and placed the #7 in storage in Korbel, where it remained until the company gave it back to the City of Arcata in 1979.

Traffic started to slack off as smaller mills started closing and as a greater percentage of the redwood industry's output went to market by truck. The A & MR still served twelve shippers at the beginning of the 1970s; by the end of the decade the number had declined to six, and annual carloadings slipped to 4,000 per year. The railroad cashed in on the incentive *per diem* boxcar boom, leasing 300 bright red boxcars from Itel Rail and a smaller number of all-door boxcars; all of these cars also carried Simpson lettering in addition to the A & MR markings.

The beginning of the end for the A & MR came in 1978, when the Island Mountain tunnel fire closed the NWP—and the A & MR—for thirteen months. When the railroads reopened, only two shippers—Simpson's Korbel mill and Blue Lake Forest Products in Glendale—remained active on the A & MR. In an average week, the railroad operated three trains delivering thirty loads to the Korblex interchange. The end arrived with the wet winter of 1982/1983, which caused numerous slides and slipouts on the NWP south of Eureka, closing the railroad many times between January and June. The NWP reopened the line on June 9, 1983, triggering the A

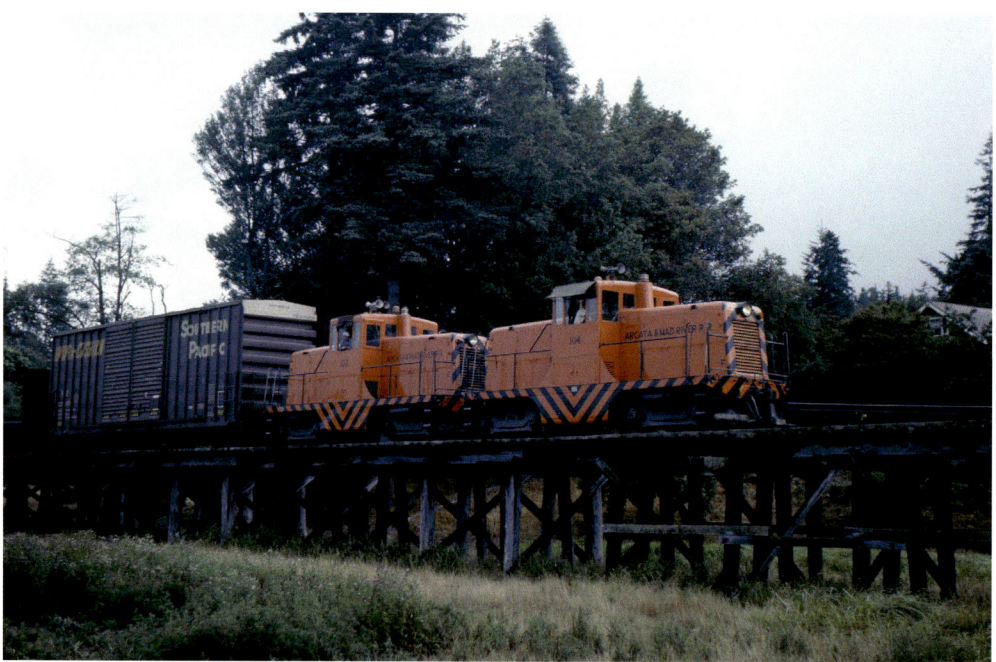

Korbel-bound Nos. 104 and 102 near Glendale. *C. G. Heimerdinger Jr.*

& MR to reopen; however, on July 18, 1983, the NWP instituted a $1,200 per carload surcharge on all traffic originating or terminating on their railroad north of Willits. The surcharge had the desired effect of driving away all remaining business, including both of A & MR's remaining shippers, and with no traffic to handle the venerable "Annie & Mary" closed up shop. Simpson started trucking much of their lumber from Korbel to a new reload they established on the McCloud River Railroad in McCloud, California (Chapter 9).

On November 1, 1984, the new Eureka Southern Railroad (Chapter 6) purchased and reopened the NWP north of Willits. However, this did not result in a resurrection of the A & MR, as Simpson deemed it cheaper to truck their lumber to a reload in Arcata served directly by the Eureka Southern. Simpson received authority to abandon the A & MR on June 13, 1985. However, Simpson made no immediate moves to salvage the railroad, and the company's equipment remained stored at Korbel.

POSTSCRIPT

The Eureka Southern purchased the A & MR properties from Simpson in September 1988 and reopened the railroad shortly afterwards; that and subsequent histories of California's first railroad are covered in the Eureka Southern chapter of this book. As this is being written, the A & MR has been reduced to an empty roadbed, and though the North Coast Railroad Authority continues to own the right-of-way it appears there is little likelihood of any future return to an active status. Blue Lake Forest Products closed in 2002, and Simpson spinoff California Redwood closed the Korbel mill in early 2015. There have been lengthy discussions

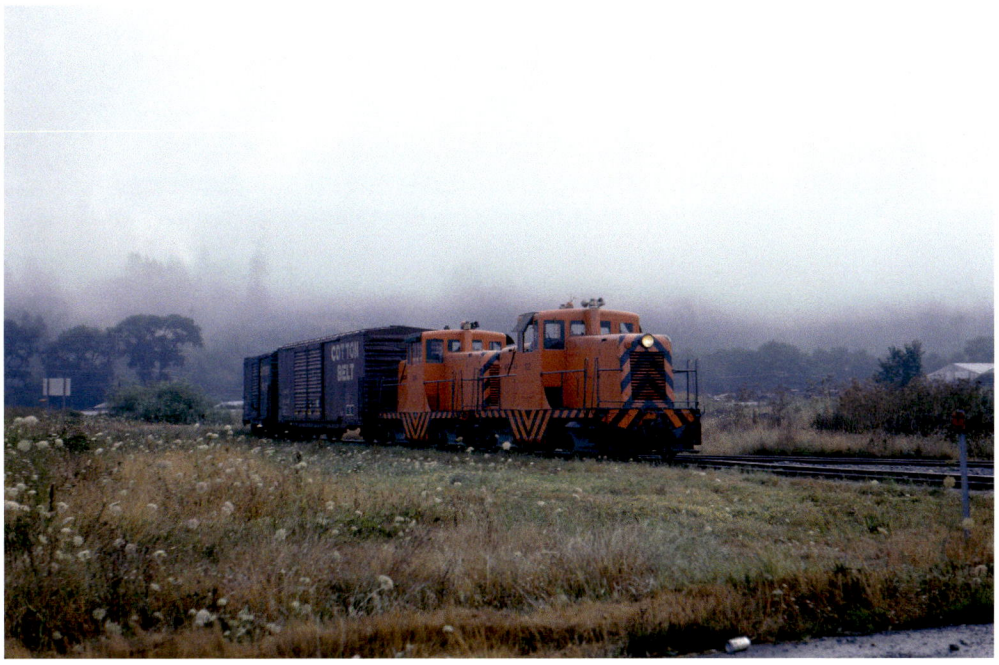

An A & MR freight switching the NWP interchange at Korblex. *C. G. Heimerdinger Jr.*

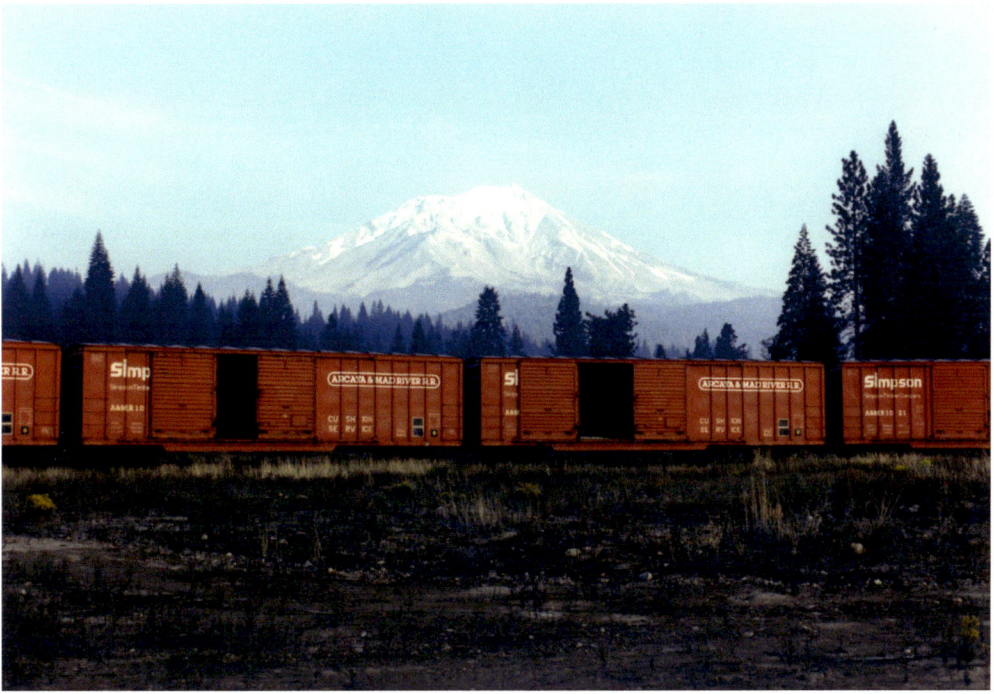

Former A & MR incentive *per diem* boxcars in McCloud, California. *Pat Driscoll photograph, Jeff Moore collection.*

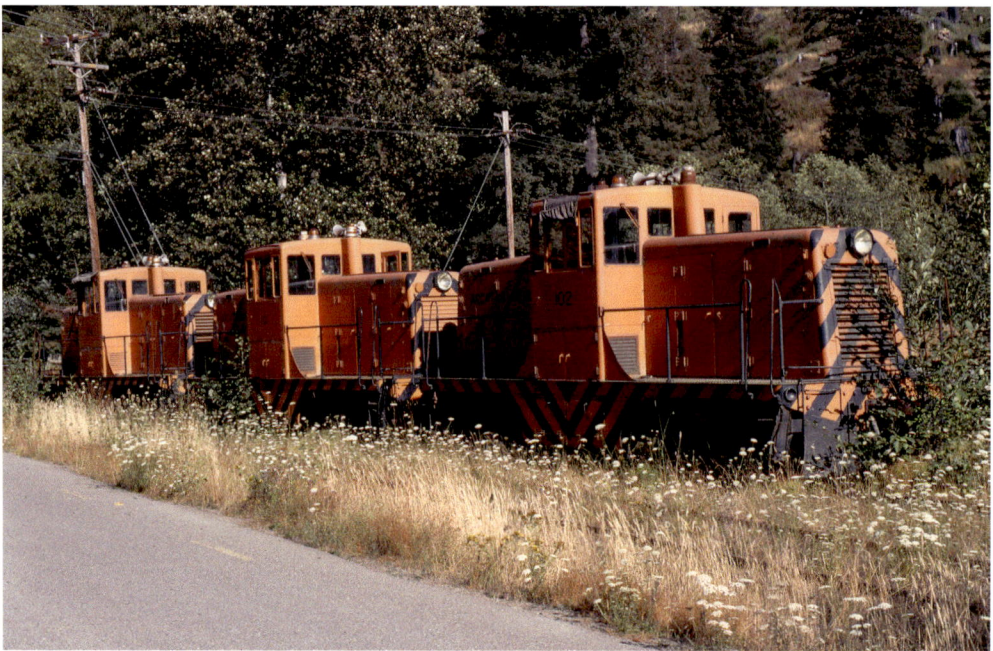

A & MR's three 44-tonners in storage at Korbel after the railroad closed. *Lee F. Hower*

of converting the grade to a trail, though neighbors have encroached upon the right-of-way in places and many of them have expressed opposition to establishing such a trail. Two significant A & MR buildings still stand, the depot in Blue Lake now housing a museum and the narrow gauge engine house in downtown Arcata, currently housing a medical marijuana cooperative. An old Burro crane is rotting away in Shively, California, not far south of Eureka, and four locomotives and a few railcars are in various museum collections or otherwise on display. The railroad does live on in several ways: the City of Arcata named its municipal bus system the Arcata & Mad River Transit System, and every July the City of Blue Lake hosts an annual "Annie and Mary Days" community event.

LOCOMOTIVE ROSTER

Narrow Gauge

1—0-4-0T geared steam. Named *Black Diamond*. Built 1875, either by Eureka Iron Works or by local mechanics. Retired and scrapped *circa* 1881.

2—Porter 0-4-0T, c/n 469, Built 1881. Named *Arcata*. Renumbered #1 1903. Retired and scrapped 1932.

3—Golden State & Miners 0-4-4T, Built 1882. Named *North Fork*. Rebuilt to 0-4-2T. Re-numbered #2 1903. Retired and scrapped 1932.

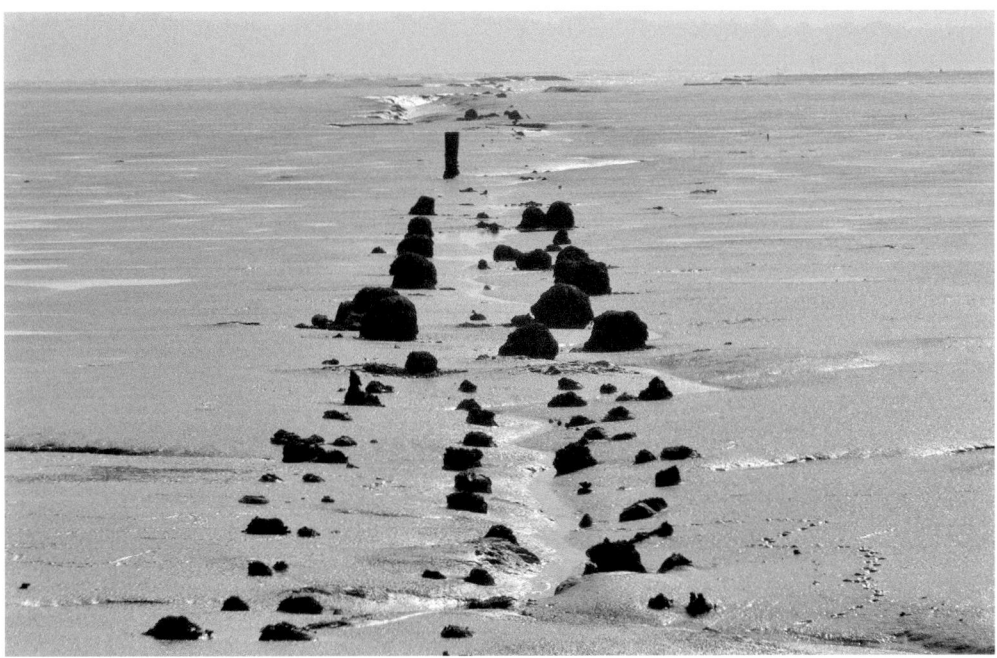

Piling stubs are all that remain of A & MR's Arcata wharf. *Jeff Moore*

4—Golden State & Miners 0-4-2T, Built 1887. Named *Eureka*. Renumbered #3 1903. Retired and scrapped 1932.

5—Baldwin 2-4-0, c/n 9249, Built 1888. Named *Blue Lake*. Renumbered #4 1903. Retired and scrapped 1941.

6:1—Baldwin 2-4-0, c/n 18564, Built 1901. Named *Hoopa*. Renumbered #5 1903. Retired and scrapped 1942.

6:2—Baldwin 2-4-2, c/n 27073, Built 1905. Named *Northern*. Retired and scrapped 1942. *Standard Gauge*

7—Lima 2-truck Shay, c/n 3014, Built 1918. Originally Lamson Lumber Company #1, Darrington, Washington; to A & MR 8/1942. Retired 1957 and donated to City of Arcata. Reacquired 1968 and restored to service for passenger operations 1969-1971, then retired again; Re-conveyed to City of Arcata in 1979 and again placed on display; subsequently conveyed to Northern Counties Logging Interpretive Association (now Timber Heritage Association) and stored with their collection, first at Glendale, California, and now at the former Hammond Lumber Company roundhouse at Samoa, California.

11—Alco 2-6-2, c/n 66317, Built 1925. Originally McCloud River Railroad #23; to A & MR 7/1953. Retired and scrapped 1956.

12—Baldwin 2-6-6-2T, c/n 60870, Built 1929. Originally Hammond Lumber Company #6, Mill City, Oregon; to Hammond Redwood Company #12, Samoa, CA; to A & MR 7/1951; to Southwest Lumber Mills #12, Flagstaff, Arizona, 1956; Retired 1959 and placed on display.

101, **102**—General Electric 44-ton, c/n 30473 and 40464, Built 1950. Originally Pine Flat Dam Contractors #30473 and #30464; to A & MR 10/1953 and 2/1954. Retired 1984; to Eureka Southern 1988. #101 to MeadWestvaco Company, DeRidder, Louisiana, then donated 2000 to Timber Heritage Association and returned to Arcata in 2005; #102 to Sims Metals, Richmond, CA, and scrapped 2004.

103—Whitcomb 65-ton, c/n 60639, Built 1945. Originally U.S. Navy #65-00291; to Hyman–Michaels #7; to A & MR 3/1955; to Franko Railroad Contractors #103 1960.

104—General Electric 44-ton, c/n 18197, Built 1945. Originally New York, Ontario & Western #103; to Fernwood, Columbia & Gulf #D-3; to A & MR 2/1960. Retired 1984; to Eureka Southern 1988; to North Coast Railroad 1992; subsequently conveyed to Chris Baldo, Willits, California; to Roots of Motive Power, Willits, CA.

Northern Redwood Lumber Company owned four 2-truck Heisler type geared steam locomotives that periodically saw service on the A & MR, all purchased new: **2**—c/n 1113, Built 1906; **3**- c/n 1193, Built 1910; **4**—c/n 1447, Built 1921; and **25**—c/n 1471, Built 1922. In 1921 NRLCo renumbered the first three 22, 23, and 24. All four converted from narrow to standard gauge in 1925. Locomotive retired and scrapped in 1951, 1945, 1943, and 1952 respectively. NRLCo had several other locomotives used on its private logging railroad, some of which may have seen service on the A & MR.

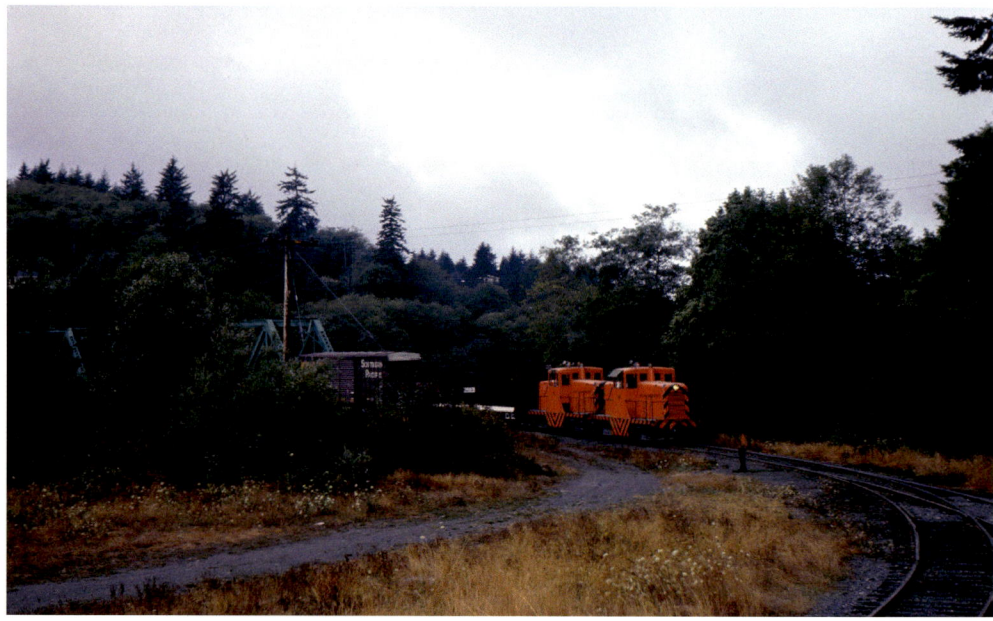

Nos. 104 and 102 rolling off the Mad River Bridge and are entering Glendale. *C. G. Heimerdinger Jr.*

4

CALIFORNIA WESTERN

BACKGROUND

By 1852, the whine of primitive sawmills could be heard up and down the California coast. The appearance of these mills upset the local natives, who started raiding some of them and otherwise harassing the pioneering European settlements. In 1856, the U.S. Government created the 25,000 acre Mendocino Indian Reservation, and on June 11, 1857, the U.S. Army established a military outpost a mile-and-a-half north of the mouth of the Noyo River to administer the reservation. The Army concurred with post founder Lt. H. G. Gibson to name the post Fort Bragg in honor of Captain Braxton Bragg, later a general with the Confederate army during the Civil War. The fort remained active until October 1864, when the military abandoned the post. Two years later the government abolished the Mendocino Indian Reservation, moved its inhabitants to the Round Valley Indian Reservation, and opened the lands to settlement.

The containment and then forced removal of the natives opened the door for the redwood lumber industry. The small Noyo Bay at the mouth of the river provided a rare semi-protected harbor where ships could be loaded, and the earliest sawmills in the immediate area were concentrated along the banks of the Noyo River. Floods and the native backlash outline above claimed the earliest mills. In 1858, one A. W. MacPherson erected another mill cutting up to 35,000 feet a day. Sometime later Henry Weatherby joined MacPherson, and together the pair boosted the mill's daily output to 40,000 board feet. Nine miles to the north, the Ten Mile River emptied into the Pacific, and by 1875 a sawmill built by the Field Brothers commenced operations up that river; however, the mill burned in 1877, after which the Stewart & Hunter Lumber Company, incorporated by Calvin Stewart and Jamed Hunter, purchased the site and built a new mill. Ten Mile River did not have a bay, and Stewart & Hunter built a small doghole port called Newport on the coastline just north of the river's mouth.

EARLY RAILROAD DEVELOPMENT

In 1881, MacPherson and Weatherby incorporated the Noyo & Pudding Creek Railroad, which subsequently invested $30,000 building a two mile long railroad from Noyo towards Pudding Creek. The same year, Charles Russell Johnson arrived in California and, upon hearing tales of the redwoods, travelled north in 1882. Johnson quickly fell in with Stewart & Hunter and, using

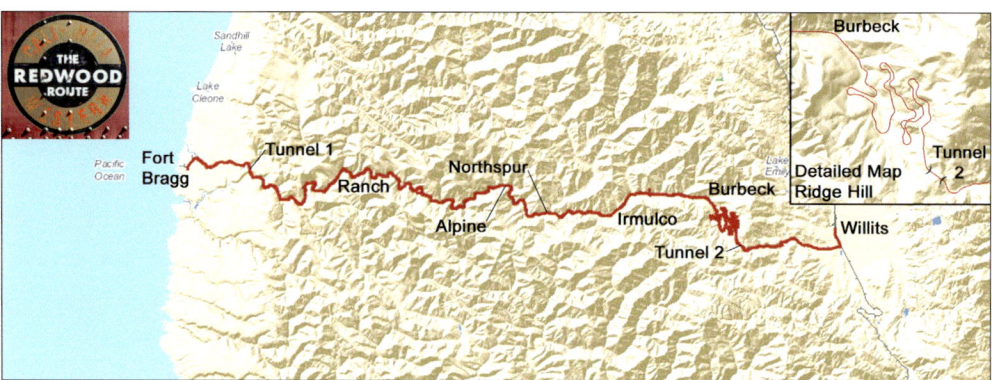

money fronted by his father, bought into the company, making it Stewart, Hunter & Johnson in the process. Johnson implemented many innovations in the mill, including starting a night shift. However, Johnson found his plans frustrated by the small size of the mill and the poor port facilities at Newport.

Johnson quickly settled on the old Fort Bragg grounds as being ideal for his expansive plans, and in 1884 he launched the Fort Bragg Redwood Company, formally incorporating the company on July 7th of the following year. The Fort Bragg Redwood Company immediately made two large purchases, the first to acquire the Stewart, Hunter & Johnson company, and the second consisting of most of MacPherson & Weatherby's lands around Fort Bragg and up both Pudding Creek and the Noyo River, together with the Noyo & Pudding Creek Railroad. Johnson promptly renamed the railroad the Fort Bragg Railroad and started extending it up Pudding Creek into the timber. Meanwhile, the Fort Bragg Redwood Company built a wharf into Soldier Harbor to facilitate delivering sawmill machinery. Construction progressed quickly, and the sawmill entered operation on November 16, 1885. The first mill lasted but three years, being destroyed by fire on April 18, 1888. Johnson secured enough financing to quickly rebuild the mill; in the midst of this, Johnson also had time to plat the Fort Bragg town site, and was elected as the first mayor upon the city's incorporation in 1889.

The Fort Bragg Railroad's principle function lay in bringing logs harvested from the Pudding Creek watershed down to the new mill. A converted San Francisco street car arrived in one of the first equipment purchases, allowing the railroad to start offering passenger service, including special weekend and holiday picnic excursions into the redwoods. The rails advanced up the creek as needed, with 6.6 miles in place by 1887. The railroad established its end of track at the station initially named Glenela and later Glen Blair, where the Pudding Creek Lumber Company had built a mill the previous year. The Pudding Creek company quickly renamed itself the Glen Blair Redwood Company, and it built its own logging railroad extending generally north from the mill site. The Glen Blair company added lumber traffic to the railroad's traffic mix, shipped from the mill down to the wharf.

TUNNELING TO THE NOYO

The Fort Bragg Redwood Company exhausted its available timber in the Pudding Creek watershed by 1891. The company had extensive timberlands up the Noyo River, but quickly determined an expensive tunnel would be required to access them. To raise capital, Johnson interested another company with holdings along the river, C. L. White and W. P. Plummer, to join with him, and together they incorporated the Union Lumber Company on August 17, 1891. The new company acquired the holdings of all previous companies and had sufficient resources to punch a 1,129-foot tunnel through the watershed divide. To dig the tunnel, Johnson eventually had to bring in a gang of experienced Chinese laborers, causing a certain amount of civil unrest amongst the local Europeans. Johnson had to enlist the services of the local Sheriff "Doc" Standley to protect the gangs, who completed the bore in 1893.

Logging and railroad building began anew once the rails entered the Noyo River watershed. The railroad advanced slowly up the Noyo River, reaching Little North Fork in 1898 and Alpine, 18.1 miles from Fort Bragg, in 1904. The railroad gained another lumber shipper, the Alpine Lumber Company, who started shipping lumber down to the wharf. Alpine also lay not far from Sherwood, itself at the end of the California Northwestern Railway main line running northwest from Willits, and the Fort Bragg Railroad commenced offering passenger and express service from Fort Bragg to Alpine, with a stage line bridging the gap between Alpine and Sherwood.

Johnson considered his transportation holdings as the 1900s dawned. On June 24, 1901, he incorporated the National Steamship Company to own and operate a small fleet of steam schooners providing scheduled lumber and passenger service between Fort Bragg and San Francisco. Four years later, on June 30, 1905, the Union Lumber Company incorporated the California Western Railroad & Navigation Company, which formally replaced the Fort Bragg Railroad the following day. Among the Articles of Incorporation were provisions authorizing the road to construct a railroad "*from the eastern terminus of Alpine, up the Noyo River along the most practicable route to a point in or near the City of Willits.*" However, two events immediately set these plans back. The great San Francisco earthquake on April 18, 1906, wrecked the Fort Bragg mill and much of the town, and then a major flood event the following winter severely damaged the railroad, closing it for three months. However, rebuilding San Francisco created a huge demand for lumber, giving the Union company ample resources to repair the damage and continue building east.

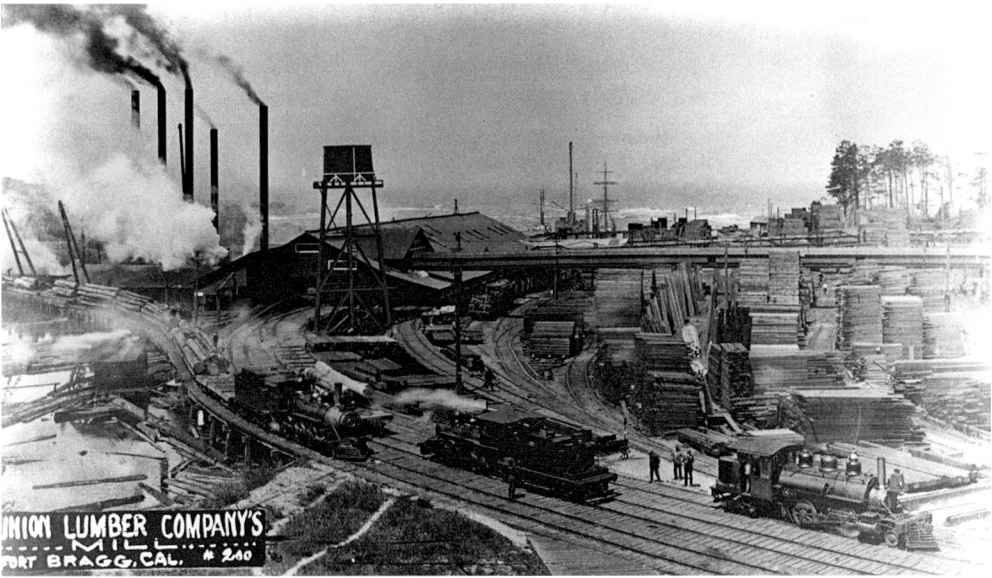

Three early CWR locomotives gathered at the Fort Bragg mill. *Tom Moungovan collection.*

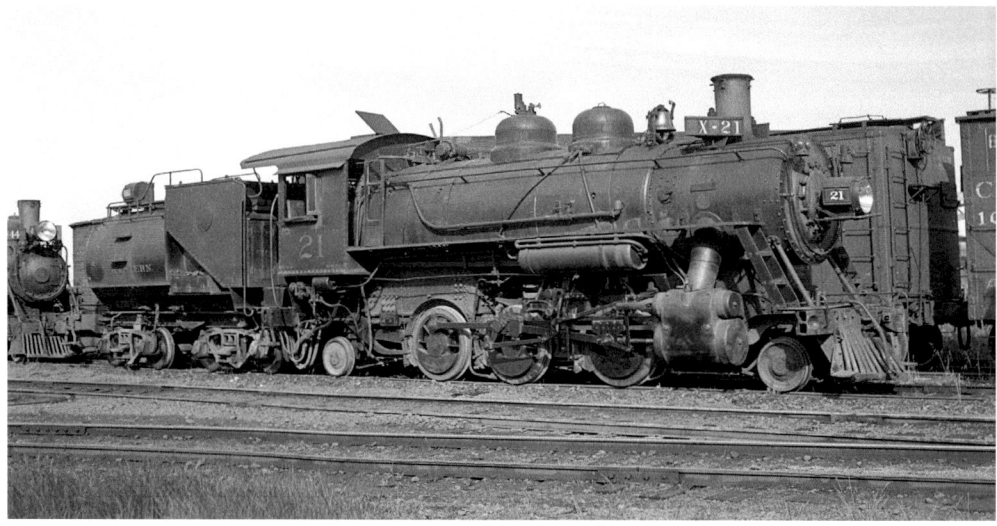

No. 21, one of three nearly identical Baldwin-built Prairie-type locomotives. *Don Hansen collection*

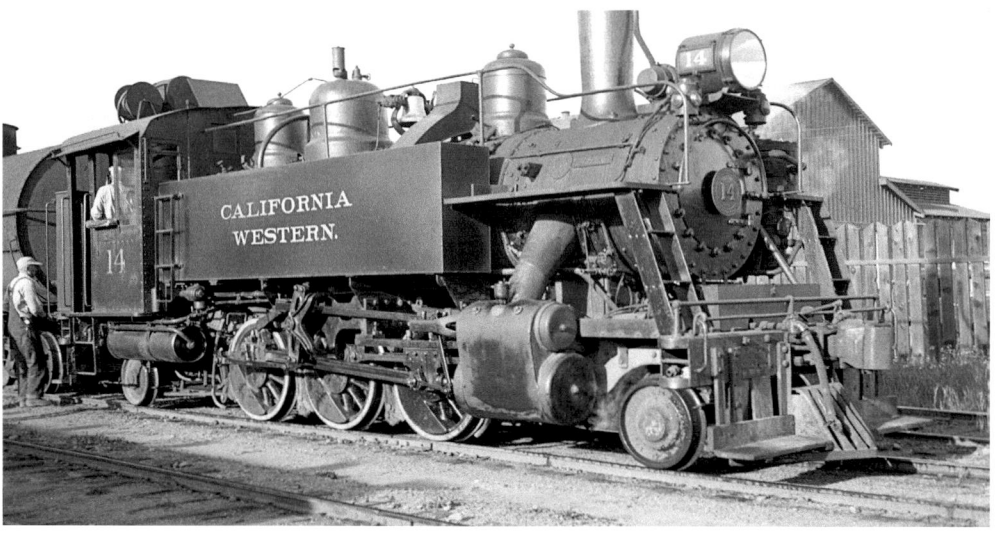

No. 14 switching at Fort Bragg. *Don Hansen collection*

THROUGH RAILROAD TO WILLITS

Work on connecting the railroad from Alpine to the Northwestern Pacific—successor to the California Northwestern—at Willits began in earnest after the earthquake and storm damage had been repaired. By 1908 the California Western reached Irmulco at Milepost 23.9, location of a sawmill operated by Irvine & Muir Lumber Company; another two years of construction brought the railhead to Burbeck, Milepost 27.8. Burbeck lay only five and a third miles as the crow flies from Willits, but a steep sided ridgeline separated the two places. Construction on a railroad line bridging the gap commenced in 1910; in addition to its own forces working

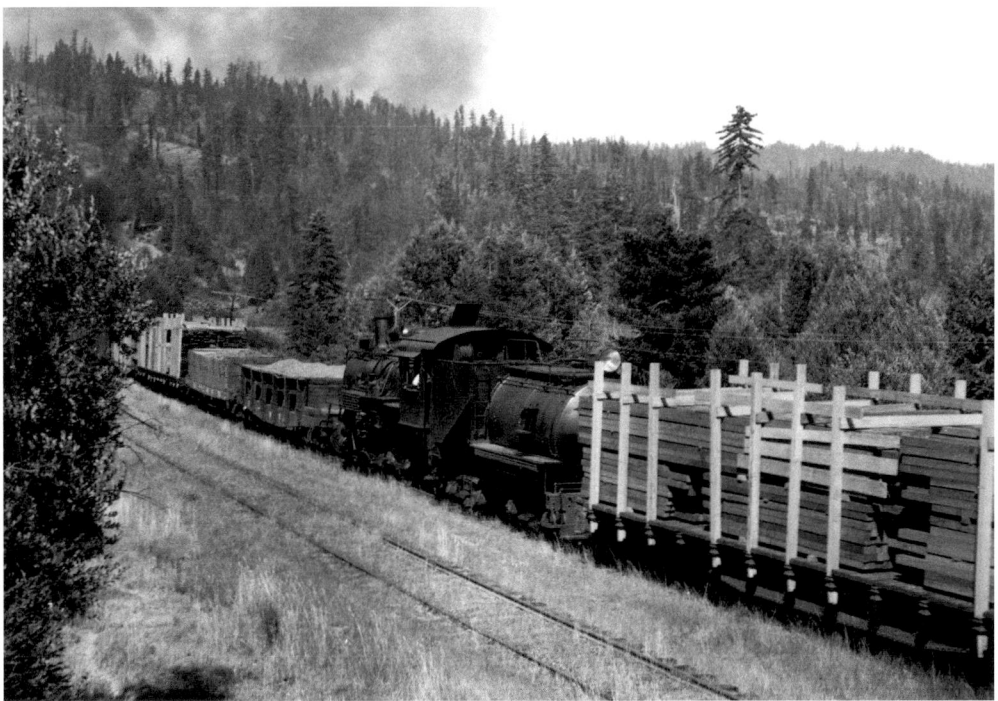

One of the Prairies cut into the middle of a freight bound for Willits. *Tom Moungovan collection*

uphill from Burbeck, the CWR & N rented Northwestern Pacific crews and equipment to start building the line up the east side from Willits. The railroad determined to not have a ruling grade over 3 percent, and to achieve that the line up the west face looped back on itself six times while climbing up the mountain. In order to minimize grades the railroad determined a 790-foot tunnel—designated #2—would be needed to pierce the top of the ridge, and in April 1911 the P. Nelson & Company of San Francisco started digging the bore, working in from each end. The two crews met on November 4, 1911, and quickly thereafter completed the bore. The railroad built 12.2 miles of track connecting Burbeck and Willits. By the end of the month the CWR & N had a completed railroad running forty miles between Fort Bragg and Willits, crossing 115 trestles in the process.

Finishing the outside connection brought a strong sense of relief, hope, and optimism to the people along the Mendocino Coast. For decades the only way into or out of the country was on the shallow drafted lumber schooners on rough seas or by stage over the often uncertain trails over the mountains to the east. On December 19, 1911, the first through passenger train traveled from Fort Bragg to Willits, where a brass band led almost the entire population of Willits in welcoming the first train from the coast. Issues with settling the roadbed, more flood damage, and the need to repair arson-caused fire damage to Tunnel #2 prevented the CWR & N from initiating regular passenger service until August 1, 1912. In 1916, the CWR & N and NWP completed their joint passenger depot in Willits, with the design and redwood lumber principally provided by C. R. Johnson.

On May 22, 1921, the CWR & N and NWP jointly launched through Pullman sleeping car service between Fort Bragg and Sausalito; the California Western, for its part, put on a special night passenger train for the movement in addition to the day passenger train the company already operated. In 1925, the railroad purchased from the Mack Moto Car Company a rail bus to replace the day passenger train; locals along the line promptly dubbed the car with the "Skunk" nickname, reportedly because one could smell the gasoline fumes the car produced before the car itself could be seen. The Pullman sleeper lasted until 1929, when its service was cut back to Willits.

Over on the freight side, the CRW & N settled down to a routine of handling outbound lumber from various sawmills owned by the Union Lumber Company and other concerns to Willits, along with fuel oil, general merchandise, and any other freight offered to it. Westbound log traffic complemented the outbound lumber as the Union Lumber Company continued harvesting its holdings up the Noyo River. In 1916, the Union Lumber Company commenced constructing its Ten Mile Branch logging railroad, extending from Fort Bragg northward along the coast line to the Ten Mile River, where the line turned east into vast holdings the company had in that watershed. At places the line ran right along the top of the beach. Union Lumber operated this line with CWR & N locomotives. Between 1919 and 1926 the Northwestern Pacific operated its own log trains over the eastern part of the CWR & N, from Irmulco to Willits.

The Depression hit the companies hard, though Union Lumber was able to keep the Fort Bragg mill in continuous operation by lowering production. The company also had acquired several other mills along the coast through the years, and closed most of them during the tough times. Passenger service continued to dwindle; in 1930, the Sausalito-Willits Pullman service ended, prompting the CWR & N to consolidate its night passenger and freight trains into a single mixed train. A second rail bus arrived on the property in 1934, complementing the original rail bus in the day service. The night mixed train lasted until 1937, when the railroad dropped the passenger service and operated the train only for freight. Dwindling lumber shipments also affected Union Lumber's shipping line, with its last voyage occurring in 1939.

As the end of the Depression approached, the Union Lumber and CWR & N companies marked a significant passing. Charles R. Johnson retired from the operations in 1939, after a career spanning fifty-seven years. The leadership torch passed to Otis R. Johnson, his son. C. R. Johnson enjoyed his retirement for less than a year, as he passed away at the age of 81 in February 1940.

WAR AND MODERNIZATION

The onset of the Second World War pushed lumber production to new heights, boosting traffic over the railroad. A third rail bus arrived in 1941 to help with the passenger runs. Freight trains continued operating at night; weight concerns did not allow more than one locomotive at a time on most of the bridges, and the railroad would get around this by dispatching two freights ten minutes apart eastbound out of Fort Bragg, each consisting of a locomotive, around ten lumber loads, and a caboose. At Northspur, the trains would be assembled into one, which would head east. Somewhere above Shake City the train would be cut in two, with each section taken up to Summit in turn.

In the years after the war the CWR & N invested heavily in replacing as many bridges as it could with either fills or minor re-alignments, reducing the number of trestles from 115 to 35. On December 19, 1947, the railroad changed its name, simplifying it to just the California Western Railroad. Freight traffic continued strong, as did passenger traffic as tourists started discovering the "Skunk" rail bus service. The railroad also provided the only transportation to many points along the line, and the company provided passenger and mail service to many of these outlying communities. Rail enthusiast groups also discovered the railroad, and from the 1930s through the 1960s the line hosted many special "Weekend in the Redwoods" excursions, usually consisting of chartered passenger trains operating as round trips from various points around the Bay Area to Fort Bragg.

The year 1949 would prove to be momentous in several ways. First, Union Lumber Company decided to replace its Ten Mile branch with off-highway trucks. The last log train rolled along the beach and into Fort Bragg on June 18, 1949. Then, at the end of the summer, the California Western accepted the delivery of two Baldwin 750-horsepower diesel electric switchers, which immediately assumed almost all duties on the railroad. By 1952, only one steam locomotive remained on the roster, and a third Baldwin switcher acquired in 1956 put it out to pasture as well. Freight traffic continued to climb, averaging 7,500 loads a year through the middle 1950s. In addition to the traffic from Fort Bragg, the railroad also switched a couple sawmills in Willits, along the first mile or so of its mainline in town.

RETURN TO TOURISM

Unlike almost all other small railroads, California Western's passenger business remained strong. Ridership on the "Skunk" rail buses averaged 24,000 a year through the 1950s. The growing popularity of this passenger service and the ever increasing tourism economy of the Mendocino Coast, together with the railroad management's awareness of the popularity of steam passenger excursions elsewhere in the west, prompted the company to start evaluating the potential of expanding its tourist railroad offerings. In the meantime, the railroad purchased and placed into operation a fourth rail bus in 1963 to help accommodate the ever growing demand; it arrived just in time, as in 1964 the original two rail buses met in a head-on collision, damaging the original rail bus beyond repair and forcing a complete rebuild of the other.

By 1964, the railroad firmly decided to enter the steam excursion business and launched a search for appropriate locomotives and equipment, resulting in the purchase of a steam locomotive from Medford, Oregon. The hunt for short steel passenger cars took longer, but the railroad eventually located four Erie-Lackawanna Railroad coaches. The railroad assembled the newly acquired equipment in Fort Bragg, performed needed repairs, and painted the train in a brilliant vermillion, cool red, gold, and black scheme designed by Water Lander and Associates, a San Francisco-based industrial design firm. On July 9, 1965, the "Super Skunk" made its debut run, making Fort Bragg-Willits round trips. The train had a capacity of 320 people and sold out nearly every trip.

The inauguration of the steam program shined an even greater spotlight on the road, and its tourist business continued to grow each year. The railroad purchased additional passenger coaches, cutting the tops off several to make open air cars. In 1969, the railroad purchased a second steam locomotive and brought to Fort Bragg for restoration, and by 1970 the Super Skunks had two steam locomotives available to pull the trains.

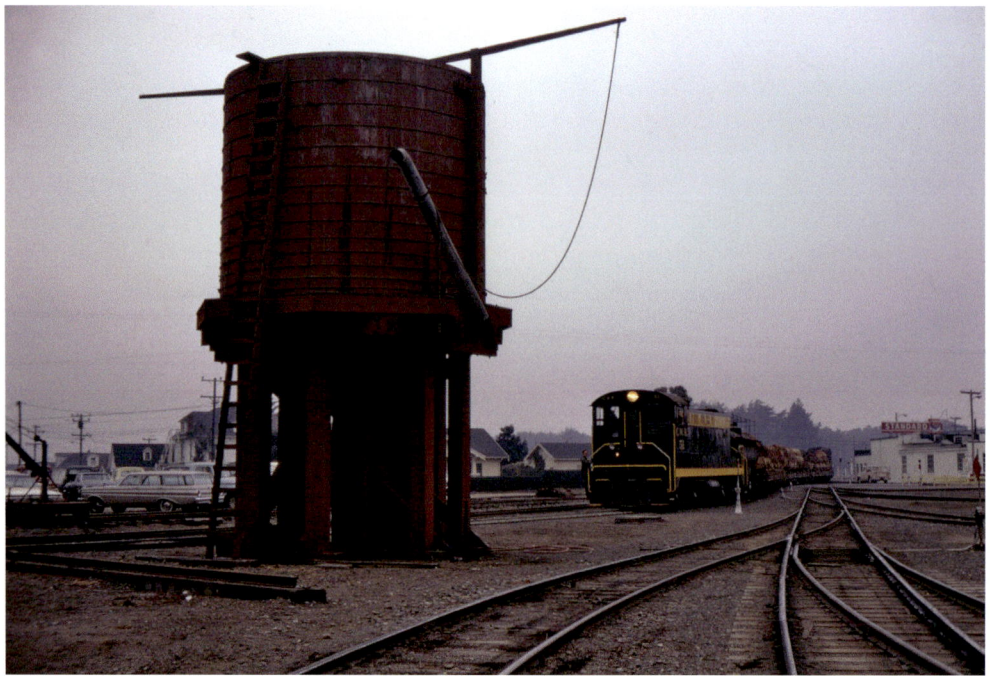

No. 51 leads a westbound train through the redwood region's famous "liquid sunshine" into Fort Bragg in September 1967. *Tom Moungovan*

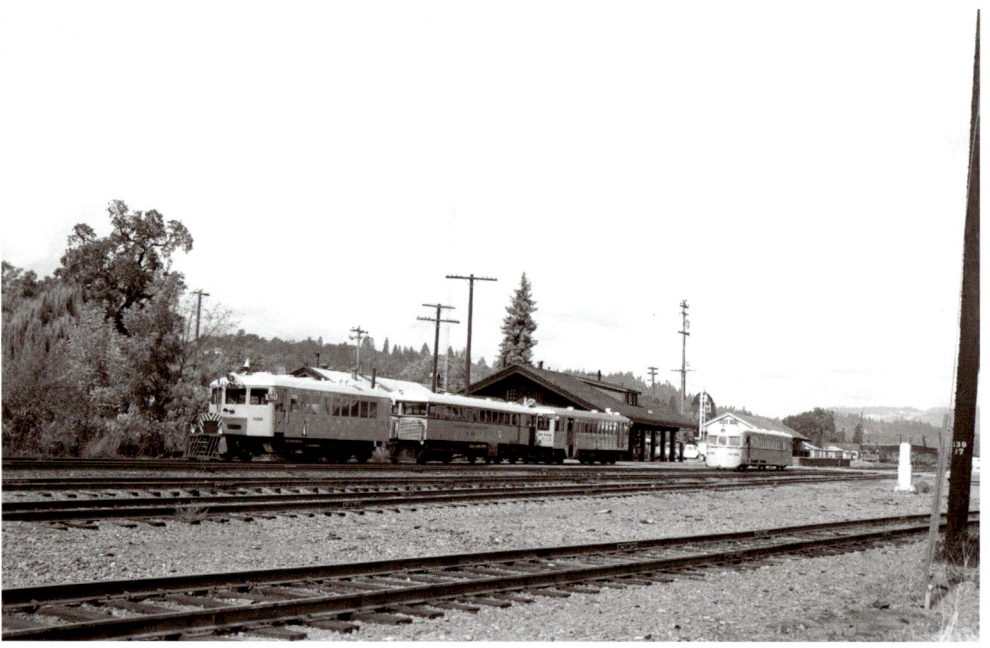

All four CWR railbuses in front of the Willits depot on 10/6/1963. *Don Hansen*

A WRECK AND OWNERSHIP CHANGES

Like the tourist business, freight traffic remained strong and continued increasing as the 1960s waned. By 1968, the nightly freight usually required all three diesels, and the railroad purchased a fourth Baldwin switcher to provide them with operational stability should one or more of the other locomotives be unavailable. Inbound propane and intraline log shipments from isolated logging operations and/or storm cleanups along the Noyo supplemented the outbound lumber traffic into the late 1970s.

The Union Lumber Company continued in existence until January 1969, when timber industry giant Boise Cascade purchased the company, including the California Western Railroad. The transaction initially changed very little, though it did mark the passage of one of the longest running companies in the California timber industry.

One of the most serious wrecks to ever occur on the railroad happened on the night of January 14, 1970. Three of the Baldwin diesels pulling twenty-seven lumber loads departed Fort Bragg around 5:00 p.m., arriving at Shake City in due time. The crew left half of its train there and proceeded to Summit with the other half, placing the loads in the siding. The conductor and brakeman started tying hand brakes on the loads while the engineer and fireman uncoupled the locomotives from the train and moved back onto the mainline, where they waited for the other half of the crew to finish their chore so they could start back towards Shake City. At just after 10:00 p.m., the locomotive brakes failed, and they started rolling on their own towards Willits. The engineer and fireman desperately tried to stop the locomotives but quickly determined it was a lost cause, at which point both jumped, receiving moderate injuries in the process. The two men walked down to Highway 20, where a passing motorist took them into the Willits hospital. Back on the mountain, the three locomotives raced downhill on their own for almost a mile, reaching an estimated sixty miles per hour before derailing. The three partially overturned into the side of the cut and then slid along for a considerable distance before coming to rest.

Repair work started immediately, with a shoe-fly around the wrecked diesels completed in nineteen hours. The railroad leased a locomotive from the Southern Pacific, using it to move cars between Summit and Willits while the lone remaining switcher worked round the clock delivering loaded cars to Summit and taking empties back to Fort Bragg. To remove the wrecked units, the California Western borrowed NWP's Eureka-based steam wrecking crane. The railroad deemed the three switchers damaged beyond repair and immediately searched for replacements, resulting in the lease and then purchase of two Baldwin road switcher locomotives, followed by another switcher.

Boise Cascade owned the Fort Bragg operations only until February 14, 1973, when they sold the sawmill and railroad to Georgia Pacific. G-P carried on operations, but freight traffic started a precipitous decline. Tourism started slowing down as well, but at a slower rate than the freight business. The railroad also suffered through other periodic calamities, such as the night of April 23, 1975 when the NWP inadvertently interchanged to the road Cotton Belt #61291, a hi-cube boxcar. In the darkness of night in the Willits yard the CWR crew failed to note the car's excess height and included it in the consist for the westbound trip. The boxcar made it through the newer Tunnel #2, but upon entering Tunnel #1 it started tearing through the bracing, causing a partial collapse of the bore. The train crew quickly brought the things to a halt, and once they determined the problem they uncoupled the train ahead of the boxcar and headed for Fort Bragg, leaving the boxcar and the rest of the train partially buried in the tunnel. Work on excavating the trapped cars extended until May 30th, and the offending boxcar

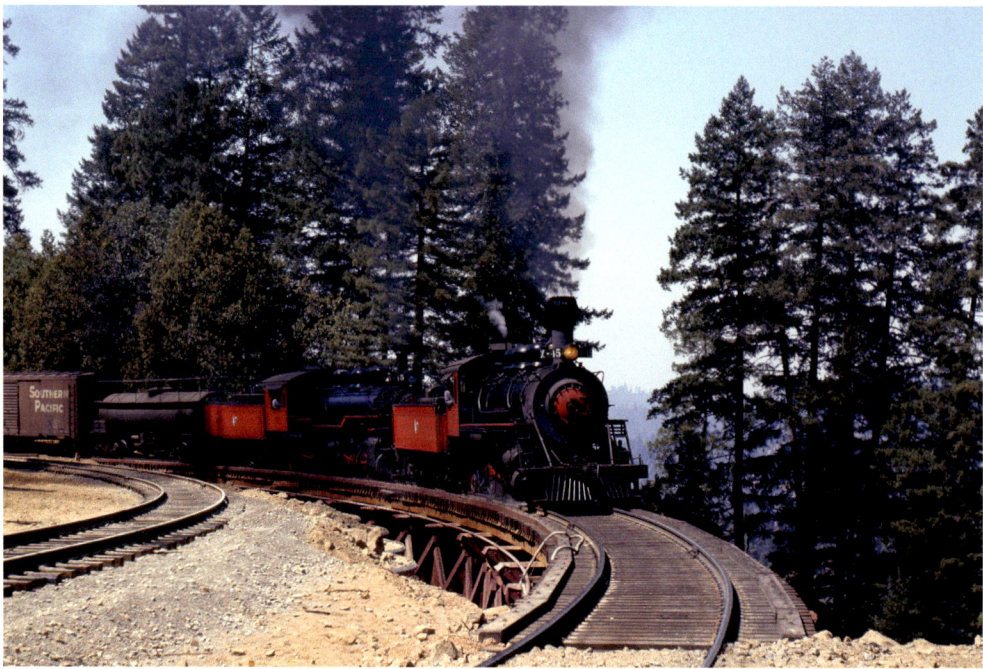

Nos. 45 and 46 climbing Ridge Hill with a freight bound for Willits in 1973. The fill on the left will shortly replace the trestle. *C. G. Heimerdinger, Jr.*

had to be scrapped in place to get it out. No sooner had the last of the cars been removed when the entire bore collapsed. The railroad supplemented its own forces with crews loaned from the NWP and G-P, and together they rebuilt the tunnel and reopened the railroad on July 10th. In the meantime, G-P and the railroad's other shippers trucked their freight to Ranch, a station not far east of the tunnel, and the CWR operated its freights from there using leased NWP locomotives. The railroad also periodically suffered from landslide and flood damage, especially during the wetter winters.

THE KYLE YEARS

In 1977, G-P inked a deal with Kyle Railways, a shortline owner and operator, to lease and operate the CWR. Kyle established The Mendocino Coast Railway, Inc. to operate the railroad. Kyle eventually gained permission to operate the line, but not before sparking a legal battle resulting in some precedent-setting decisions affecting efforts to end employee unions in certain shortline sales.

Unfortunately, both freight and passenger traffic significantly fell off after Kyle took over. Kyle did transfer some additional passenger equipment in from some of its other operations, and purchased three Alco road switchers to replace the aging Baldwin diesels; however, the Alcos proved to be hard on the track structure. The steam program did not last; in the face of rising operating and maintenance costs, Kyle sidelined both steam locomotives in 1980. The absence was to be short-lived, however, as in 1983 a movie studio fronted the $30,000 to bring the Mikado back into operation so it could be used in the movie "Racing With The Moon". The other steam locomotive needed more work than what the company could afford, and the railroad donated it off to a museum.

By the middle 1980s the railroad faced grim times. The operation lost $510,000 in 1984 and $650,000 in 1985 before taxes and sought permission to end its requirement to run daily passenger operations year round, which would free-up some money to improve its offerings during the busier times of the year. Freight business, which had been upward of 7,500 loads annually in the 1960s, fell off to around 1,000 loads a year by the middle 1980s. By 1986, freight trains only ran an average of twice a week. The railroad only handled 17 percent of the output of the Fort Bragg mill, and freight revenues dropped $100,000 between 1984 and 1985. Despite the declines, in 1987 Kyle exercised a clause in its agreement with G-P to purchase the railroad—but not the right-of-way—from Georgia Pacific, and then in the same year Kyle located two EMD GP-9 type locomotives for the road, replacing all but one of the Alco road switchers.

INDEPENDENCE

The CWR continued on with minimal changes into the middle 1990s, when Kyle decided to exit the railroad business. Kyle was actively marketing the railroad by 1996, and with no other serious parties interested in the property and abandonment being discussed as a real possibility a group of local businessmen put together a plan to save the railroad. A group of twelve principal investors formed the California Western Railroad, Inc., which took possession of the property. The new ownership invested substantially in the road, including purchasing two more locomotives, repainting equipment, rehabilitating the roadbed, and making other

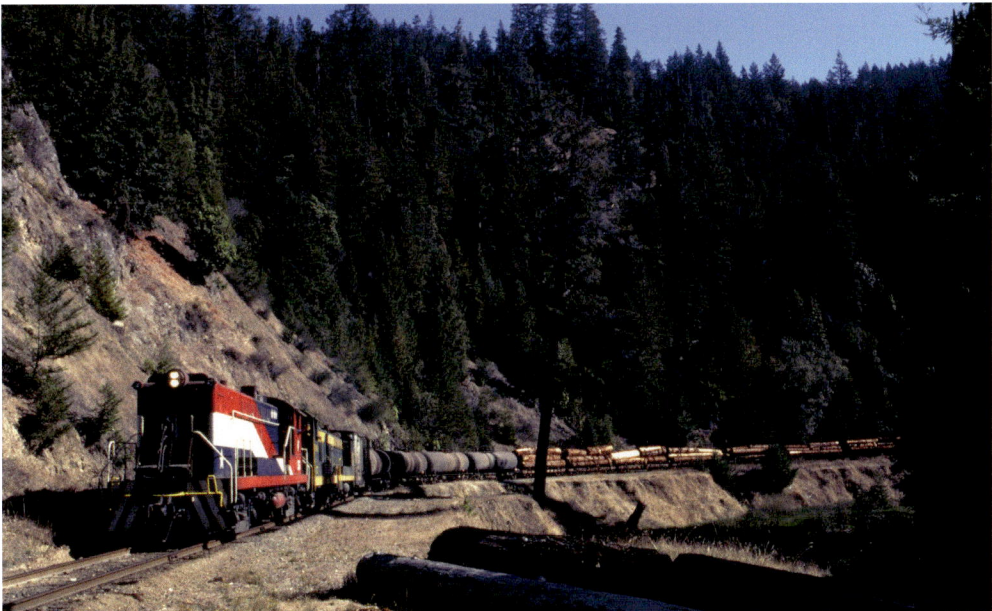

No. 55, wearing a paint scheme honoring the Nation's Bicentennial, westbound along the Noyo River in October 1978. *Henry Brueckman photograph, Tom Moungovan collection*

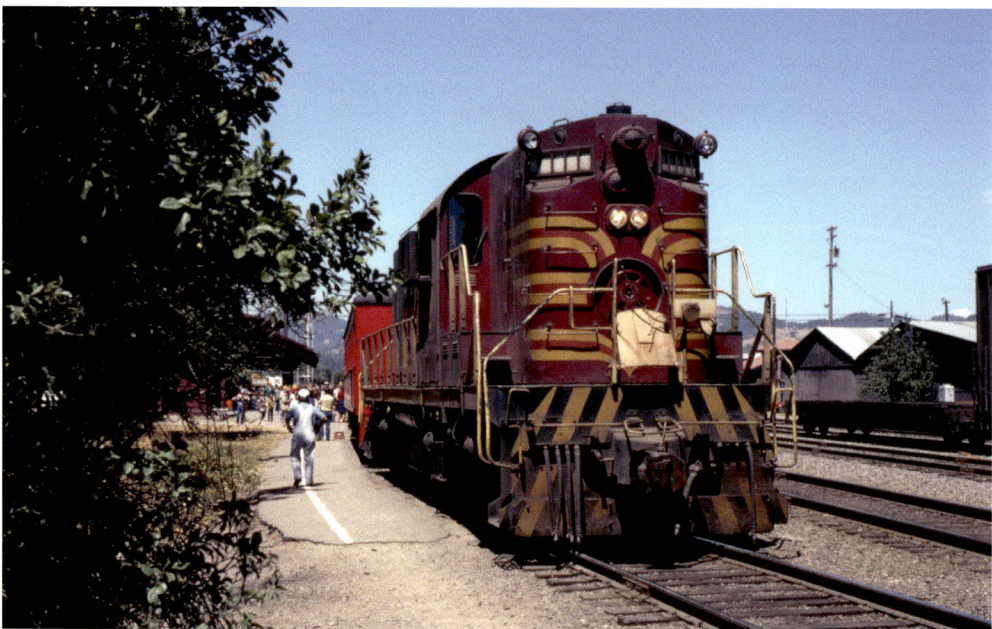

Alco-built No. 62 preparing to depart Willits with a passenger train. *Lee F. Hower*

improvements. The railroad also started exploring other available steam locomotives, with an eye towards returning the excursion trains to all-steam operations. In March 1998, the management announced a public stock offering, hoping to raise $4.6 million to perform additional track and bridge upgrades, improve equipment, and retire debt. The railroad's board held initial discussions considering possible expansion opportunities.

The new ownership also focused on improving the freight business, which had finally bottomed out at around 700 loads a year through the 1990s. The railroad started heavily marketing its services, with a goal of generating at least 1,000 loads a year; however, before any of these could really start bearing fruit, the Federal Railroad Administration issued an emergency order in late November 1998 closing the NWP, depriving the CWR of its only outside connection. Compounding this was extensive storm damage inflicted to the road in the winter of 1997–1998. The local ownership group struggled on until 2002, when the company finally gave up hope and declared bankruptcy; this action cost the company its mail contract, one of the last such U.S. Mail rail movements.

Once again the CWR teetered on the brink, but once more a savior appeared. The owners of the Sierra Railroad of Oakdale, California, purchased the railroad from the bankruptcy court. The railroad subsequently purchased its right-of-way, giving it some measure of security, and then in 2009 an internal reorganization of the Sierra companies conveyed the railroad to the Mendocino Railway, Inc. The company continues to experience periodic setbacks, including a massive mudslide in 2006 that closed the railroad and cost a lot to repair, followed by a manhunt for a murder suspect in 2011 that shut the railroad down for a month and scared a lot of tourists away, eventually costing the company $200,000 in lost revenues. The biggest recent blow came in May 2013, when a substantial portion of Tunnel #1 collapsed. The future of the railroad hung in doubt for a while until Save the Redwoods League purchased the timber harvesting rights the railroad held along its right-of-way, in the process giving the company sufficient funds to repair the damage.

As of this writing the railroad continues to be a tremendous tourist draw to the Mendocino coast, providing one of the better train ride experiences in North America and serving as the area's top attraction outside of the various redwood and beach state parks. Half-day round trips out of Willits or Fort Bragg provided by trains or the two remaining railbuses continue to be the railroad's bread and butter, with a large number of special event trains operated throughout each year. The revitalized NWP continues to discuss reopening their line north towards Willits as a long term goal; however, should the California Western ever regain a connection to the outside world, any future return of freight business would require new industry, as Georgia-Pacific closed the Fort Bragg mill in 2003 and has since removed all structures from the site.

LOCOMOTIVE ROSTER

1—Baldwin 2-4-2T, c/n 7831, Built 1886. Purchased new by Fort Bragg RR; to CWR & N #1; To Standish & Hickey 1906; to California Lumber Company #2.

2:1—Baldwin 2-4-4T, c/n 8852, Built 1887. Converted to 2-4-2T when trailing truck swapped with #3. Purchased new by Fort Bragg RR; to CWR & N #2:1; to Irvine Muir Lumber Company #2 1910.

2:2—Baldwin 0-4-2T, c/n 18618, Built 1901. Originally California State Belt #2; to CWR & N prior to 1912; Scrapped 1920.

3—Baldwin 2-4-2T, Built 1884. Converted to 2-4-4T when trailing truck swapped with #2:1. Purchased second hand by Fort Bragg RR; to CWR & N #3; to Mendocino Lumber Co. #2.

4—Hinkley 4-4-0, Built 1883. Purchased second hand by Fort Bragg RR 1904; to CWR & N #4; Scrapped 1914.

5—Schenectady 4-6-0, c/n 1301, Built 1880. Originally Southern Pacific of Arizona #22; to Southern Pacific #102, then #1605, then #2042; to CWR & N 1906; Scrapped 1923.

6—Mason 0-4-0, c/n 245, Built 1867. Originally California Pacific #1; to Southern Pacific #1114, then 1002; to CWR & N 1906; Scrapped 1915.

7—Baldwin 2-6-2T, c/n 33390, Built 1909. Purchased new; Renumbered #17 1924.

8—McKay & Aldus 4-6-0, Built 1867. Originally Central Pacific #39; to Southern Pacific #1529, then #2002; to CWR & N 1910; Renumbered #38 1924.

9—Lima 3-Truck Shay, c/n 2547, Built 1912. Originally Norman B. Livermore & Company (Dealer), San Francisco, CA; to CWR & N 1912; to F. S. Rolandi Construction Company #9 1914; back to Norman B. Livermore & Company; to White River Lumber Co. #9, Enumclaw, Washington; Scrapped 1941.

11—Baldwin 2-6-2T, c/n 39551, Built 1913. Purchased new; Scrapped 1947.

12—Baldwin 2-6-2T, c/n 41922, Built 1915. Purchased new; Scrapped 1950.

14—Baldwin 2-6-2T, c/n 58050, Built 1924. Originally California Fruit Exchange #1, Graeagle, CA; to CWR & N 1938; to Burt Rudolph, Willits, CA, 1956; Donated 1991 to Roots of Motive Power, Willits, CA; Leased to California Western for return to operation *circa* 1998, but work not completed and locomotive moved back to Roots of Motive Power facility in Willits.

17—Renumbered from #7; Scrapped 1938.

21, **22**, **23**—Baldwin 2-6-2s, c/n 53277, 54898, and 57553; Built 1920, 1921, and 1923. Purchased new; #21 to Pan American Engineering 1950, then Ferrocarril Mexico del Pacifico #6, where it may still exist; #22 scrapped 1952; #23 scrapped 1950.

36—Baldwin 4-6-0, c/n 9298, Built 1888. Originally Colorado Midland #36; to CRW & N 1918; to Little River Redwood Company #7 1929.

38—Renumbered from #8; Scrapped 1942.

41:1—Baldwin 0-6-0, c/n 18760, Built 1901. Originally Arizona & New Mexico #16; to El Paso & Southwestern #30; to CWR & N 1922; Scrapped 1937.

41:2—Baldwin 2-8-0, c/n 18760, Built 1920. Originally Sierra Railroad #22; to CWR & N 1950; Scrapped 1950.

44—Baldwin 2-8-2, c/n 61306, Built 1930. Originally Lamm Lumber Company #3, Modoc Point, Oregon; to CWR & N 1944; Scrapped 1952.

45—Baldwin 2-8-2, c/n 58045, Built 1924. Originally Owen-Oregon Lumber Company #3, Medford, Oregon; to Medford Corporation #3; to California Western #45 1964. In service.

46—Baldwin 2-6-6-2T, c/n 62064, Built 1937. Originally Weyerhaeuser Timber Company #110, Longview, Washington; to Rayonier, Inc. #111, Railroad Camp, Washington; to California Western #46 1968. Rebuilt as a 2-6-6-2 by CWR, and tender converted from slope back to square. To Pacific Southwest Railway Museum, Campo, California, 1984, where locomotive is on display.

51, **52**—Baldwin DS-4-4-750, c/n 74408 and 74409, Built 1949. Purchased new; Wrecked 1/14/1970 and scrapped.

53—Baldwin DS-4-4-1000, c/n 74193, Built 1949. Originally U.S. Army Corps of Engineers #W8380; to Pan American Engineering Company; to CWR 1956; To John Bradley 1984, who moved the locomotive to Dos Rios, California, for possible use on the Eureka Southern, then moved to Willits; to Chris Baldo 1993; to Roots of Motive Power 1995. Presently on display in the Roots of Motive Power facility in Willits.

54—Baldwin S-12, c/n 75823, Built 1953. Originally Wabash #307; to CWR 1968; Wrecked 1/14/1970 and scrapped. Cab of locomotive may still be on hillside below wreck site.

55, **56**—Baldwin RS-12s, c/n 76024 and 76105, Built 1955. Originally McCloud River Railroad #32 and #33, McCloud, CA; to Chrome Crankshaft 1969; to CWR 1970. #55 scrapped 1992; #56 to Traveltown Museum, Los Angeles, CA, *circa* 1992, where locomotive displayed.

57—Baldwin S-12, c/n 75916, Built 1953. Rebuilt by Chrome Crankshaft using parts from two former Southern Pacific S-12 switchers, #2148 and 2146; to CWR 1973; to John Bradley 1984; to Chris Baldo 1995; to Roots of Motive Power 1995. Cannibalized for parts and scrapped.

61, **62**, **63**—Alco RS-11, c/n 83411, 83416, and 83490, Built 1959. Originally Southern Pacific #5849 (#2914), #5854 (#2919), and #5870 (#2935); to CWR 1979. #61 to Martin Murietta #61 by 1991; #62 to Napa Valley Wine Train #62 *circa* 1998; #63 to Kankakee, Beaverville & Southern Railroad #324, Iroquois, Illinois, *circa* 1992, then to Delaware & Lackawanna #324, Scranton, Pennsylvania.

64—EMD GP-9, c/n 20132, Built 1955. Originally Southern Pacific #5607, then #3444, then #3311; to Kyle Railway #1750; to CWR 1987. In service.

65—EMD GP-9, c/n 19997, Built 1954. Originally Texas & New Orleans #416; to Southern Pacific #3428, then #3411; to Kyle Railroad #1758; to CWR 1987. In service.

66—EMD GP-9, c/n 22053, Built 1956. Originally Chesapeake & Ohio #6145; to Golden Spike Railroad Services #6145; to Buffalo & Pittsburg; to CWR 1998. In service.

67—EMD GP-9, c/n 19554, Built 1954. Originally Bangor & Aroostook Railroad #77; to CWR #67 1998, but never delivered; to New Castle Industrial #77, New Castle, Pennsylvania.

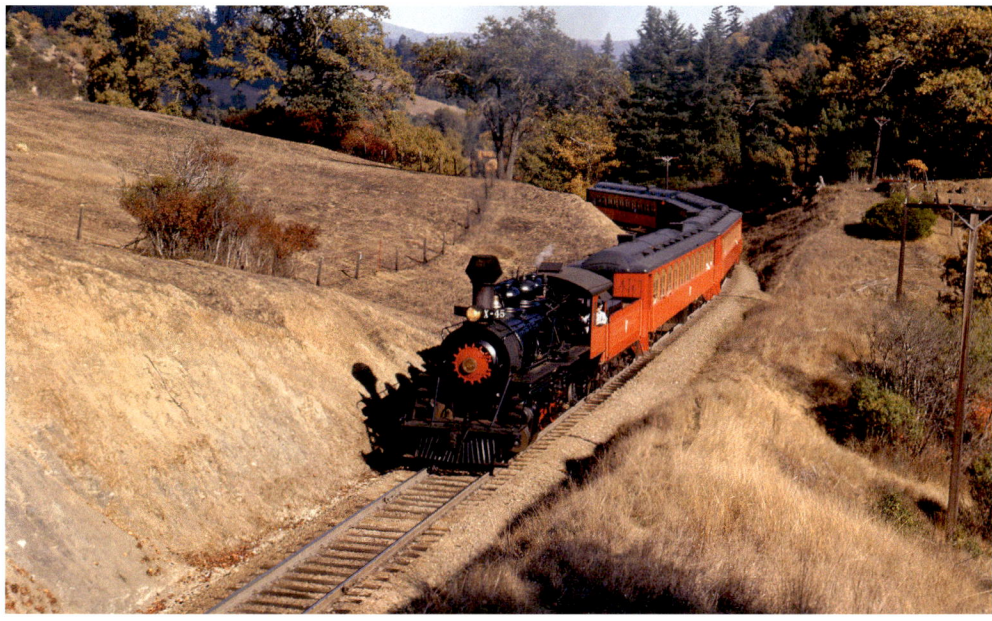

No. 45 leading the Super Skunk up Ridge Hill. *C.G. Heimerdinger, Jr.*

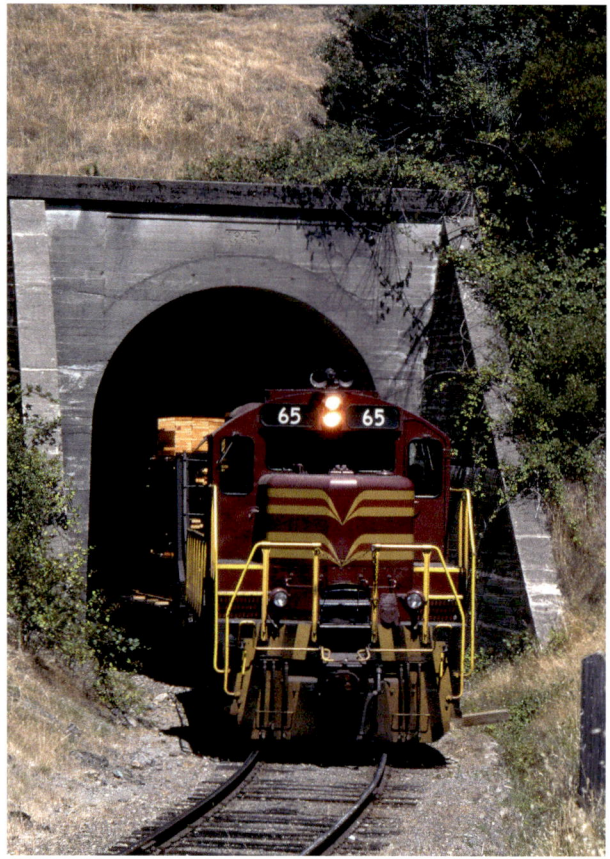

Left: No. 65 and a freight emerging from Tunnel #2. *Sean Zwagerman*

Below: No. 64 spotting lumber loads in the Willits yard. *Sean Zwagerman*

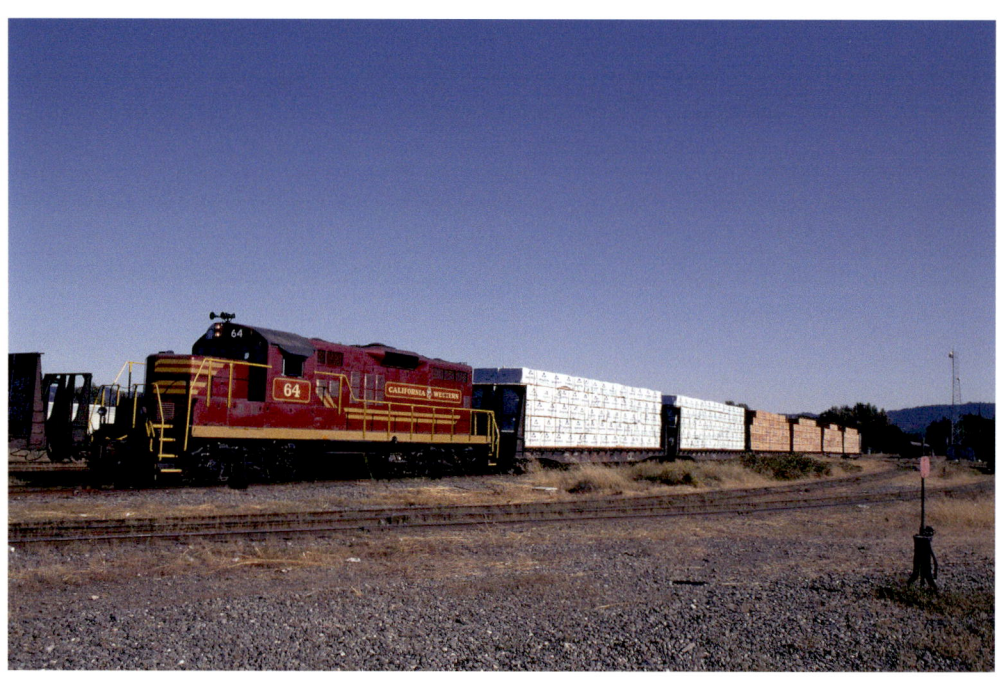

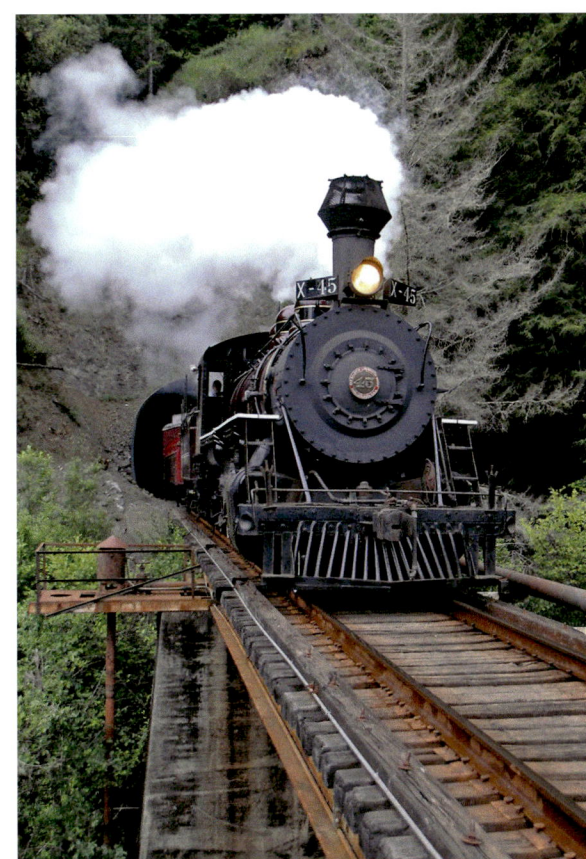

Right: No. 45 blasting out of Tunnel #1 for a photographer's special in 2009. *Drew Jacksich*

Below: Railbus M-100 and No. 65 between runs in the Willits yard in March 2015. *Jeff Moore*

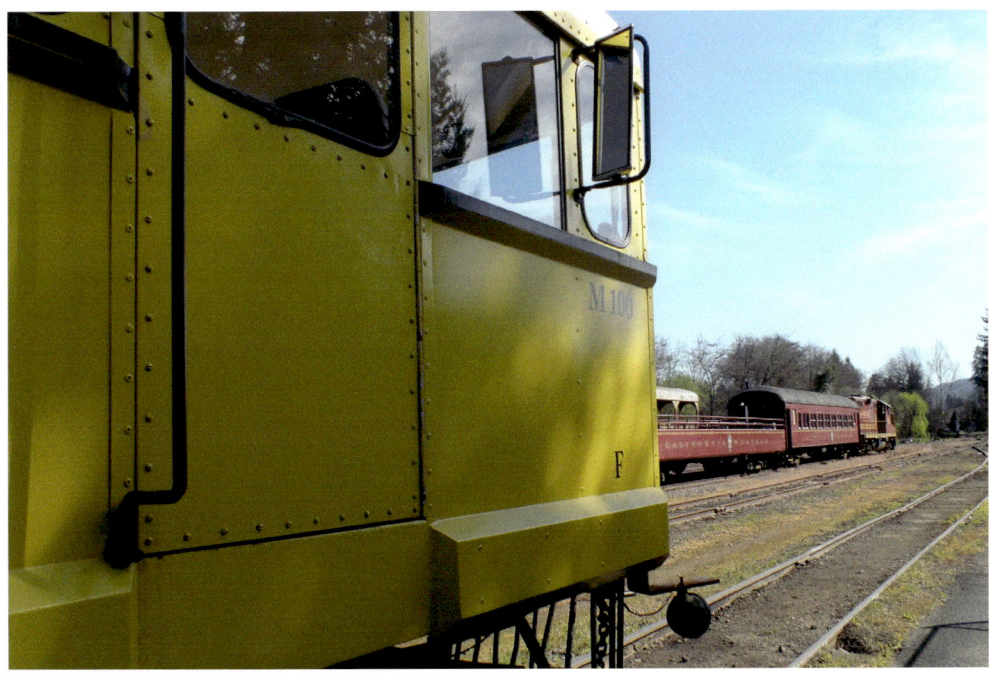

5

CAMINO, PLACERVILLE & LAKE TAHOE

BACKGROUND

At the start of the gold rush, the quickest route into the mines ran by ship through the Golden Gate into the burgeoning port of San Francisco, followed by a trip on riverboats up through the Delta to Sacramento. Smaller riverboats could take one farther north and east up the Feather River to Marysville. The growing cities of Sacramento and Marysville quickly became the preeminent inland communities supplying the mining camps in the mountains to the east; however, transportation from Sacramento to Marysville, and from either city east into the gold diggings, could be problematic, especially in winter. To compound the issue, hydraulic mining occurring upstream from Marysville pushed a lot of sediment into the river and severely disrupted water flows, often rendering it impossible to dock or unload boats anywhere in the city. Businessmen quickly foresaw a railroad would greatly expedite transportation through the valley, and on August 4, 1852, a group of them incorporated the Sacramento Valley Railroad with plans to build a rail line connecting Sacramento with Marysville. The new company had to overcome many obstacles before it could start construction. Grading out of Sacramento finally commenced in February 1855, with the first rails laid early the following August. Construction continued through the following winter, with the first twenty and a half miles to Folsom completed on February 22, 1856. However, by this point the railroad was in serious financial trouble, caused partially by construction costs far exceeding estimates. The Sacramento Valley would build no farther.

Meanwhile, tent city mining camps appeared in all parts of the mountains, and a few of them started to become permanent communities. These settlements habitually acquired rough and often unseemly monikers in their earliest days, only to take more socially acceptable names as the camps matured into cities. One of them, located forty miles northeast of Sacramento, initially took the name Dry Diggins, only to be shortly renamed Hangtown due to the large number of hangings occurring in and around the camp. The more respectable elements of the community finally got their way in 1854 when the town was incorporated as the City of Placerville. By this point Placerville had become the third largest city in California and the center of much of the commercial activities in the mining districts. By the early 1860s, Placerville had become a permanent community clamoring for railroad service; however, it would be slow in coming. The Placerville and Sacramento Railroad started contemplating a line from a connection with the Sacramento Valley Railroad east to Placerville; it was not long before the two railroads

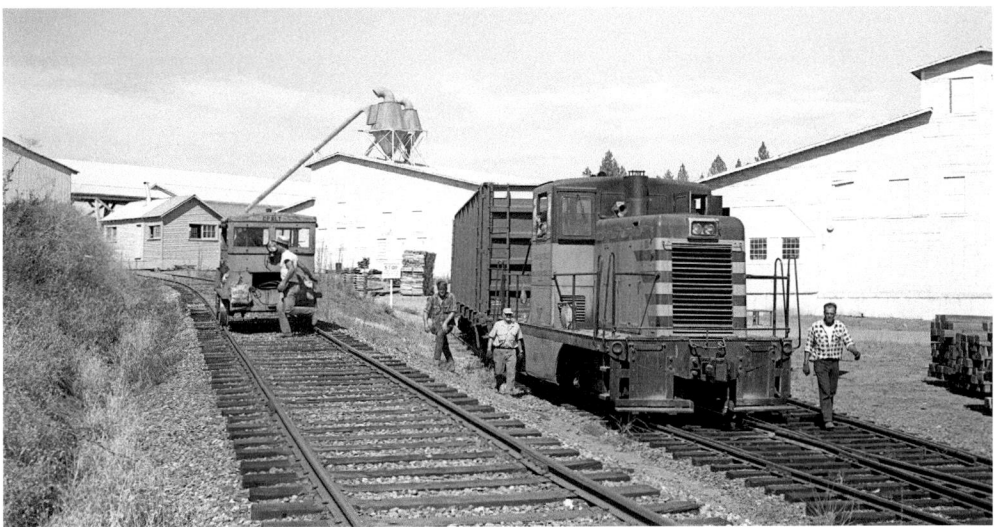

No. 101 switching Camino on 8/10/1964. *Don Hansen*

back up the hill, but was moving at a slow enough speed at the point it reached its crew to allow one of them to climb aboard and bring the locomotive to a stop.

THE FINAL YEARS

The railroad lived out a quiet existence, serving as little more than an a shipping department of the sawmill. Very little other business came the railroad's way other than outbound forest products from the Camino mill. The road's first diesel served the railroad for almost two decades, and as the 1970s dawned the company went shopping for a second locomotive, resulting in the 1971 purchase of a second 44-tonner originally from the Chicago, Burlington & Quincy. The unit operated in full CB & Q colors for well over a year before being repainted into its new owners colors, at first black and orange and later on green and white. The railroad shortly afterwards started cannibalizing the original diesel for parts.

The railroad's equipment roster had always been small, consisting of two cabooses, the homebuilt passenger coach, and a few work cars; all this changed in the 1977, when the railroad jumped into the incentive *per diem* boxcar market, at first leasing fifty double door boxcars from Itel, supplemented in 1980 with an additional fifty cars subleased from the McCloud River Railroad. CP & LT's original cars were painted green, with the logo prominently displayed in the upper right hand part of the cars.

By the early 1980s, the CP & LT faced a dim future. The railroad was not capable of handling the larger freight cars coming into use, and the potential traffic base did not justify the costs to upgrade the road. Mich–Cal shifted almost all of its products to trucks by 1984. If the shortline had any cars to move, both SP and CP & LT would run one train a week into Placerville; however, almost all of this traffic consisted of CP & LT's boxcars being returned to the road, and they quickly filled almost every available track, including most of the Placerville and Camino yards and the old Placerville Lumber Company mill spurs.

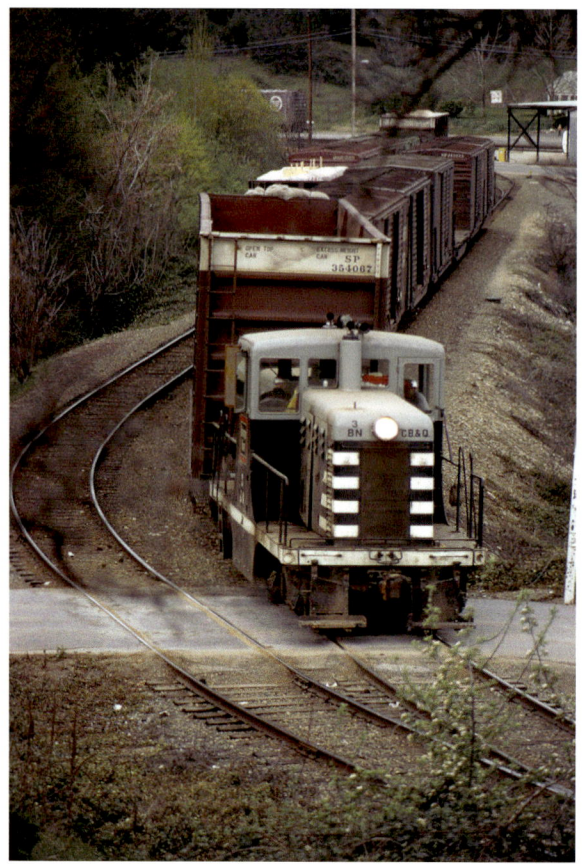

Left: No. 102, still in full CB&Q paint, departing Placerville on 3/31/1972. *Dave Stanley*

Below: No. 101 out of service at Camino in August 1972. *Lee F. Hower*

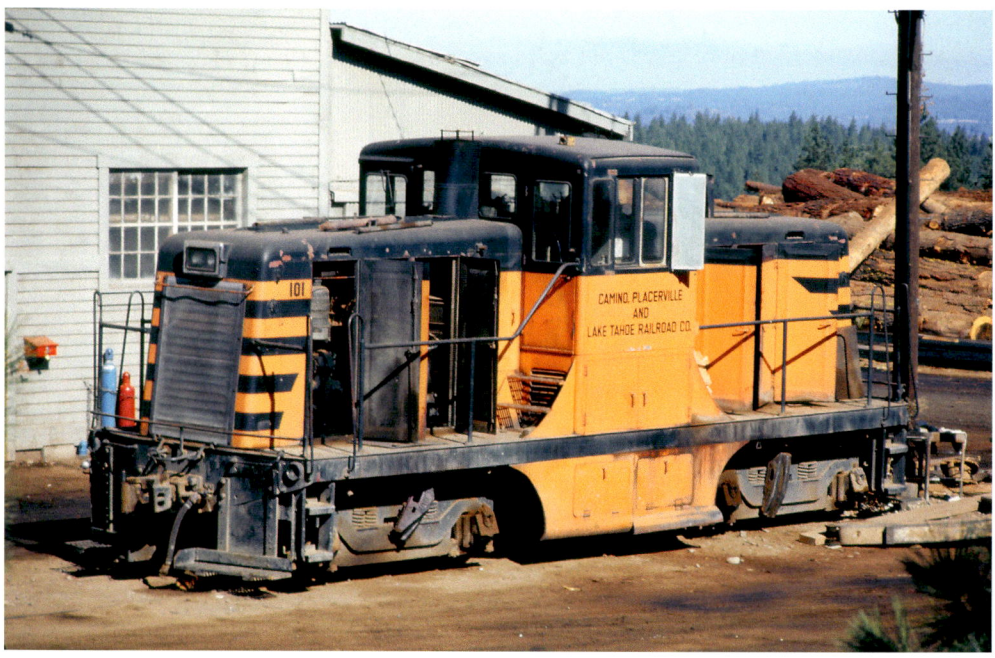

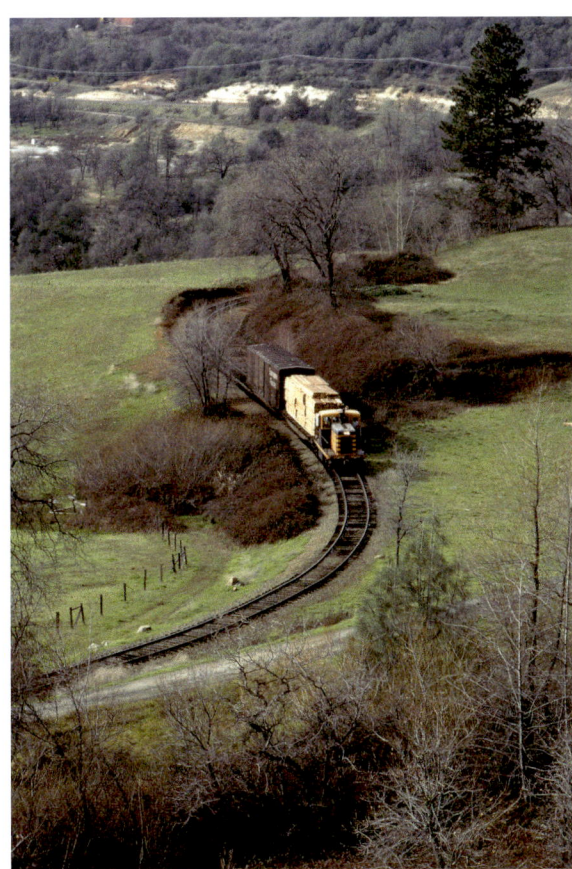

Right: No. 102 descending towards Placerville on 2/1/1978. *Dave Stanley*

Below: No 102 switching Placerville Lumber Company at Smith Flat. *Wayne I. Monger*

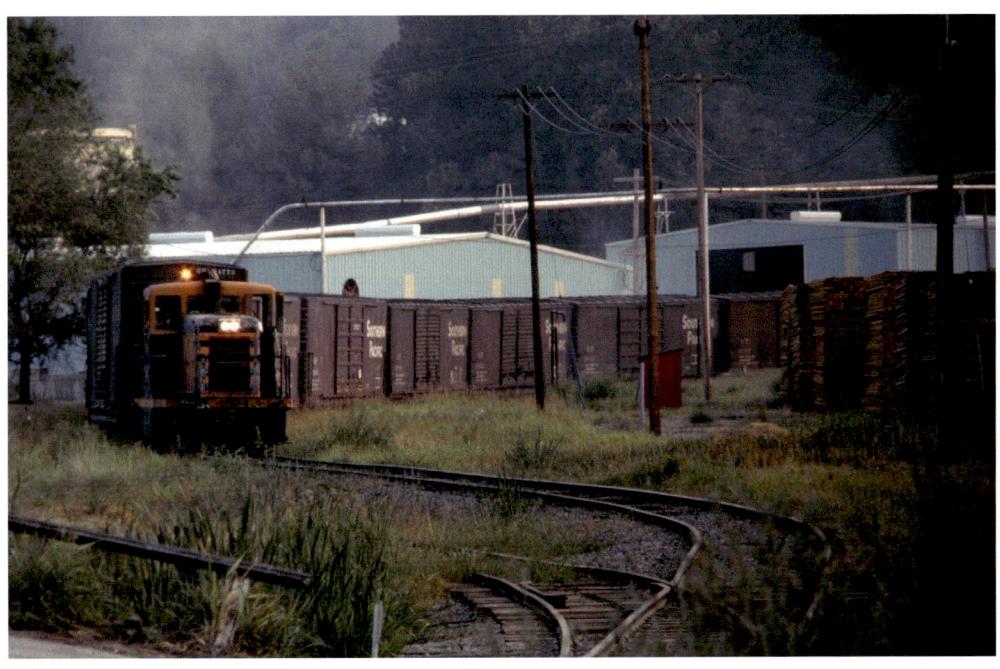

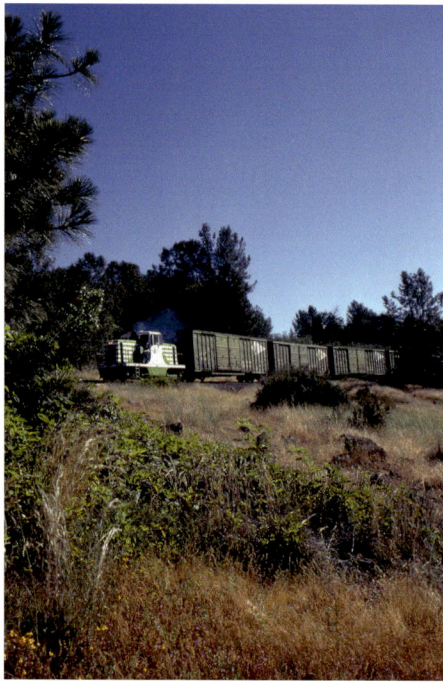

Left: No. 102, wearing its final green and white paint, rolling empty boxcars towards Placerville on 6/17/1986. *Dave Stanley*

Opposite: One of CP&LT's incentive *per diem* boxcars. *Wayne I. Monger*

Mich–Cal finally threw in the towel as SP initiated abandonment proceedings on its Placerville branch. The CP & LT turned all of its boxcars back to Itel in November 1985, though they remained stored on the property. On May 26, 1986, the CP & LT filed for abandonment. The job of cleaning the cars off the line started on June 11, when SP pulled 30 boxcars out of Placerville, opening some yard tracks. CP & LT delivered 26 more boxcars to Placerville on June 13 and attempted to remove its last cars on June 17, but could not complete that run as SP had yet to move the cars interchanged on the 13th. The CP & LT made its last run on June 19, delivering the last 17 boxcars to Placerville. The SP made its last run into Placerville on June 21. Approval to abandon the CP & LT came quickly, and the last movement of any kind happened on October 14, 1986, when Jim Dobbas Company—the firm hired to scrap the shortline—moved the CP & LT's diesel down to Placerville just before salvage began. The diesel remained in Placerville until April 21, 1987, when Dobbas loaded it onto a truck for delivery to its new owner.

POSTSCRIPT

Michigan-California Lumber Company sold out to Sierra Pacific Industries in 1994. SPI continued operating the mill until consolidating its operations into another mill at Lincoln, California, in 2009. Most of the buildings have since been removed from the site.

The ICC denied SP's Placerville branch abandonment application in late 1987. SP continued operations as far as Diamond Springs until March 7, 1989, when the last shipper there closed. The ICC finally authorized the abandonment of the 4.87 miles from Diamond Springs into Placerville in 1990, and subsequently local interests converted most of the SP and CP & LT grades from Diamond Springs to near Camino into the El Dorado Trail. SP subsequently sold

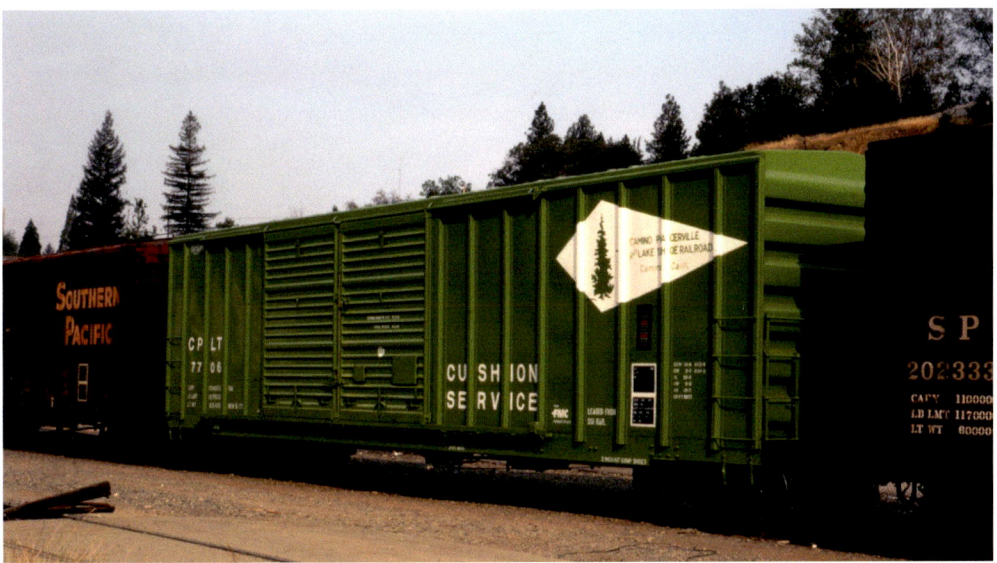

the rest of the branch to the Sacramento Placerville Transportation Corridor Joint Powers Authority, and two preservation organizations—the El Dorado and Sacramento Historical Railroad Association (operating as the Placerville & Sacramento Valley Railroad) and the El Dorado County Historical Museum (Ed Dorado Western Railroad) are both working on tourist railroad operations and/or museums on the line, while other trail concerns are lobbying for the conversion of much of the railroad into an expansion of the trail.

Besides the trail, other remnants of the CP & LT can be found. Shay #2 is part of the Travel Town Museum collection at Griffith Park in Los Angeles. Some of the road's old incentive *per diem* boxcars are still earning a keep, though the cars are now butting up against the 40-year age limit for cars in interchange service. A couple speeders also survive, as does caboose #2, presently under restoration at the El Dorado Western.

LOCOMOTIVE ROSTER

1—Lima 3-Truck Shay, c/n 885, Built 1904. Displayed at St. Louis Exposition through 1904, then to El Dorado Lumber Co. #8; to Placerville & Lake Tahoe #1; to CP & LT #1. Scrapped 1955.

2—Lima 3-Truck Shay, c/n 3172, Built 1916. Originally Little River Redwood Company #4, Crannel, CA; to Hammond & Little River Redwood Co. #4; to CP & LT #2. Donated 1955 to Travel Town Museum, Los Angeles, where it remains on display.

101—General Electric 44-ton, c/n 31231, Built 1953. Purchased new; Cannibalized for parts and later scrapped.

102—General Electric 44-ton, c/n 12951, Built 1941. Originally Chicago, Burlington & Quincy #9106; to Burlington Northern #3; to CP & LT #102; to Napa Valley Railroad #50; to Sims Metal #5004; Scrapped *circa* 2010.

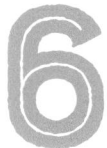

EUREKA SOUTHERN/NORTH COAST/ CALIFORNIA NORTHERN/ NORTHWESTERN PACIFIC

BACKGROUND

The redwood region on California's north coast was the last major part of California lacking a railroad connection to the rest of the world. By 1900, a relatively dense network of independent railroads not otherwise covered in this book had been built, mostly to bring logs or lumber down to Humboldt Bay and other ports to be loaded on ships. Other railroads stretched north through Marin and Sonoma counties, including an extensive narrow gauge system built near the coast. Around 1900, the Atchison, Topeka & Santa Fe commenced purchasing some of these independent companies, prompting the Southern Pacific to do the same. Both the ATSF and SP plotted lines connecting Humboldt Bay with the rest of the state; however, both railroads soon realized the potential business would only support one railroad, and on January 8, 1907, the SP and ATSF jointly incorporated the Northwestern Pacific Railroad, into which the big roads consolidated all of the independent roads they acquired. The NWP then built a new line up the Eel River canyon, completed on October 23, 1914. Lacking a direct connection to the NWP, the Santa Fe relied on rail barges across San Francisco Bay to effect a connection with the NWP, and because of this was never able to fully integrate the road into its system; this finally caused the road to sell its half interest to the SP in 1929. The NWP carried on from that point as a subsidiary of the SP.

The NWP remained both a major headache and a source of substantial revenues to the SP. Even through the slack times in the lumber industry in the 1920s and 1930s the NWP generated substantial traffic, only to have business explode at the start of the Second World War. On the negative side, the railroad ran through some of the most geologically unstable country found anywhere, and as such was very susceptible to frequent closures due to landslides, slipouts, tunnel fires, and flood damage; however, the volume of business the road handed off to the SP fully justified the enormous maintenance and repair costs associated with keeping the railroad open.

The situation started to change dramatically in the late 1970s. The amount of timber available for harvest declined, due to a combination of excess logging in early years and substantial timberlands being placed off limits to logging in the creation and then expansion of Redwood National Park. Then, in 1978 the 4,314-foot long tunnel at Island Mountain burned, closing the railroad north of Willits for thirteen months, and traffic afterwards never recovered, mostly due to increased use of trucks and the depressed lumber market. Revenues plunged, and when the winter of 1982–1983 closed the line north of Willits again for most of the first half of 1983

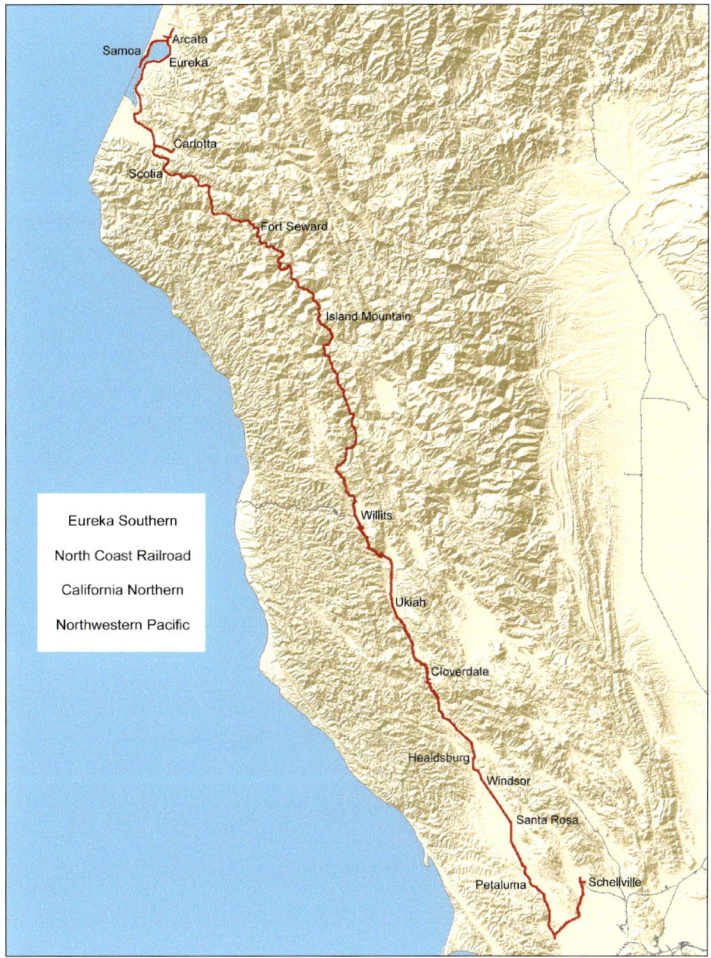

the SP reached the end of its rope. On July 18, 1983, the NWP instituted a $1,200 per carload surcharge on all traffic moving north of Willits. All freight to and from the North Coast shifted to trucks, and the railroad fell silent save for occasional work trains.

EUREKA SOUTHERN IN BORN

On September 1, 1983, the NWP formally applied to abandon the 165.87 miles of railroad north of Willits. Substantial local and state level backlash caused the ICC to deny the application in February 1984; however, the surcharge remained in place, keeping traffic negligible. Unable to abandon the line, the NWP did the next best thing and placed it up for sale. Bryan Whipple, formerly with the SP and several shortlines, became interested, and by the later part of 1984 he and the NWP had a deal. On October 31, 1984, Whipple's Northwestern Pacific Acquiring Corporation purchased the entire railroad beyond Milepost 142.5, three miles north of Willits, for $5 million, financed mostly through loans from GATX Leasing and other sources. This company in turn leased the property to the Eureka Southern Railroad (EUKA) for operations, which commenced the following day.

Whipple devoted substantial time and effort to contacting old rail shippers and potential new customers, resulting in significant lumber traffic being handled over the road from the beginning. The railroad initially leased a pair of GP-9 type locomotives from the SP while searching for its own power, which arrived near the end of 1984 in the form of four ex-Conrail GP38- type diesels. Initial operations consisted of crews departing both Willits and Eureka, meeting at Fort Seward to swap trains, plus a local job in Eureka that switched the branches around Humboldt Bay. Ten sawmills and a particle board plant provided the bulk of the traffic base, along with inbound carloads of cement into a dealer in Eureka and occasional outbound butter loads from the creamery at Fernbridge. New traffic the railroad developed included a special movement of stone blocks from Island Mountain to Samoa for use in a jetty enhancement project.

NORTH COAST DAYLIGHT

Establishing some form of tourist railroad through the Eel River canyon had long been a goal of local planners and officials, and the EUKA welcomed such an operation. San Francisco based Great Western Tours formed Redwood Coast Railway Company, which launched the *North Coast Daylight* on May 25, 1985, using EUKA power and Great Western cars. The *Daylight* operated weekends through the summer months, traveling from Willits to Eureka Saturdays and returning to Willits on Sundays. Passengers overnighted in Eureka hotels. Great Western and affiliated parties brought in three diesel locomotives purchased from the Central California Traction to help out as needed, and a local railfan had two other locomotives available for lease. EUKA preferred to operate with its own locomotives when possible, but did periodically take advantage of some of these privately owned locomotives.

Despite the apparent success of the 1985 season, financial problems forced Great Western Tours and Redwood Coast Railway into bankruptcy at the end of January 1986. A new operator, North Coast Daylight, Inc., immediately assumed the passenger operation; however, by the end of February a series of strong Pacific storms battered the EUKA, closing the line until early April. North Coast Daylight proposed starting the 1986 season in May, but shortly before the scheduled first run they cancelled the entire season due to problems purchasing liability insurance.

BANKRUPTCY

The 1986 storms significantly hurt EUKA finances, further compounded by low business levels. Before the railroad opened, potential shippers projected enough business to keep the line viable, but despite the railroad's best efforts actual carloads shipped never approached the lofty predictions. The EUKA cut service to trim costs but still found itself facing mounting financial problems as the end of 1986 approached. On December 15, 1986, the railroad declared bankruptcy with a $4 million debt. The court overseeing the railroad named Jerry Gregg, formerly with the Kansas City Southern railroad, as trustee.

The first part of 1987 saw a flurry of action in the bankruptcy courts. GATX Leasing moved to take possession of the track materials so they could salvage their investment. However, on April 21, 1987, the judge placed a three-year stay of liquidation on the property, and furthermore relieved EUKA of paying GATX for use of the line.

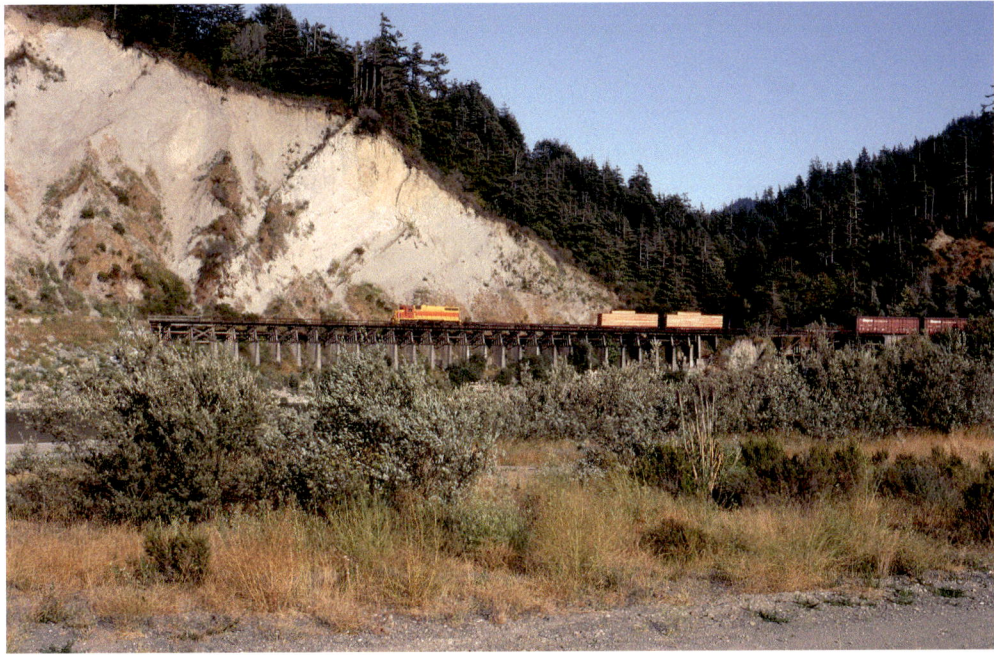
EUKA No. 31 heading north along Scotia Bluffs. *Lee Hower*

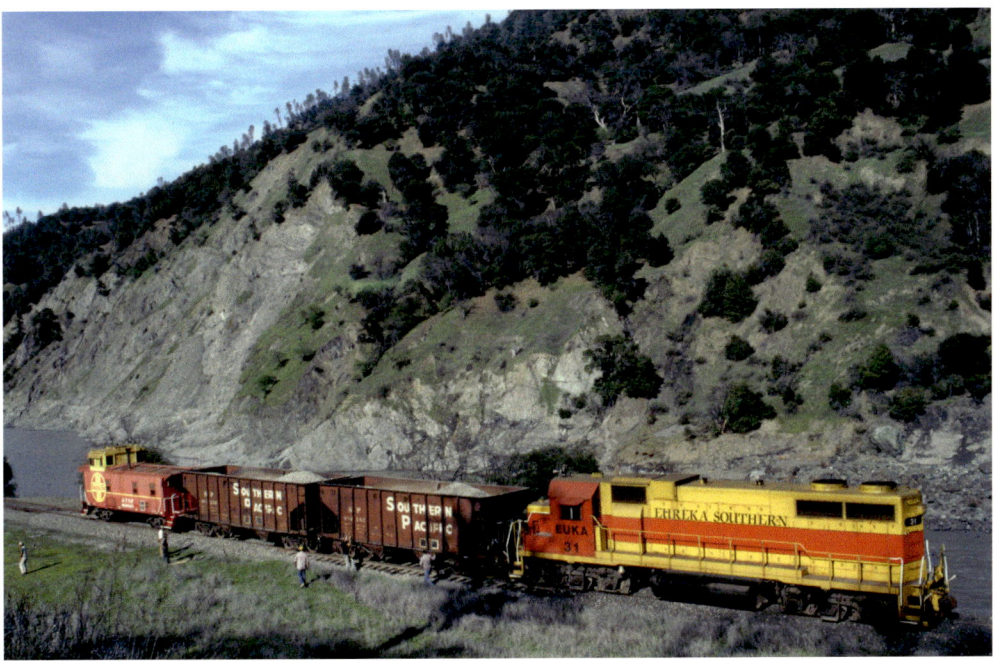
A work train dumping ballast on 3/1/1986. *Tom Moungovan*

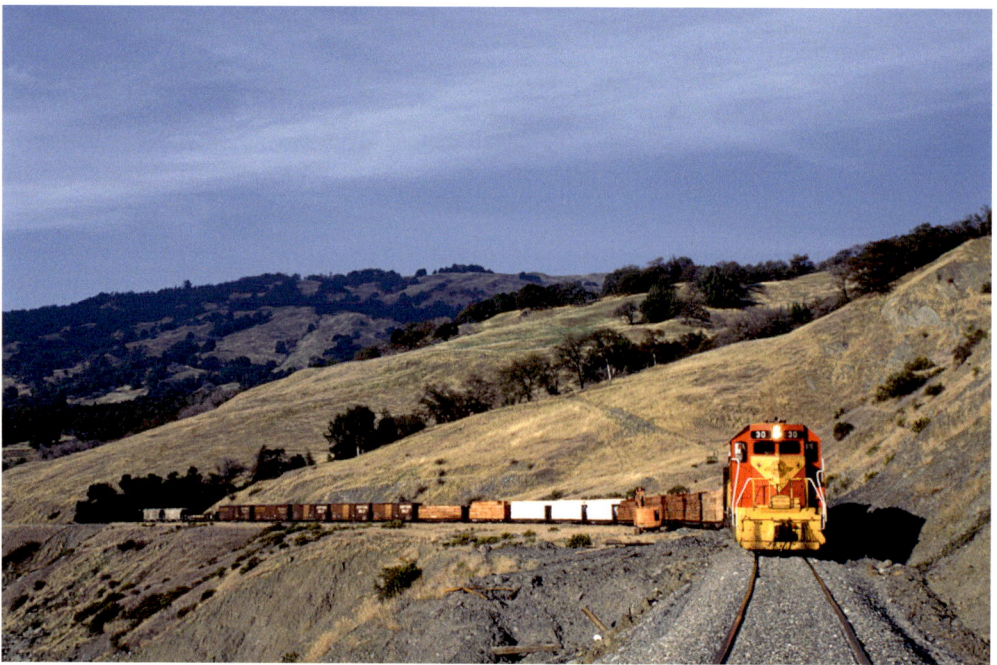

A southbound EUKA freight along the Eel River on 10/21/1986. *Tom Moungovan*

The court actions gave trustee Gregg some breathing room. Gregg implemented a major operations change, moving the northern base of operations from Eureka to Scotia. Southern Pacific still owned the land underneath the extensive Eureka yards and shops, the capacity of which greatly exceeded EUKA's needs. EUKA operated local trains north out of Scotia to switch out customers. The financial stability associated with not making payments to GATX allowed Gregg to make other investments; in mid-May EUKA purchased Great Western's passenger cars and started a dedicated log train running north from Island Mountain. *North Coast Daylight* service resumed in June with a few runs out of Eureka, followed in July by full round trips to and from Willits.

EUKA had a busy year in 1988. The *Daylight* returned for a full season of round trips out of Willits. In May the railroad purchased one of the privately owned ex-CCT diesels and placed it in service working local freights out of Arcata, and then on September 16th EUKA purchased the Arcata & Mad River Railroad, ending several years of negotiations with Simpson. The railroad's track gangs reopened the A & MR, allowing EUKA in the spring of 1989 to start serving the two sawmills located on that line directly instead of through reloads in Arcata. Track crews also removed almost all passing sidings and spurs on the line along with the Eureka yards.

California's prolonged drought through the late 1980s stabilized EUKA's roadbed, allowing the road to avoid crippling storm repairs. Despite this, 1988 was the last year for passenger operations over the entire road; no excursions operated in 1989 or 1990, with Eureka–Fort Seward trips and local excursions around Humboldt Bay resuming in 1991. The dry conditions created another problem, fires set by trains, resulting in the state fire agency levying hefty fines against the company and ordering its closure for several weeks until courts intervened.

EXIT EUREKA SOUTHERN, ENTER NORTH COAST AND CALIFORNIA NORTHERN

The three year stay on liquidating the EUKA expired in early 1990, bringing the courts back into the picture. In November 1990, Gregg filed a reorganization plan calling for either a sale to a new entity or outright liquidation of the property; however, the courts ruled the plan inadequate. Meanwhile, the political forces interested in preserving the railroad got down to work, and in 1989 the California state legislature passed a bill creating the North Coast Railroad Authority (NCRA), owned by Humboldt, Mendocino, and Trinity counties. Despite the governor vetoing a companion bill funding the agency, NCRA scraped together enough funds to tender Gregg a $5.26 million offer for the railroad in November 1991. The bankruptcy court ordered the sale to go through the following month, and NCRA took over on April 1, 1992.

NCRA established the North Coast Railroad (NCR) to operate the line. NCR purchased two locomotives, the passenger cars, and work equipment from EUKA, and started operations with locomotives provided by the SP on short term leases until its own power, six ex-SP locomotives on a long-term lease, arrived. NCR's ability to secure funding through non-traditional sources benefitted the road greatly, allowing the new railroad to start improving track conditions. Sporadic Eureka to Fort Seward passenger excursions continued, as did shorter trips around Humboldt Bay. NCR's dependable service brought shippers back to the rails, boosting the finances and allowing the road to declare profits in its first years. One setback occurred about 1993, when North Coast suspended operations over the old Arcata & Mad River due to terrible track conditions, the weakened status of the trestles, and an undermined pier on the Mad River bridge.

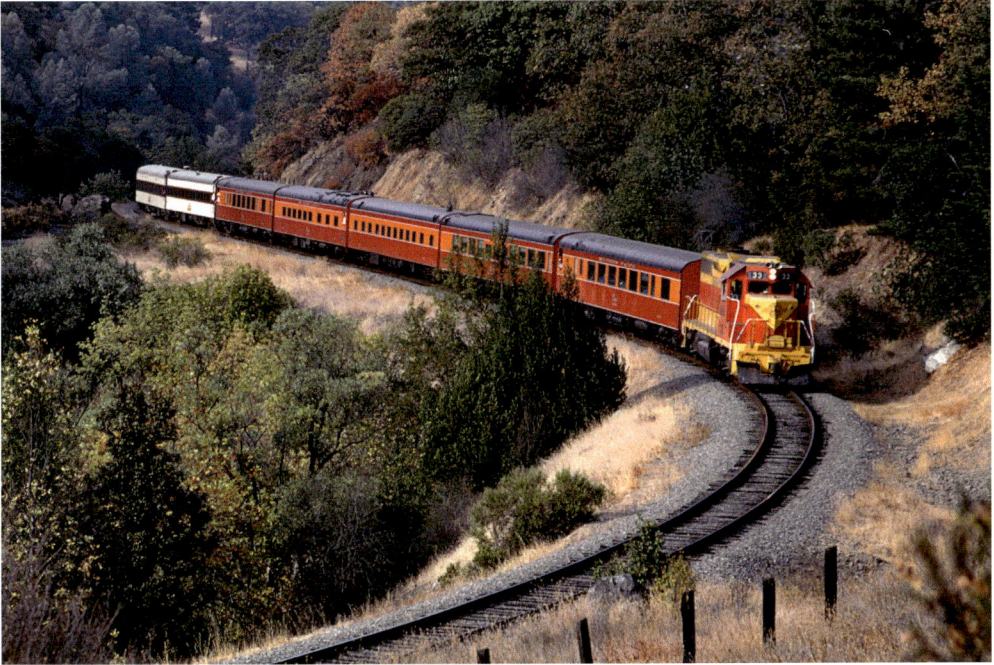

The North Coast Daylight on 10/11/1987. *Tom Moungovan*

Meanwhile, in 1993, Southern Pacific announced a major push to lease out its California branchlines to new shortline companies. SP packaged the south end of the Northwestern Pacific and its connecting branchline, extending from Suisun City to Willits, along with its West Valley secondary mainline (Davis–Tehama) and West Side line (Tracy–Los Banos). Parksierra Corporation won the bidding, and their California Northern Railroad (CFNR) assumed operations of all these lines on September 26, 1993.

Unfortunately for both NCR and CFNR, their startup coincided with the beginning of an abnormally wet cycle along the coast. The winters of 1994–1995 and 1995–1996 were substantially wetter than normal, resulting in substantial storm and flood damage closing both railroads for extended periods of time. The Federal Emergency Management Agency did reimburse the railroad for the damage, but only substantially after the fact, and NCR found itself stretched ever thinner with each wet winter.

NORTHWESTERN PACIFIC RESURRECTED, THEN CLOSED

Both CFNR and NCR were destined to have short lives on the NWP. Establishing commuter rail service on the old NWP's south end had long been a priority for the various commuter agencies, and in the middle 1990s their plans started falling into place. NCRA's ownership expanded to include Sonoma County, and state legislation created the Northwestern Pacific Railroad Authority, owned by NCRA, Marin County, and the Golden Gate Bridge District. On June 22, 1996, the two authorities paid SP $27 million for the south end of the NWP, extending from Schellville to Willits. NCRA extended its ownership south to Healdsburg, and NWPRA took possession of the line south from there. The deal included the Northwestern Pacific name

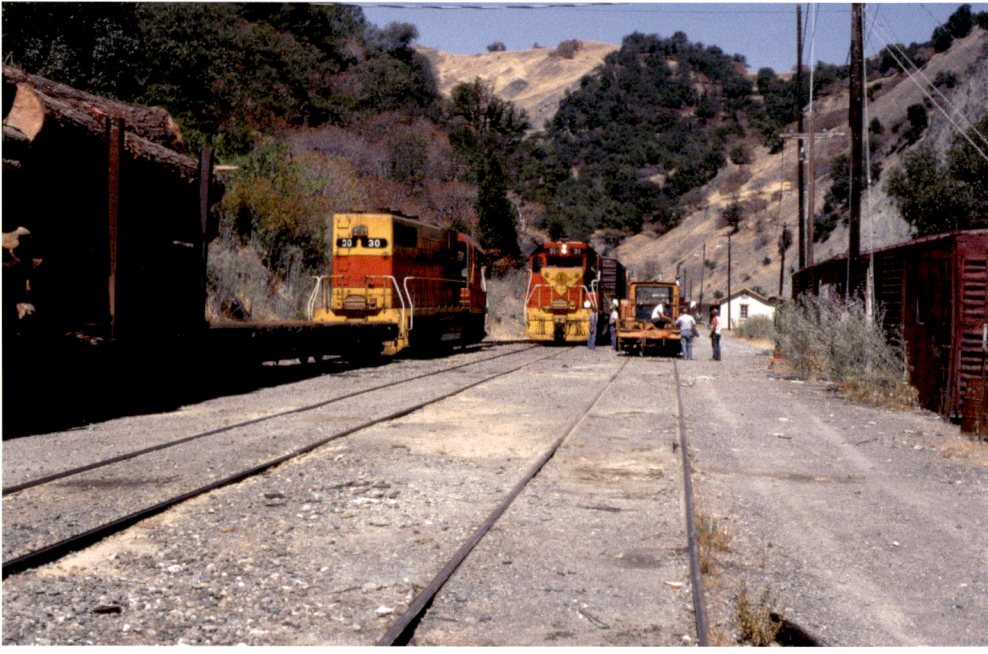

Crews from Scotia and Willits swapping trains at Island Mountain. *Lee Hower*

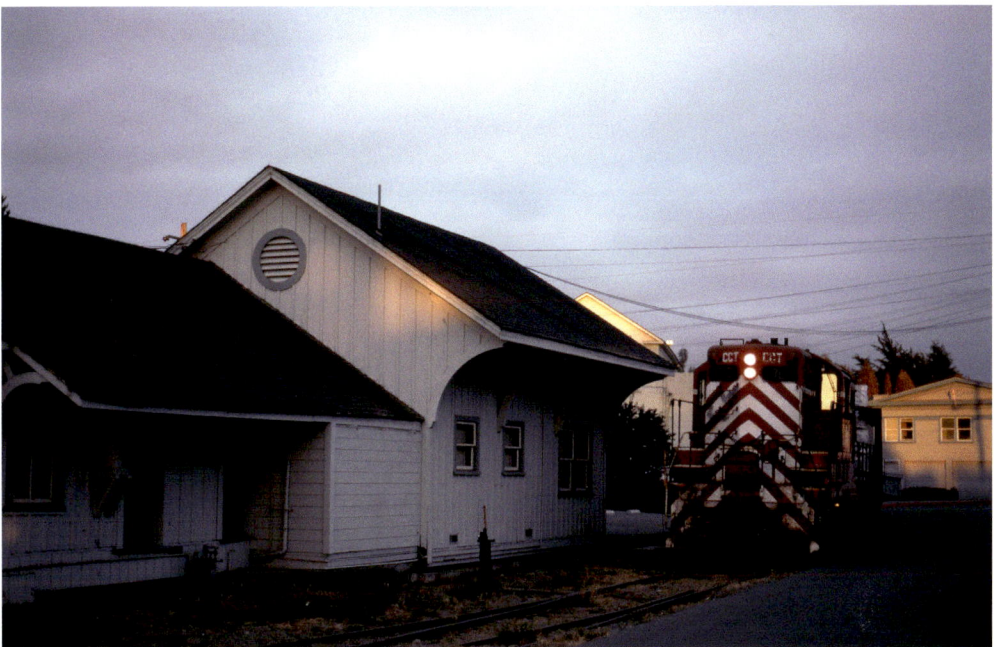

No. 70 rolling by the former Arcata & Mad River depot in Blue Lake. *Sean Zwagerman*

and logo; North Coast Railroad promptly changed its name to the Northwestern Pacific and extended its operation to the entire Schellville-Eureka line. CFNR retreated to the former SP lines east of Schellville.

Much fanfare and good press accompanied the NWP's launch. The railroad went after additional business, including gravel mined from the Eel River not far north of Willits and upscale wine tasting and other excursions on the Healdsburg–Willits line. However, the wet winters continued unabated; the 1996–1997 winter closed the railroad north of Willits for 72 days and caused $5 million worth of damage, not counting the lost revenue.

The railroad inherited a dedicated and talented workforce from the predecessor roads; however, that was about the only high point. Derailments, bad, track, and near constant mechanical failures beset the railroad, and the Federal Railroad Administration took an ever increasing interest in the operation. By the summer of 1997, increasingly poor track conditions caused the FRA to end all passenger operations save for some limited trips in the Eureka-Arcata area, followed by a second order restricting almost the entire line to 10 m.p.h. The NWP experienced ever increasing difficulties paying its bills, to the point the railroad allowed A & K Railroad Materials to salvage the rails from the old A & MR as payment for services and supplies that company rendered.

Then came the winter of 1997–1998. Another series of severe storms struck in the first days of 1998. The last NWP freight south from Scotia only made it to Island Mountain with its eleven loads of lumber before slides ahead of and behind the train stranded it. As in previous years, repair work commenced as soon as the waters receded; however, NWP shortly ran into trouble. As noted, FEMA reimbursed storm damage costs for the previous winters; however, NCRA/NWP had been forced to use the FEMA money to meet payroll and pay other bills for which the monies

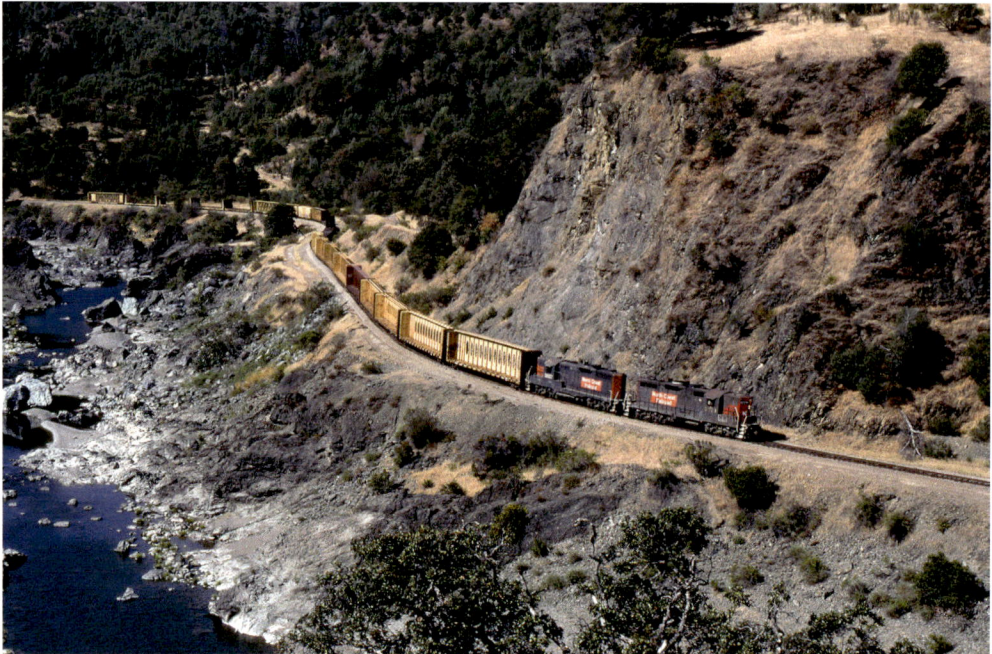

A northbound NCR freight along the Eel River. *Sean Zwagerman*

could not be legally used, a situation compounded by the railroad's lack of any sort of accounting procedures capable of tracking where FEMA money had been spent. FEMA held up any further storm related reimbursements until such time as NCRA could provide a full accounting of previous disaster relief funds received and implement systems to track future payments. NWP exhausted its cash reserves trying to patch the line back together enough to resume operations to Willits and almost made it, but the money ran out too quickly. The north end fell silent by early summer.

The economics of the railroad as a whole were based on the lumber traffic from Eureka, but even with it the NWP had been losing money at an alarming rate. Several Eureka sawmills established reloads at Willits after the north end closed, but only shipped a trickle of what the intact railroad once handled. The NWP's economic tailspin amplified, but the road struggled on until November 25, 1998, when the FRA issued Emergency Order #21, closing the NWP until specified track repairs and programs could be completed.

SMART AND NEW STARTS

NCRA started efforts to comply with the requirements of FRA's order, working in tandem with Rail-Ways Inc., a private company the agency had already hired to take over management of the railroad. NCRA also received $60 million in state funds to finance the repairs and pay off accumulated debts, mostly related to storm damage repairs going back to the middle 1990s. Rail-Ways incorporated the Northwestern Pacific Railway Company LLC (NWPY) as an operating company. Repairs to the south end consumed several years, and the FRA lifted the order covering 40.8 miles of track, from Schellville to near Petaluma, on February 1, 2001.

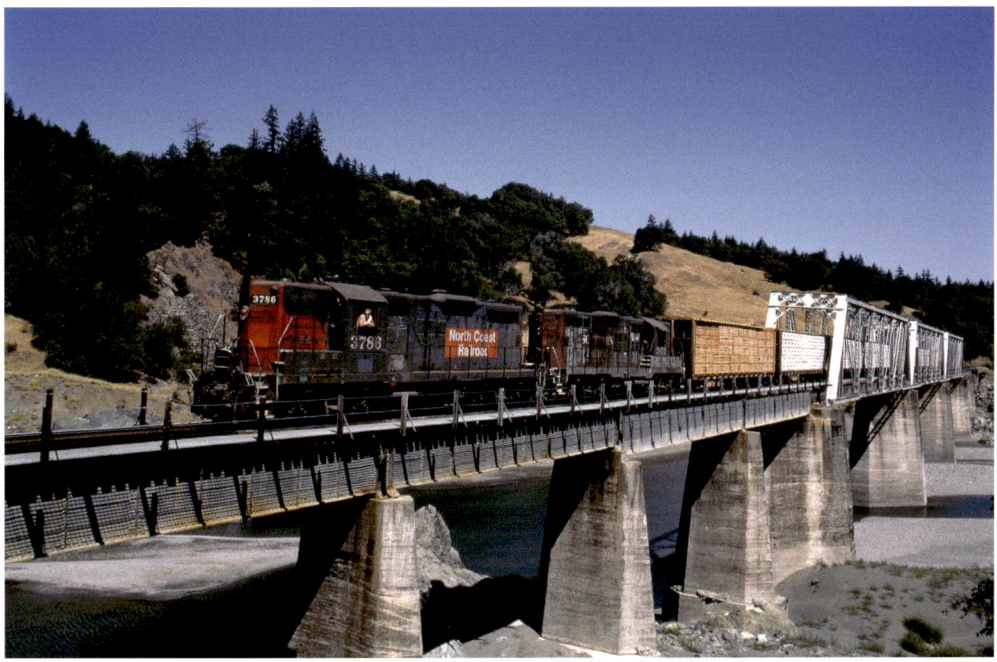
Southbound loads crossing the Eel River. *Sean Zwagerman*

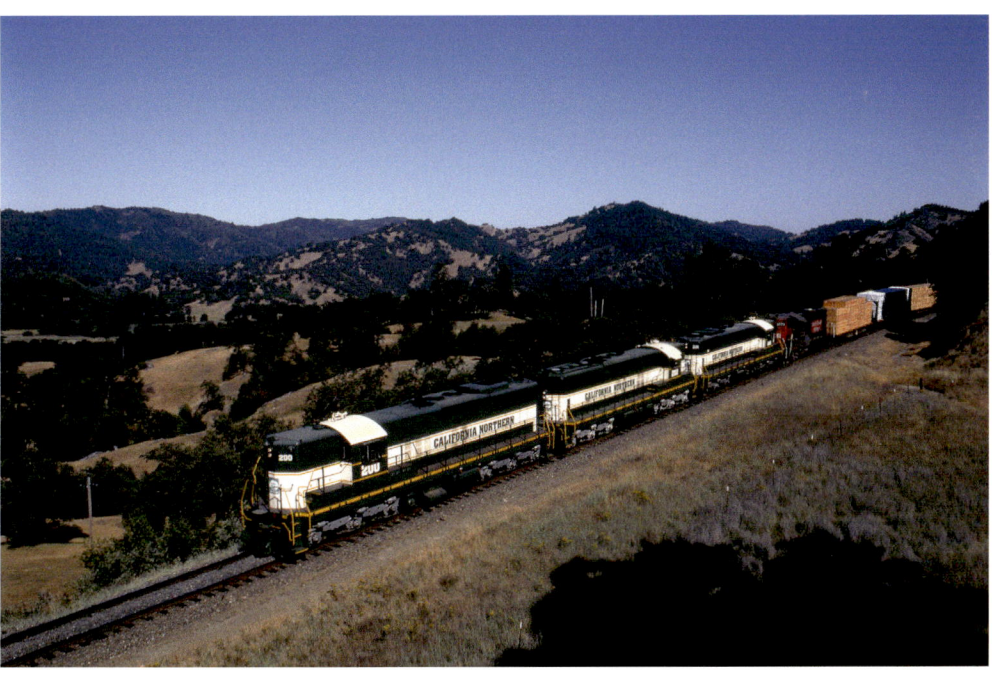
A California Northern freight descending the south side of Ridge Hill. *Sean Zwagerman*

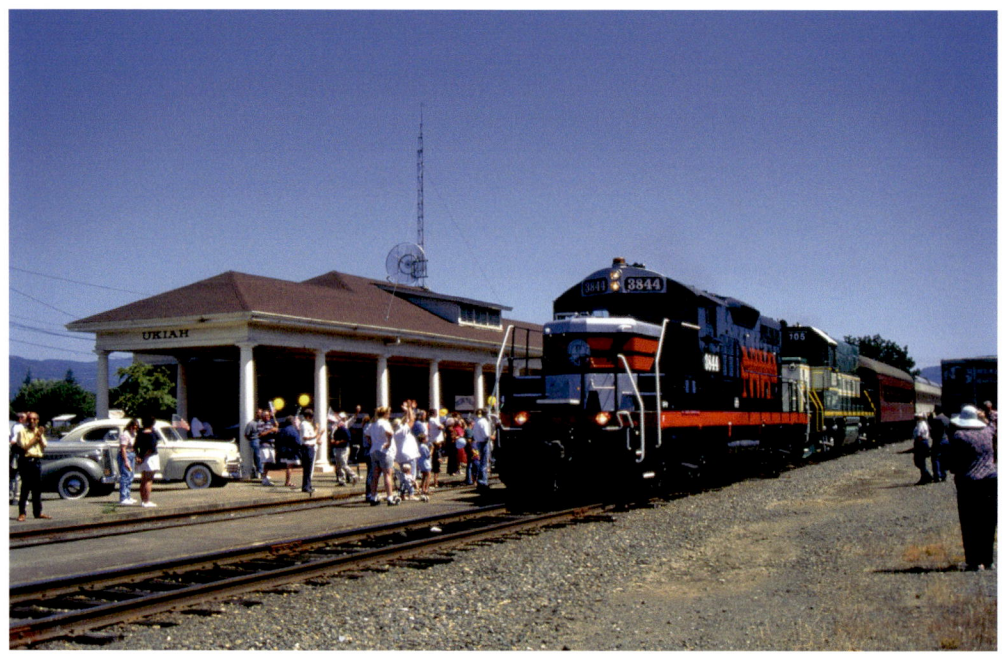

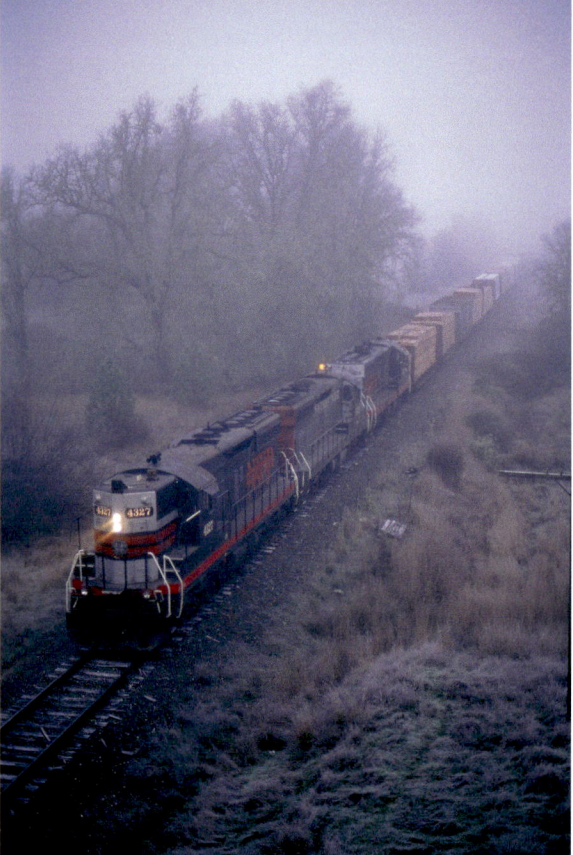

Above: The passenger excursion celebrating the new Northwestern Pacific at Ukiah. *Wayne I. Monger*

Left: Southbound lumber loads rolling through dense fog on the NWP's south end. *Sean Zwagerman*

NWPY commenced operations on that part of the line on February 14, 2001, hauling mostly inbound chicken feed. NCRA and NWPY announced plans to have the railroad reopened to Willits by the end of the summer; however, before that could come to pass, relationships between the agency and its operator broke down over some bitter contract disputes, resulting in NCRA removing NWPY from the property by September 2001.

The railroad again lapsed into inactivity and a period of protracted litigation. In the meantime, the commuter rail plans continued progressing, and on January 1, 2003, the Northwestern Pacific Railroad Authority sold its part of the line to the Sonoma–Marin Area Rail Transit (SMART). NCRA retained its freight easement over the line.

In 2005, prospects for the railroad started to look up again, helped immensely by some $20 million in new funding and debt forgiveness included in a major Federal transportation bill. NCRA started a search for a new operator, resulting in the 2006 selection of NWP, Inc. Required permitting, environmental reviews, and clearing legal hurdles consumed the next several years. Work trains started running in 2009, repairing the 62 miles of track from Schellville to Windsor. On May 10, 2011, the FRA lifted its Emergency Order covering the line as far as Windsor, and NWP, Inc. operated its first freight on July 15, 2011. Traffic handled over the new line is primarily inbound chicken feed, supplemented by some outbound loads trucked from a sawmill in Cloverdale to a reload in Windsor.

PROSPECTS FOR THE FUTURE

As of this writing, NWP Inc. had made a good start on their operations. SMART is actively rebuilding portions of the south end for their commuter rail operations, which will coexist with NWP's freight operations. NCRA and SMART continue planning future extensions of SMART service to Cloverdale and freight operations to Ukiah. If completed, this could re-establish direct rail service to at least five sawmills. The future of the line north of Ukiah is very much an open question—the only shipper on the California Western has been long closed, and there were no other major shippers in Willits. Gravel and other aggregates from Willits or Fort Bragg could be hauled, but baring a major—and unlikely in the current political environment—comeback of the timber industry, there appears to be little impetus at the present time for resuming rail service north of Ukiah.

Resuming freight operations to Eureka remains a dream or an anathema, depending on one's perspective. As of this writing, eighteen years have passed since the last freight became stranded at Island Mountain. The lumber has been trucked out, but the railcars are still there. Most of the cars trapped in the Eureka area have been scrapped, but five locomotives moldered away in Eureka until spring 2015, when the City of Eureka issued nuisance abatement orders forcing their removal. Only three of the eleven forest product plants in operation when the railroad closed in 1998 remain, and one of those announced its imminent closure in early 2016. Developing Humboldt Bay into a major west coast port remains a goal of many, and reopening the rail line—either a rebuild of the existing line or constructing an entirely new railroad over the mountains to the east—is seen as an inextricable part of any such efforts. Timber Heritage Association already offers speeder rides out of Samoa and would be satisfied if they could get a tourist railroad established around the bay, and trail groups covet the right-of-way as well. Down in the Eel River canyon, no maintenance and the forces of nature have obliterated the railroad in many places; tunnels have collapsed; and neighbors have encroached fences and roads onto or across the tracks.

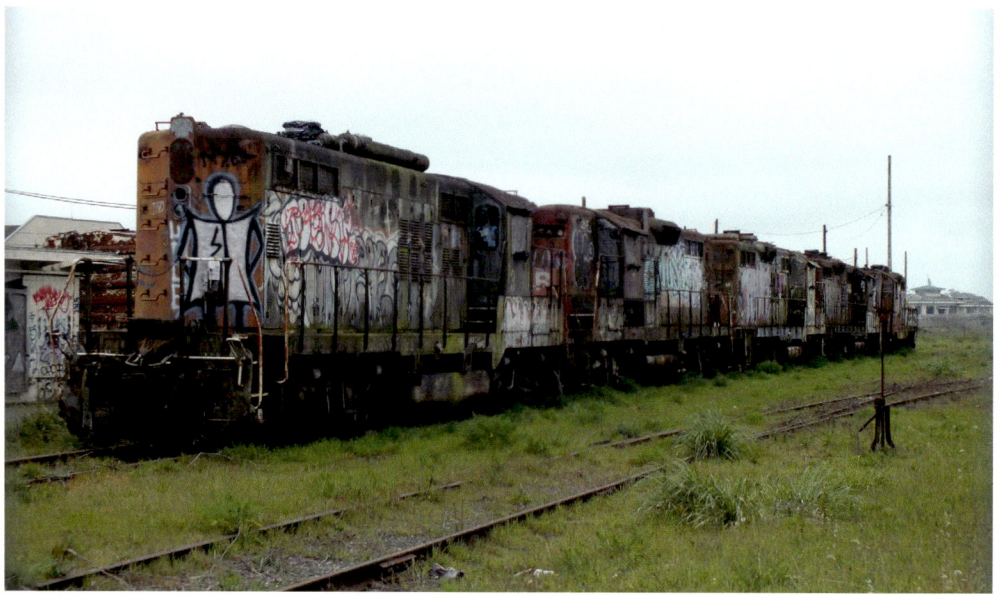

The five locomotives marooned in Eureka in March 2015. *Jeff Moore*

LOCOMOTIVE ROSTERS

Eureka Southern:

30, **31**—EMD GP38, c/n 34754 and 34755, Built 1969. Originally Pennsylvania-Reading Seashore Lines #2007 and #2008; to Conrail #7667 and #7668, to EUKA 1984. Sold 1992 to Dakota, Minnesota & Eastern #3800 and #3801.

31, **32**—EMD GP38, c/n 35449 and 35450, Built 1969. Originally Pennsylvania Central #7820 and #7821; to EUKA 1984. Sold 1992 to Dakota, Minnesota & Eastern #3802 and #3803. #3803 apparently to Helm Leasing.

70—EMD GP-7, c/n 18418, Built 1953. Originally Reading #618; to Central California Traction #70; to private owners; to EUKA 1988; to North Coast Railroad 1992; to NWP 1996. Stored in Eureka 1998-2015. Scrapped in Eureka fall 2015.

101, **102**, **104**—General Electric 44-ton switchers, formerly Arcata & Mad River. Origin and disposition covered in A & MR chapter.

North Coast Railroad:

70—EMD GP-7, same #70 as in Eureka Southern list above.

104—General Electric 44-ton, formerly Arcata & Mad River #104.

2872, **3190**, **3779**, **3786**, **3804**, **3857**—EMD GP-9, c/n 25136, 19980, 22922, 22945, 22943, 25139, Built 1956, 1955, 1957, 1957, 1957, and 1959. All former Southern Pacific, same numbers, and leased 1992 by NCR from a private party. As of 5/2015, #3786 is in Willits, #3804 is in Schellville after a long period of storage in Petaluma, and the others remain in Eureka pending removal to Stockton.

California Northern principally operated with a fleet of 14 former Chicago & Northwestern EMD GP15-1 locomotives, #100-#113; 2 former Duluth, Missabe & Iron Range EMD SD-9 locomotives, #200 and #201; and 2 former SP EMD SD-9s, #202 and #203.

Northwestern Pacific commenced operations in 1996 with the seven former North Coast locomotives, plus ten locomotives leased from Omnitrax: four EMD GP-9s (#3825, #3840, #3844, and #3850), four EMD SD-9s (#4324, #4327, #4423, and #5305), and two EMD GP35s (#6595 and #6600), all former SP same numbers save for #5305, which is from the Denver, Rio Grande & Western. #3844 and #3850 wrecked in a yard switching accident in Willits in July 1997. Five additional ex-SP SD-9s leased from another source rounded out the power until the end of operations in 1998.

Northwestern Pacific Railway operated with three locomotives leased from LLPX, ex-Appalachicola Northern EMD SW-1500 #171 and ex-Conrail SD40-2s #6412 and #6413.

NWP, Inc. presently owns a Railpower RP20BD "Genset" unit (#2009) and an ex-Northern Pacific/ Burlington Northern EMD GP-9 (#1922) and leases an ex-Santa Fe EMD GP-7u (#1322).

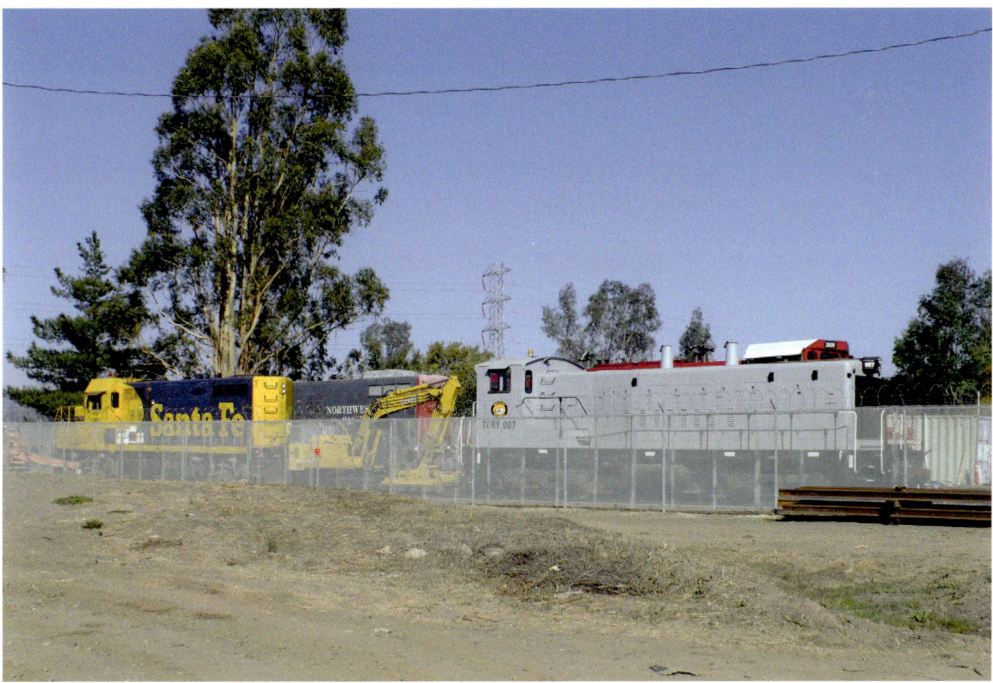

NWP's locomotive compound in Schellville. The grey switcher is privately owned. *Jeff Moore*

7

FEATHER RIVER RAILWAY

BACKGROUND

Sixty-five miles north of Sacramento a major river system empties into the valley from the east. The Spanish named it Rio De Las Plumas; Americans translated this to Feather River. The area lay near the far northern tip of the Smartville Block, and prospectors made numerous strikes in the area. Early communities the gold rush spawned included Bidwell Bar, Ophir City, and Mooretown; Ophir City morphed into Oroville in 1854. The California Northern Rail Way completed a line from Marysville north to Oroville in 1864; this line came under the control of the Southern Pacific.

Large scale exploitation of the forests along the river really began after the Western Pacific completed its mainline in 1909. Speculators and those hoping to get into the lumber industry purchased timberlands; however, even with the presence of the SP and WP lines to and through Oroville, any serious industrial development would require additional railroad construction to access the timber. In 1920, R. L. Hutchinson, a successful lumberman from West Virginia, decided to move his operation to the west, resulting in the purchase of timberlands around Mooretown, mostly on the divide between the Middle and South Forks of the Feather River. The Oroville Chamber of Commerce induced Hutchinson to locate his mill in the city by donating half the cost of the land. However, that location choice lay over two dozen miles from the timber, requiring a railroad to bring logs out of the woods.

BUILDING A RAILROAD

The Western Pacific had its hand full elsewhere, but did consent to build 2.12 miles of the needed railroad, from a connection with their mainline at Bidwell east to Bidwell Bar. The Hutchinson Lumber Company laid out a logging railroad running east from there. Grading on both parts of the railroad commenced in early 1921; the WP hired the Toughy brothers construction firm to construct their part, and Hutchinson brought in several others to work on their portion. The W. A. Bechtel company laid most of the rails for both roads, starting work in the fall of 1921 and completing the line into Mooretown on May 5, 1922. The Hutchinson company concurrently built a large sawmill at Oroville, and on May 23, 1923, R. L. Hutchinson's granddaughter flipped the switch, powering up the saws.

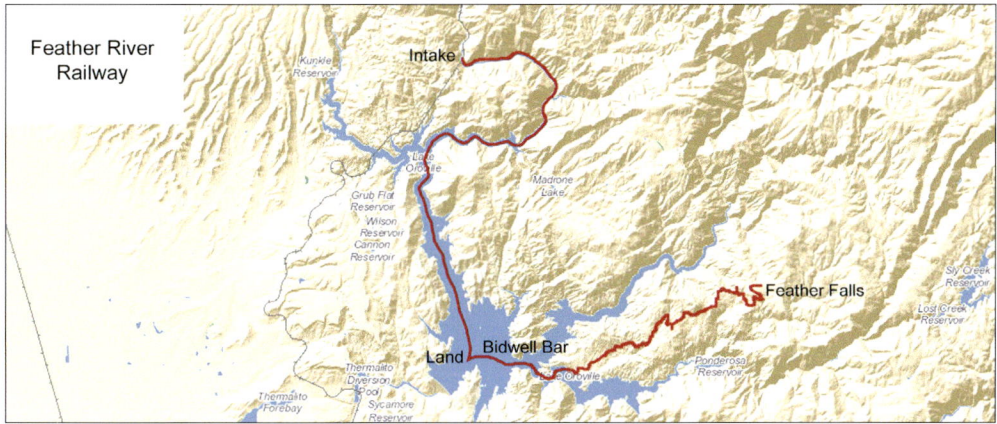

Hutchinson's line was a tough piece of railroad. The line climbed 2,600 feet in 17.4 miles, and to accomplish this the railroad climbed grades up to 5.2 percent in places. The railroad was exceptionally well engineered and built, requiring fifteen carloads of dynamite to blast four miles of grade in one stretch. In deference to the grades, the railroad used Shay-type gear driven steam locomotives on the railroad. Construction did not stop at Mooretown, as Hutchinson snaked several logging railroad lines into the woods east of there.

Unfortunately for Hutchinson, the company launched its venture right as the lumber market softened. The company accumulated a substantial debt load building the California operations, and a rash of expensive forest fires in 1924 compounded the problems. In September 1926, a West Virginia bank issued a foreclosure notice, forcing the company into bankruptcy. Andrew H. Land, formerly a partner in the Hutchinson company, purchased the assets at the liquidation auction held on the court house steps in Oroville; Land promptly conveyed them to his new Feather River Pine Mills, Inc. (FRPM). The new company suffered on for only five more months; on October 6, 1927, a massive fire wiped out the entire Oroville sawmill. FRPM received insurance payments, but almost immediately lost them due to the failure of the bank in which the funds had been deposited. Lumber markets continued to fall, and Land decided to keep the operations closed and wait until better times arrived.

RESURRECTION

The entire operations remained mothballed until 1938, when Land finally decided lumber markets had sufficiently improved. Feather River Pine Mills received a $850,000 loan from the Reconstruction Finance Corporation to rehabilitate the properties and resume operations; however, instead of rebuilding the Oroville sawmill, the company planned instead to build a new mill at Feather Falls, adjacent to Mooretown. On October 13, 1939, Land incorporated the Feather River Railway Company (FRRY) to take over the operations of the old Hutchinson and WP lines between Feather Falls and Land, where a formal interchange would be established with the Western Pacific mainline. FRPM completed the new mill and had it in operation by 1940.

The Feather River operations rode out the 1940s in fine shape. The logging railroad lasted until 1950, when the company switched entirely to truck logging and abandoned all rail operations beyond the FRRY. Unlike almost all other railroad operations, the FRRY elected to stick with its steam locomotives, largely because they generally worked better on the 5+ percent grades than any diesel electric then available.

GEORGIA PACIFIC TAKES OVER

The Land family continued their ownership until 1955, when they sold the operations to Georgia-Pacific Corporation. G-P made no substantial changes to the operations; however, as with most other timber railroads, the line started handling woodchips in addition to the lumber traffic.

FRRY never did offer passenger service. As the 1950s progressed, word got out in the railfan community that working steam could still be found at Feather Falls. The railroad hosted several large organized railfan excursions, with the largest two in October 1954 and June 1963. Over 1,100 people rode the latter trip. Several adventurous railfan photographers found their way to Feather Falls to record the anachronism the railroad was quickly becoming; the railroad put on a good show for them, dispatching three to six trains a week behind the Shays, depending on the ebb and flow of lumber traffic from the mill.

The Shays continued performing admirably on the line; however, steam's days were numbered. In 1961, G-P closed the logging railroad feeding their big mill at Samoa, California, freeing up the services of an EMD switcher. G-P sent the locomotive to Feather Falls, arriving on October 11. FRRY intended for the diesel to replace steam entirely, but the diesel immediately proved too heavy for the road and suffered a rash of derailments, forcing the railroad to fire up the Shays again until the road could be upgraded. Modifications to the diesel to help it operate better included a rail washer, useful in clearing sand off the flanges and providing a little bit of lubrication for following train cars; the most noticeable part of this apparatus was a water tank slung across the top of the cab roof. The diesel eventually proved completely adequate and substantially reduced operating costs.

THE DAM

The Feather River periodically produced devastating floods, and in 1951 California authorized building an enormous dam just above Oroville to cure this problem, as well as to produce hydroelectric power. The reservoir would require the relocation of multiple facilities, including the state highway and the Western Pacific mainline. The planned reservoir would inundate the lower six miles of the FRRY, and flood out its WP connection, which lay not far upstream from the dam site. Construction on the highway and WP mainline relocation started in 1957, and WP shifted all operations over to its new line on October 22, 1962.

Laws in place required California to reroute FRRY around the dam as well; however, the state balked at the $9 million price tag to build thirteen miles of new railroad around the south end of the lake to a new connection with the WP mainline below the dam. The state figured the existing railroad to be worth only $25,000, based on the company's assessed valuation for taxes, and initiated proceedings attempting to force the road's abandonment. G-P fought back, contending the railroad was vital to continued operation of the Feather Falls mill. On April 19, 1962, FRRY filed applications with the I.C.C. seeking authority to abandon the part of its line to be flooded and to build the new line around the lake. The I.C.C. granted both applications

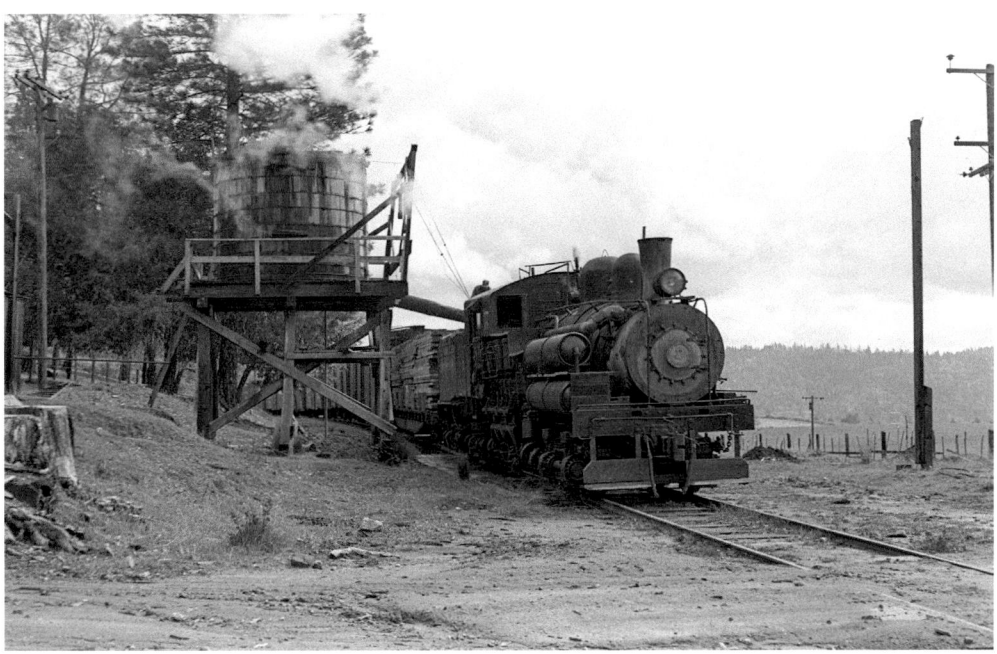

No. 2 taking on water on 3/28/1960. *Don Hansen*

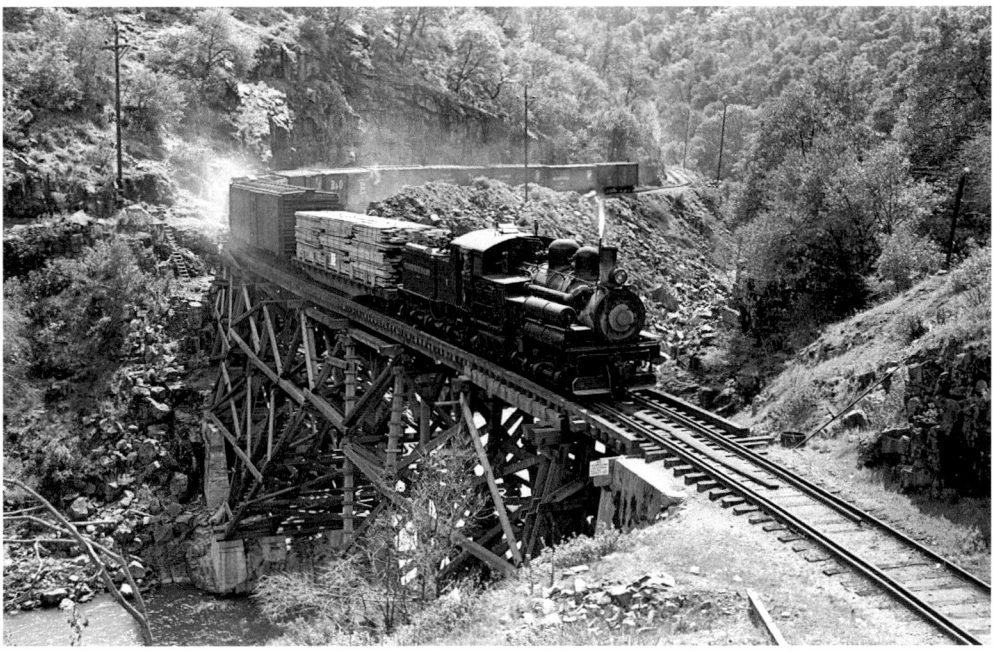

No. 2 crossing the South Fork bridge on 3/28/1960. *Don Hansen*

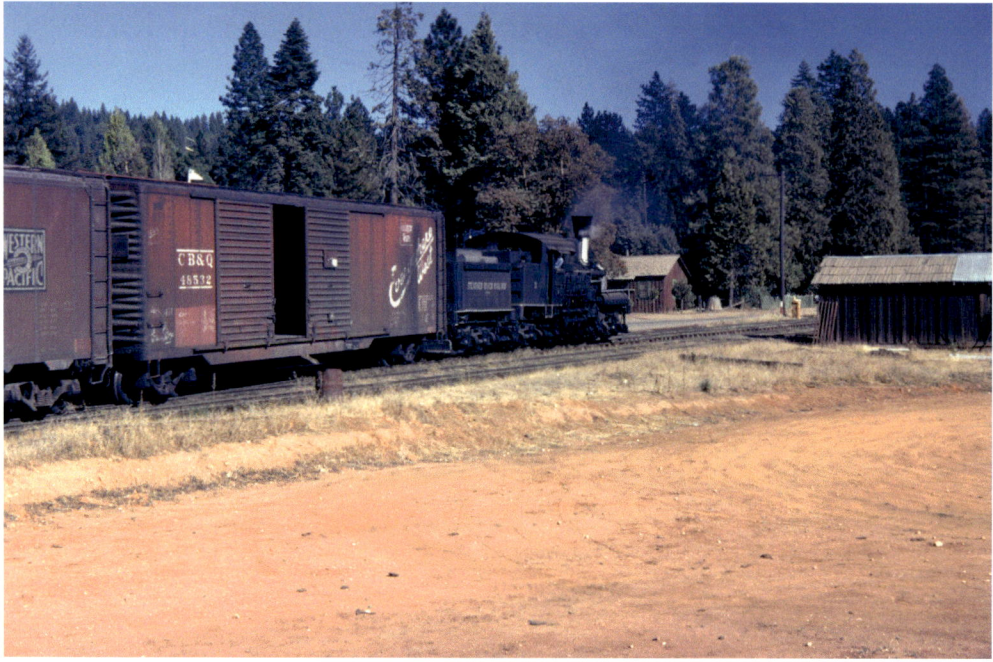

No. 3 switching boxcars at Feather Falls. *Tom Moungovan collection*

on January 16, 1964, in the process directing the State of California to build the relocation. These and other decisions started a lengthy period of litigation between G-P and the state over whether or not the new line had to be built.

In the meantime, FRRY had lumber and woodchips to haul, and once the WP vacated its main line the interchange shifted to Intake, the station at the eastern end of WP's relocation. The state gave FRRY permission to operate over 21 miles of WP's former mainline from Land to Intake, and the WP provided cabooses added to the train for each trip the shortline made. The state agreed to compensate FRRY for its increased operating and maintenance costs associated with its expanded operations.

All went well until the major storms of December 1964. The dam was under construction by this point, with the Feather River flow diverted into tunnels having flow capacities of 110,000 feet per second around the dam site; however, by the middle of the month flows far exceeded those figures, causing water to back up behind the dam. On December 21, FRRY gathered up all of its equipment in Feather Falls into three trains, which headed down to Land and then east up the old WP main to a point above the projected high water mark. The diesel brought out the last train, which included seven cars of scrap rail left on FRRY's bridge over the South Fork of the Feather River. After the bridge a couple cars derailed, and with the water rising fast the crews did not have time to re-rail them, forcing the crew to leave them behind, including several carrying finished lumber. The lake inundated the railroad with up to 100 feet of water at the deepest point for four days before subsiding, leaving the railroad covered with up to four feet of silt in some places and the roadbed washed out in others. Repair work began immediately, with a small Plymouth being used to plow out the silt. Repairing the biggest washout consumed 70,000 yards of fill. The water logged roadbed proved unable to support the weight of the diesel when the FRRY resumed operations in the last week of February, forcing the railroad to increase its cut through the silt so as to allow operations of the remaining Shays. By early March one of the Shays was back in operation, and it alone handled operations until March 19, when the railroad nearly exhausted its Bunker C fuel supplies and the roadbed finally dried out enough to support the diesel.

The railroad continued on after the floods, running almost daily trains to Intake. G-P launched a $750,000 renovation and modernization of the Feather Falls mill, indicating a stable future for the railroad—if it could find a way around the legal impasse with the state over the relocation. In the meantime, the railroad did benefit from the project, namely running concrete trains supporting construction of a relocated highway bridge over Bidwell Bar. In late 1965, G-P transferred a slightly lighter Alco-built diesel switcher from one of its Oregon operations to the FRRY; in an ironic twist of fate, the EMD switcher on the FRRY had bumped the Alco from the old Hammond Lumber railroad in Samoa, and now, six years later, the Alco got its revenge when it sent the EMD packing from the Feather River Railway.

A "RUBBER TIRED RAILROAD"

The litigation between G-P and the State of California dragged on until December 9, 1965, when the two sides reached an agreement. The state agreed to purchase the six miles of the FRRY to be flooded from G-P at a cost of $1,322,605, and to provide the FRRY with three Kenworth trucks. The FRRY, in turn, agreed to end all railroad operations by October 1, 1966. The railroad would thus be allowed to continue operations, but as a motor carrier on a specified route running from Feather Falls to a new reload to be built on the WP at Oroville.

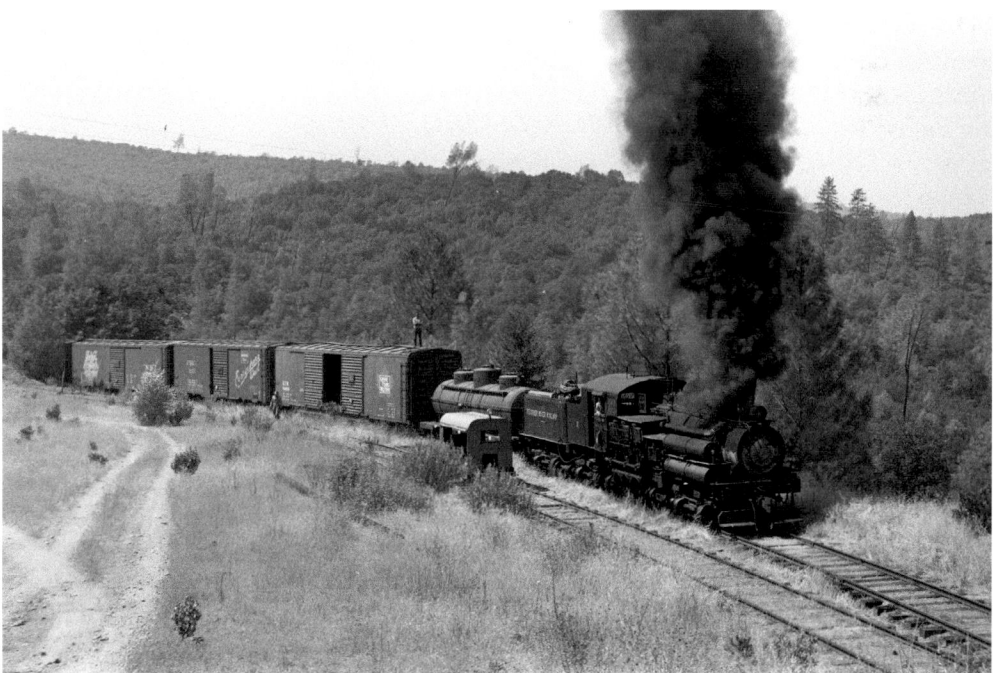

No. 2 arriving at Bidwell Bar on 8/29/1960. *Don Hansen*

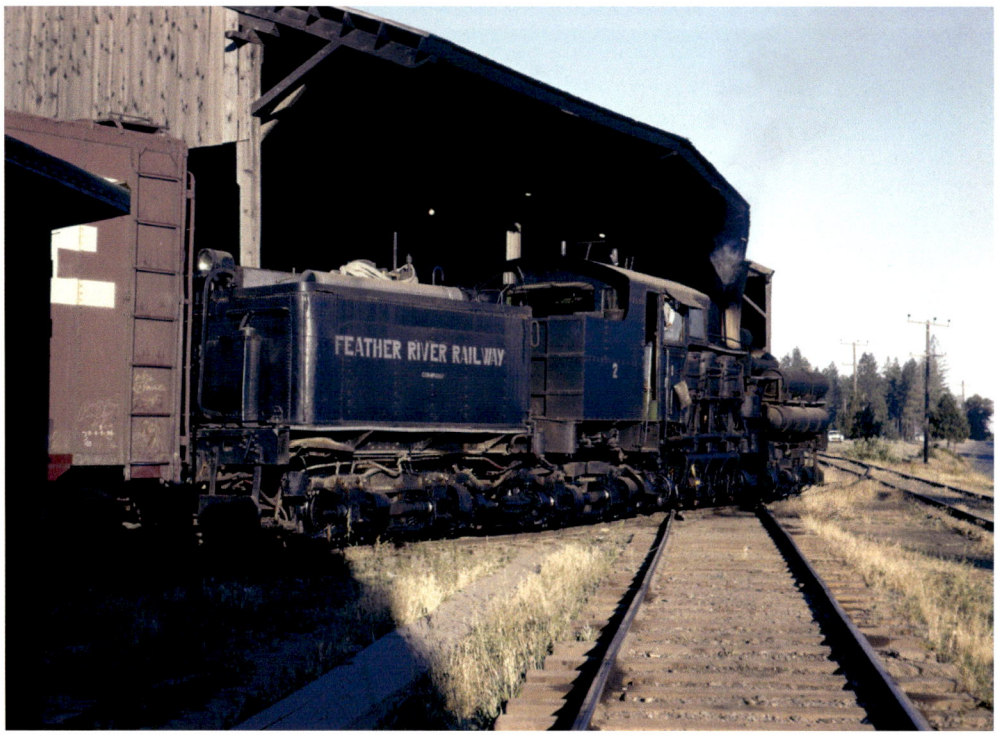

No. 2 switching the Feather Falls mill. *C. G. Heimerdinger Jr.*

Work began on building the required reload facilities commenced shortly afterwards. FRRY set late August 1966 as the target date for shutting the railroad down; however, a brush fire on August 25 burned out two and a half miles of ties on the railroad above Bidwell Bar. The new trucks were ready but the reload was not, and for a week the trucks hauled lumber to a temporary reload established at Bidwell Bar while the section gang replaced ties. The FRRY returned to Feather Falls on September 1; however, by this point the line had only a little more than a week to go. The railroad pulled its last loads from the sawmill on September 8, leaving some of the loads at Bidwell Bar. The next day, the three-man train crew ran the diesel light from Feather Falls to Bidwell Bar, picked up the last loads, and made the run up the old WP to Intake. The return trip consisted of a flatcar and three gondolas. On September 10, the FRRY became a "rubber tired railroad", using its three trucks to deliver lumber to the new reload.

Scrapping the railroad commenced even before the last trains ran, concentrating first on the Feather Falls yard and loading tracks, and then the mainline. A small crane mounted on a WP flatcar drew rails up into the gondolas, and every couple days the diesel would make a run up to Intake to deliver loaded scrap cars and bring in fresh empties. If all went well the scrappers would pick up a half mile of track a day. On October 22, 1966, the crews pulled the last FRRY rails from the ties. G-P subsequently leased the diesel to the state contractor removing the former WP tracks, the mainline from the dam to Intake and the two miles from Land to Bidwell Bar FRRY had operated, and once that job finished the diesel was returned to G-P for disposition. The state completed the dam in 1968.

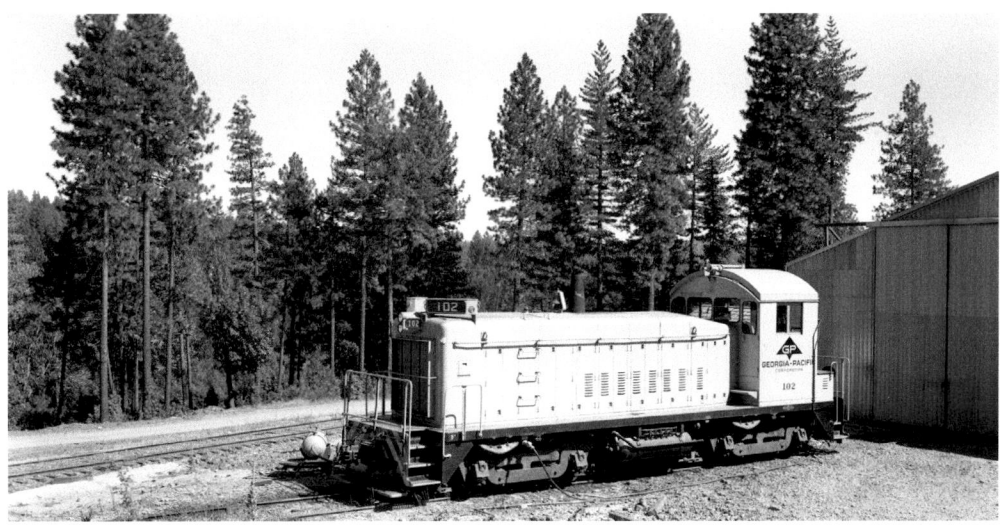

No. 102 in front of the Feather Falls enginehouse. *Don Hansen*

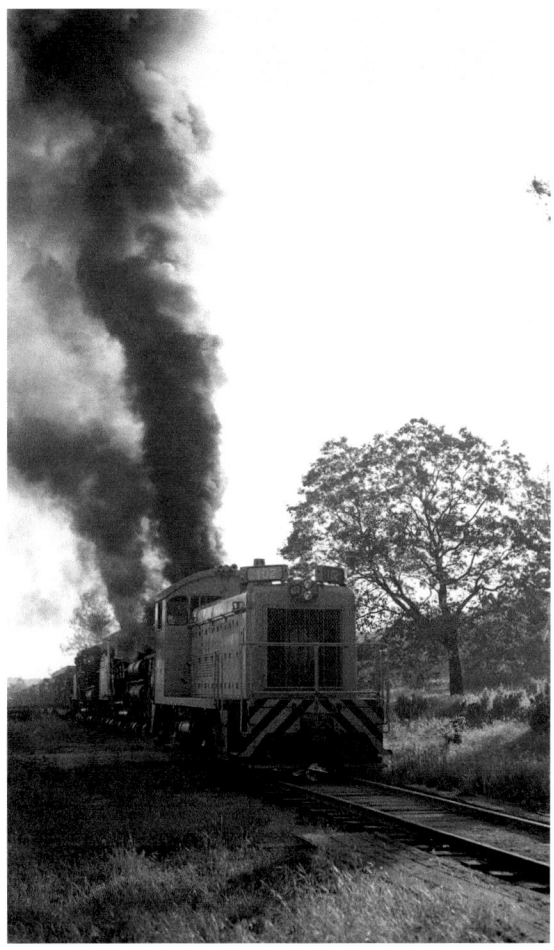

Nos. 102, 3, and 2 leading the railfan excursion on 6/1/1963. *Don Hansen*

The story of the Feather River Railway was not quite done, as the company continued in business running its trucks down to Oroville. The trucks, lettered and numbered FRRY #1, #2, and #3, were to run on a specific route from which they could not deviate without specific permission from the railroad's Feather Falls dispatcher. This situation lasted until 1971, when G-P closed the Feather Falls mill upon opening a new facility in Oroville; G-P cited the loss of the direct rail service as the principle reason for the move. FRRY sold its trucks to G-P and shortly thereafter dissolved, ending the run of one of the more interesting shortlines in California.

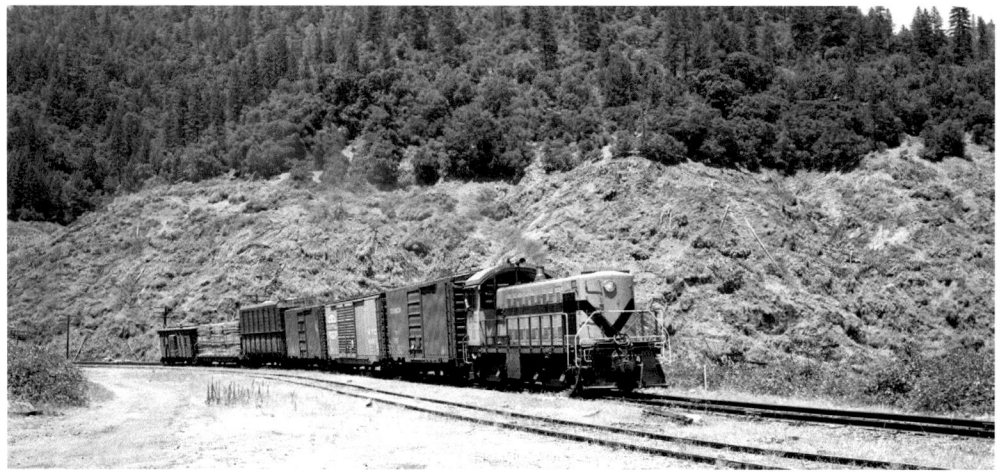

No. 101 rolling along the old WP mainline towards Intake on 7/6/1966. *Don Hansen*

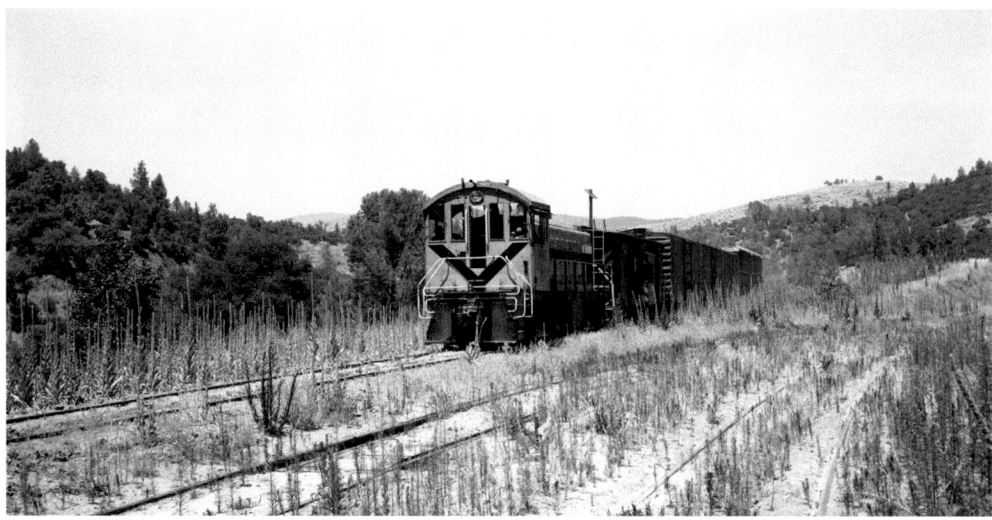

Accumulated silt from the 1964 floods is still evident at Land as the #101 adds a WP caboose to the rear of its train on 7/13/1966. *Don Hansen*

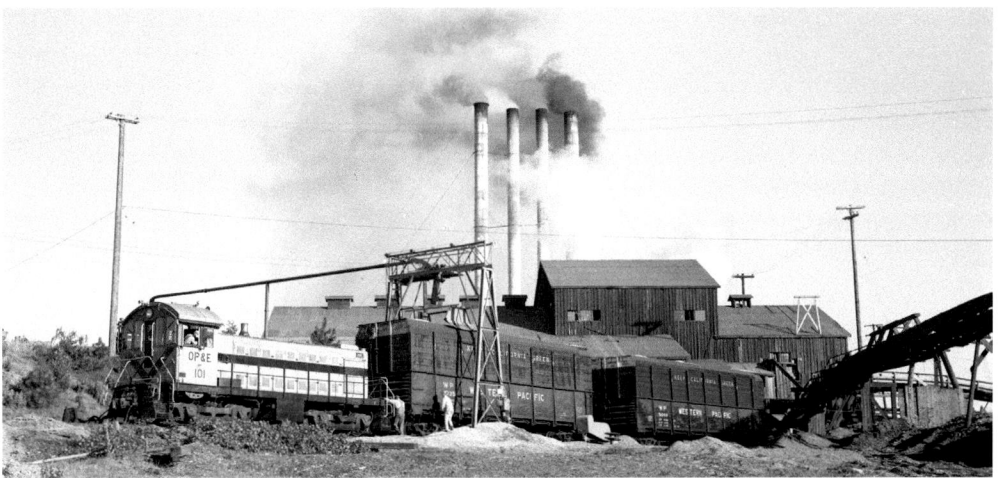

No. 101 switching WP woodchip hoppers at Feather Falls on 7/6/1966. *Don Hansen*

LOCOMOTIVE ROSTER

1—Lima 3-Truck Shay, c/n 3169, Built 1921. Originally Hutchinson Lumber Co. #1; to Feather River Pine Mills #1; to Feather River Railway #1 1959. Never lettered for FRRY. Donated 1961 to City of Oroville and placed on display.

2—Lima 3-Truck Shay, c/n 3177, Built 1922. Originally Hutchinson Lumber Co. #2; to Feather River Pine Mills #2; to FRRY #2. Retired 8/1966 and sold to State of California for display at Oroville Dam, then moved to Railtown 1897 State Historic Park, Jamestown, CA, where it is in service.

3—Lima 3-truck Shay, c/n 3221, Built 1923. Originally Hutchinson Lumber Co. #3; to Feather River Pine Mills #3; to FRRY #3; to Pacific Southwest Railroad Museum, Campo, CA, 1967; to Cass Scenic Railroad #11, Cass, WV, 1998.

4—Porter 0-6-0T, c/n 3951, Built 1907. Originally Mammoth Copper Mining #4; to Hutchinson Lumber #4; to Feather River Pine Mills #4. Never lettered for FRRY. Scrapped *circa* 1957.

5—Willamette 3-truck geared locomotive, c/n 9, Built 1923. Originally Hutchinson Lumber #5; to Feather River Pine Mills #5. Withdrawn from service after a low water event and scrapped *circa* 1957.

8—General Electric 44-ton, c/n 30791, Built 1951. Originally C.D. Johnson Lumber Co. #8, Toledo, Oregon; Leased to FRRY 9/63-7/65 for special projects associated with Oroville Dam construction, then returned to G-P plant at Toledo.

91—Lima 3-truck Shay, c/n 3322, Built 1928. Originally Polson Logging #91; to Rayonier, Inc. #91; to FRRY 1958. Could not pass California boiler inspections upon arrival and used only for a parts source until scrapped 1966.

101—Alco S-3, c/n 78140, Built 1950. Originally Hammond Lumber #101, Samoa, CA; to Georgia-Pacific #101 1956; to Oregon, Pacific & Eastern #101, Cottage Grove, OR, 1960; to FRRY 1965. Never re-lettered from OP & E. To Fordyce & Princeton #1, then #662; to Cadiz #10; to Dardanelle & Russelville #19.

102—EMD SW900, c/n 25504, Built 1959. Originally Georgia-Pacific #102, Samoa, CA; to FRRY 1961; never relettered from G-P. Transferred 1965 to Ashley, Drew & Northern #102, then #907; to Gloster Southern #907; to G-P #907; to Domtar Paper #907.

191—Lima 3-truck Shay, c/n 3343, Built 1929 for stock. To Hofius Steel & Equipment; to Polson Logging Company #191; to Rayonier, Inc. #191 1948; to FRRY 1958. Scrapped in Washington for parts.

"A"—Plymouth DLC, c/n 3476, Built 1930. Originally Garfield & Company (Dealer); to Unemployed Exchange Association; to FRRY; to Oregon, Pacific & Eastern #9, Cottage Grove, OR, then OP & E #14½. Scrapped sometime after 1983.

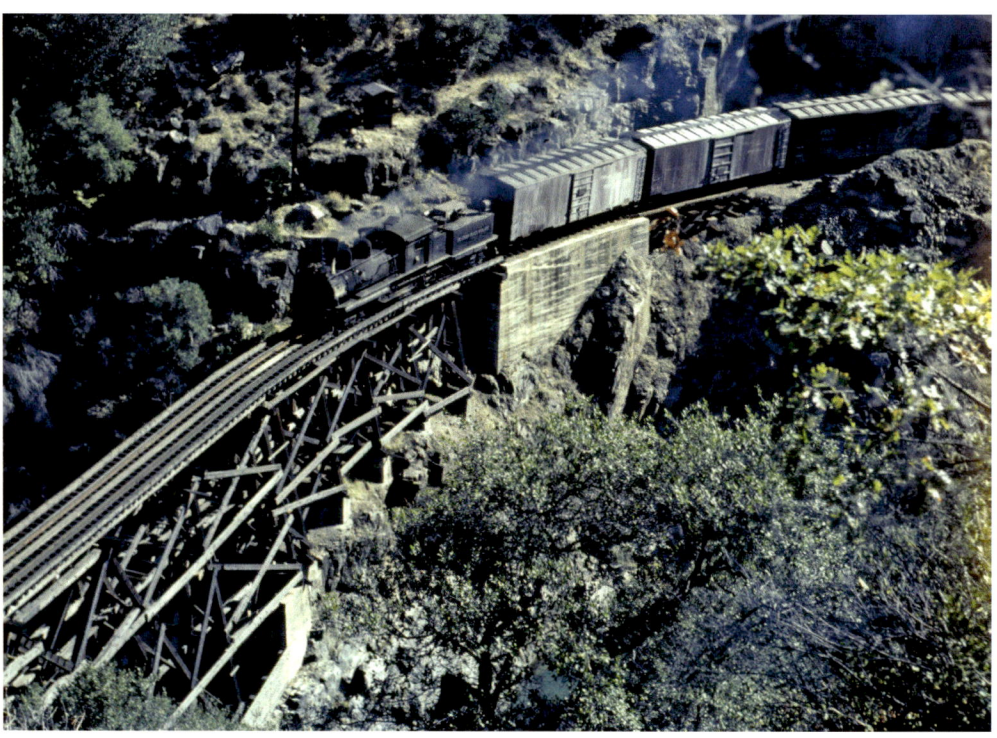

No. 3 leads a train onto the South Fork bridge. *C.G. Heimerdinger Jr.*

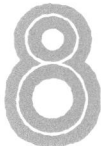

GREAT WESTERN/LAKE COUNTY/ MODOC NORTHERN/LAKE RAILWAY

BACKGROUND

The narrow gauge Nevada–California–Oregon completed its line into Lakeview, Oregon, on January 10, 1912. The company had been building north from Reno, Nevada, since 1880, heading for an eventual goal of the Columbia River; however, Lakeview would be as far as they would get. Southern Pacific purchased most of the N-C-O in October 1925, converting the line to standard gauge shortly afterwards; SP contemplated incorporating the route, along with the Oregon, California & Eastern railroad from Klamath Falls to Sprague River (both in Oregon) and then a new line built from Sprague River to Lakeview, into a shortcut for eastbound Oregon lumber traffic. However, circumstances caused SP to sell a half ownership in the OC & E to the Great Northern, and instead of building east from Sprague River SP built its "Modoc Line" from Klamath Falls southeast to Alturas, California, leaving the 55 miles of the old N-C-O between there and Lakeview as a branchline.

The Lakeview branch survived principally on livestock traffic until the late 1930s, when the U.S. Forest Service opened the nearby Fremont National Forest to logging. By 1940, no less than eight sawmills and remanufacturing plants operated on the line, and a Sustained Unit established in the Fremont forest both guaranteed a minimum log supply and insulated the Lakeview mills from having to compete for logs with the larger mills in eastern Oregon.

SP operated local freights between Alturas and Lakeview six days a week to keep traffic flowing. Despite this, starting in the early 1950s a combination of sawmill closures and increasing truck use cut deeply into business the line handled. By the early 1980s, the customer base declined to three sawmills and two moulding plants shipping less than 1,500 loads a year, and SP managed at most two trains a week. SP gave up on the line, and by August 1985 the I.C.C. blessed a SP abandonment petition.

N-C-O DIVISION OF THE GREAT WESTERN

Local officials in Oregon's Lake County grew increasingly concerned as SP's abandonment application gained traction. The remaining forest products plants needed the railroad to remain competitive, and the line would also be essential for future industrial development. County officials came up with a list of possible options for preserving rail service, the top two of which

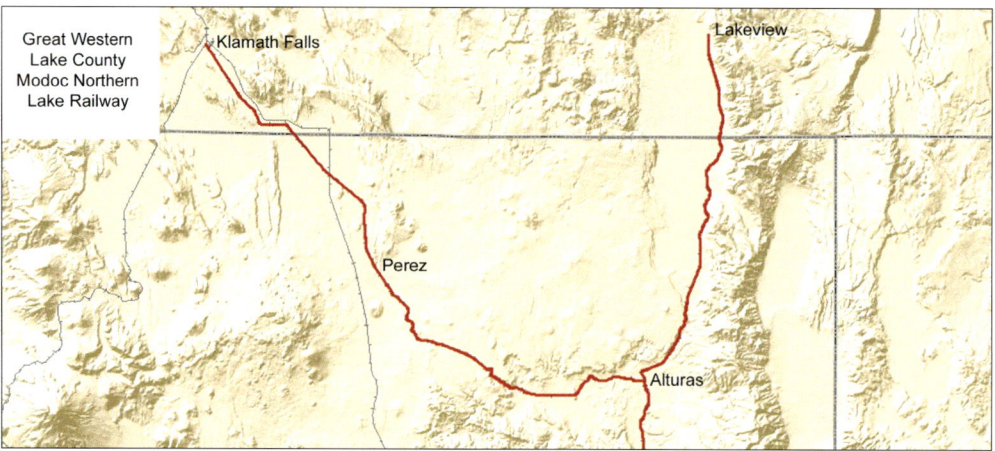

involved levying a per-carload surcharge on traffic the line handled to fund improvements or interesting a shortline operator to buy or lease the line. The first option ran into problems gaining support, and the remote location and dicey economic prospects scared potential shortline operators away.

Lake County did not want to purchase the line, but time clearly running out forced their hand. Three primary obstacles had to be overcome for the county to buy the line, namely (1) state laws prevented local governments from owning property outside the State of Oregon, (2) the county did not have the money to finance the purchase, and (3) the county did not want to operate the railroad themselves. Work began to solve all of these problems; the state legislature enacted a law permitting local governments to own property outside of the state, and then the Oregon State Lottery agreed to fund up to 85 percent of the purchase price. This left only the issue of finding an operator, and the county initially reached an agreement with Kyle Railways; however, those negotiations failed, and the county instead struck a deal with Great Western Railway (GWR) to operate the line on a contract basis. GWR got its start in 1901 serving the sugar industry around Loveland, Colorado, and was looking for expansion opportunities.

SP received authority to abandon the line before the county had all the details worked out, but agreed to continue providing service until the deal either finalized or failed. The Oregon State Lottery came through with a $474,150 grant, and the by now four remaining forest products plants in Lakeview each contributed $21,000. With the money in hand, Lake County was able to tender SP an acceptable offer, and SP ran their last train to Lakeview on January 17, 1986. The next day Great Western had two of their locomotives in Lakeview spliced by a SP flatcar, upon which state, county, GWR, and SP officials held formal ceremonies marking the ownership transfer. The sale became official on January 22.

Operations lasted less than a month before the major storms of February 1986 hit the railroad hard, with damage including 25 slides, three major washouts, and one bridge destroyed. Lake county applied for $229,565 in emergency aid offered by the Federal Railroad Administration, allowing for repairs to be made.

After surviving the first test, the county and GWR got down to the business of running a railroad. Years of deferred maintenance left the property in poor shape, and the county secured additional grants to fund various improvements, including track rehabilitation, constructing an engine house/shop building in Lakeview, and installing short spurs at Davis Creek and Willow Ranch. GWR ran two trains a week over the line to keep the flow of loads and empties going.

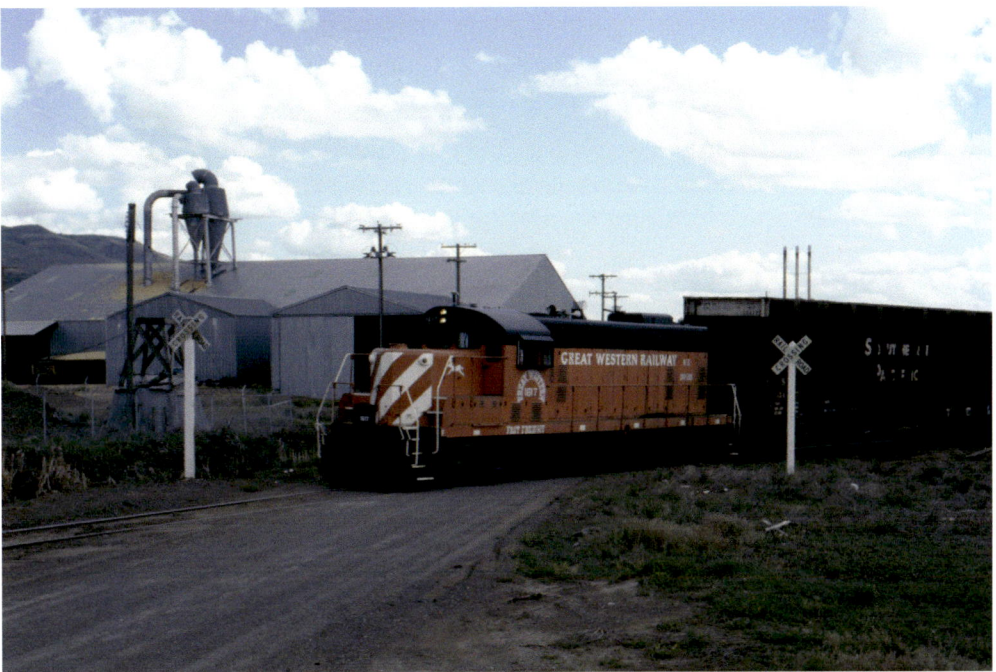

No. 1617 switching at Lakeview. *C. G. Heimerdinger Jr.*

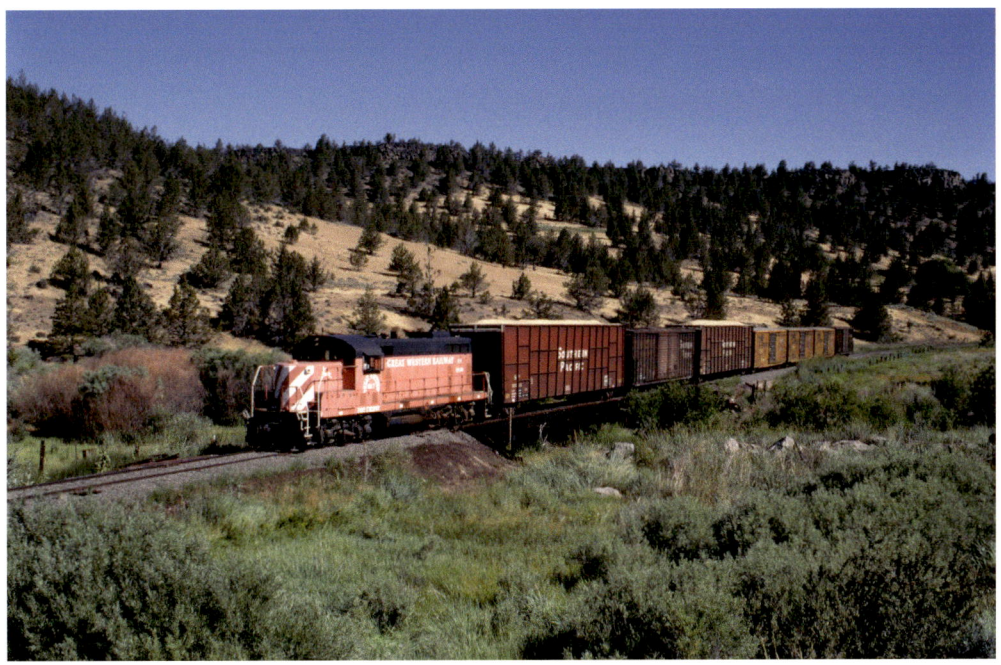

GWR No. 1617 approaching Alturas on 7/20/1988. *Tom Moungovan*

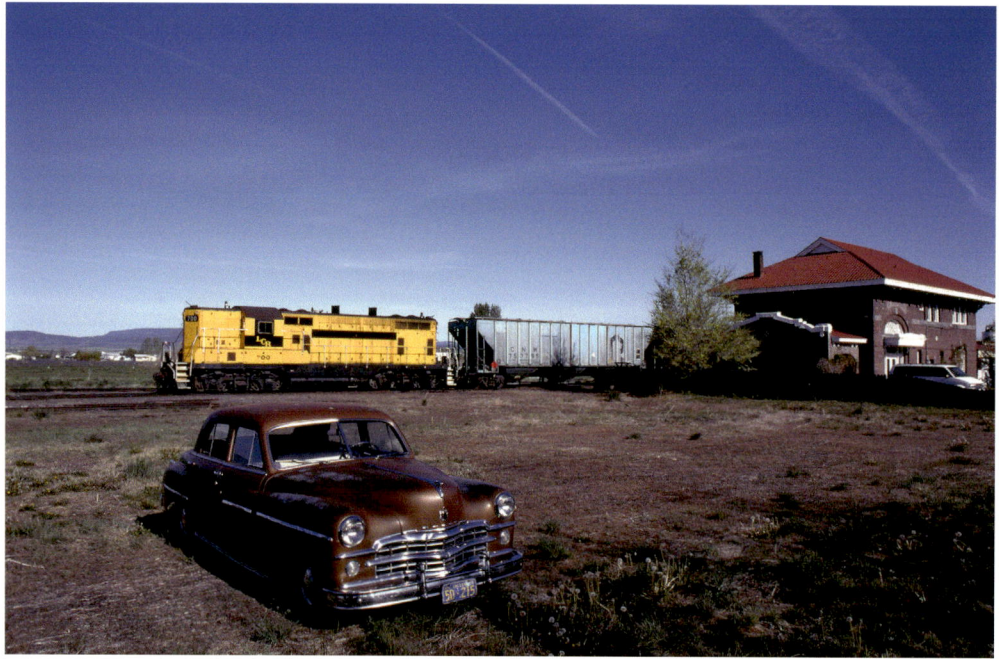

LCR No. 700 passing the old N-C-O depot at Alturas. *Sean Zwagerman*

However, freight traffic continued to drop, as the on-going recession in the timber industry during that time, coupled with increasing logging restrictions on National Forest lands, forced more mill closures in Lakeview. GWR did go after other business as it presented itself, including a couple carloads of lumber Snow Mountain Pine trucked to Lakeview from their big mill in Hines, Oregon, but before that could get going the Wyoming/Colorado Railroad reopened direct rail service to Hines, cutting any further business from this source off. By 1990 only three shippers remained in Lakeview, further reduced to two by 1991. SP at the end of its tenure handled 1,500 loads each year out of Lakeview; by the early 1990s GWR only managed two thirds of that. GWR cut service to one train a week, usually operated late Friday afternoons.

LAKE COUNTY RAILROAD

GWR grew unhappy with the line's performance but continued operations. Lakeview and Lake County desperately needed the railroad to keep what little industry it had left, and as early as 1989 the county contemplated taking over direct operations. However, the arrangement lasted until December 1996, when the operating contract ended and GWR pulled out. Lake County set up the Lake County Railroad (LCR) to take over direct operations. LCR purchased one of the locomotives GWR used on the line, but had trouble purchasing other equipment from the former operator.

Lake County's timing could hardly have been worse. One of the remaining sawmills soon closed, leaving Fremont Sawmills—a Collins company—as the only remaining shipper. To compound problems the railroad immediately experienced extreme difficulties obtaining empty

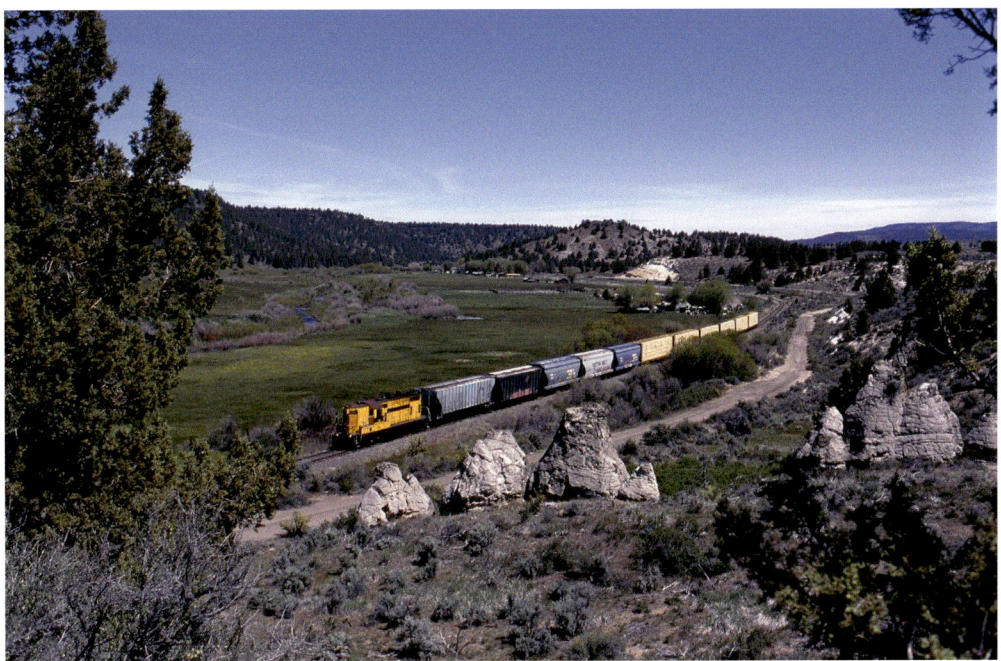

Perlite and lumber loads following the No 700 southbound. *Sean Zwagerman*

cars from Union Pacific. Service over the line dropped to once a week or less. The railroad's only locomotive developed serious health problems, requiring the company to lease one of the GWR locomotives still on the property for a while until a suitable used locomotive could be located.

The county soon came to a critical point with their railroad. Tight car supply kept shipments from the Fremont mill at next to nothing, and the railroad lost money at an alarming rate. The county did not have the resources to subsidize operations, and some in the government advocated shutting the line down and liquidating its assets. However, at literally the last minute a savior arrived on the scene in the form of a Cornerstone Minerals perlite mine located in northern Lake County, near the small community of Paisley. The perlite mine had been trying to start operations for a few years, and they finally got the leadership and financial backing to go into full scale production by late 1998. The Lake County Railroad was on the verge of closing when the first Perlite loads moved, and the new traffic literally saved the railroad.

The Perlite traffic quickly placed LCR on a firm financial footing, but the sharp increase in traffic and heavy perlite loads played havoc with the increasingly tired track structure. The new business allowed LCR to invest heavily in its physical plant, with the biggest project occurring in 2003/2004 when the road replaced several miles of rail with heavier steel salvaged from the abandoned portion of SP's Modoc Line south of Alturas.

MODOC NORTHERN

Declining lumber production in the Pacific Northwest and changing traffic patterns significantly reduced Southern Pacific's use of the Modoc Line, and by the end of January 1987 it had been

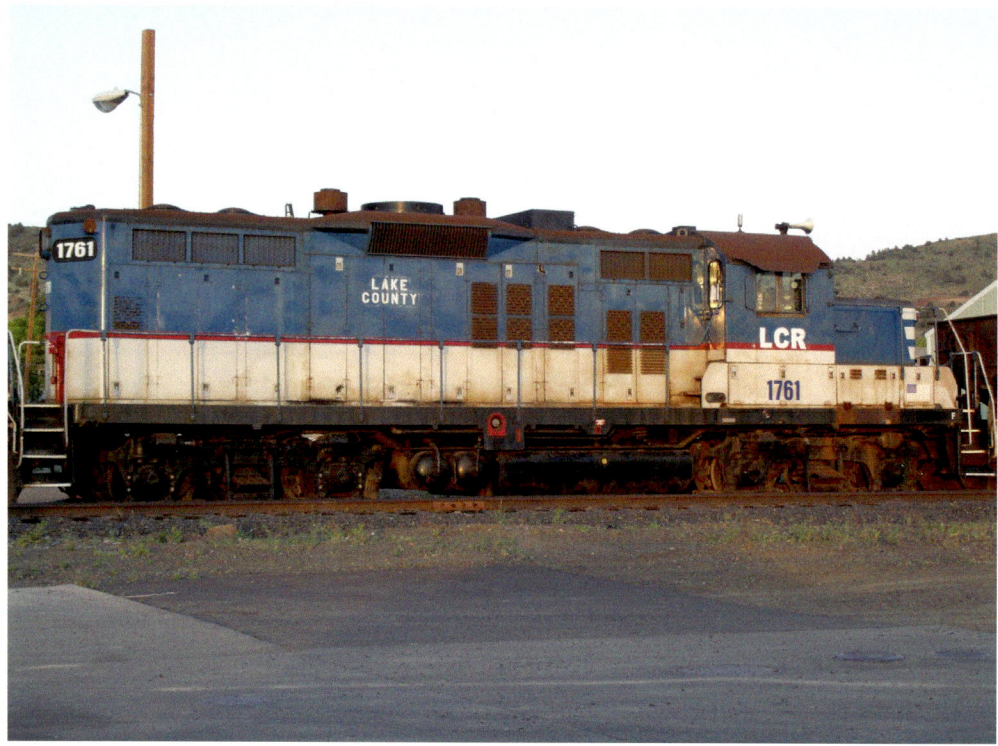

LCR No. 1761 in Lakeview. *Jim Heringer*

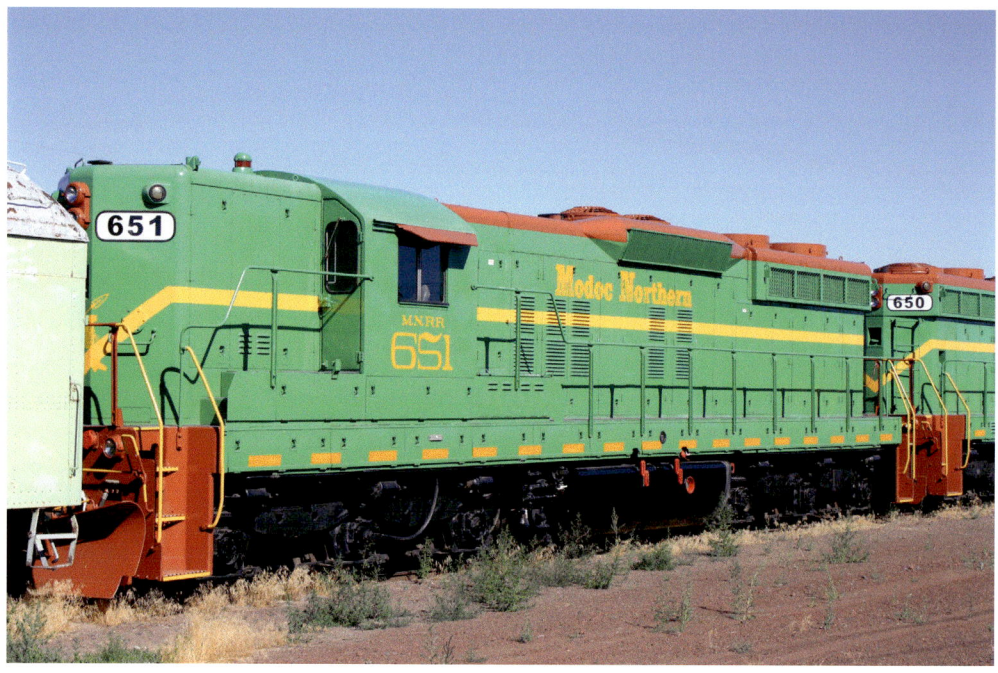

MN No. 651 in Tule Lake. *Jim Heringer*

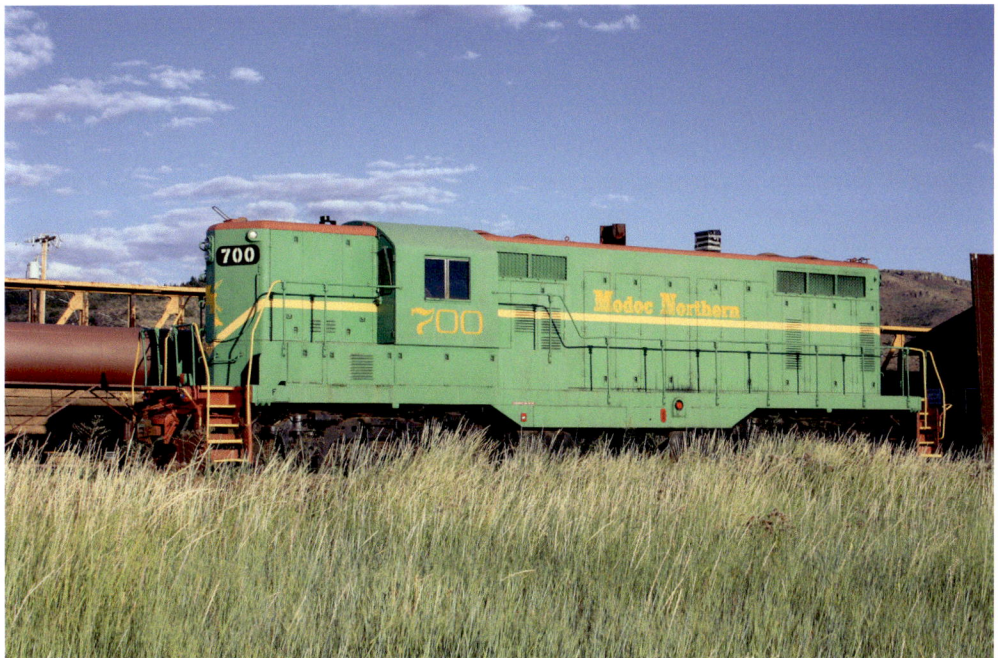

MN Nos. 700 and Lakeview. *Jim Heringer*

closed as a through route. SP continued running a local job from Klamath Falls to Alturas to maintain interchange with GWR. In 1988, the Denver & Rio Grande Western completed its acquisition of the SP, and the new management immediately reopened the line; however, traffic never grew to envisioned levels, and Union Pacific shut the line down again in June 1997. UP continued operating a weekly freight to Alturas to maintain the LCR interchange.

The situation lasted until November 1, 2005, when UP leased the Klamath Falls to Alturas line to the new Modoc Northern Railroad (MN). This line once generated substantial local traffic from the agricultural fields in Oregon and lumber mills in Alturas, but by this point the line handled very little other than the LCR interchange traffic. MN worked hard to drum up new business, meeting with some success. By the spring of 2006 LCR was using the technical expertise and some equipment the MN provided, and these dealings eventually prompted Lake County to lease their railroad to the MN for continued operations. The MN inherited one of the two locomotives with the lease.

Unfortunately, MN would have a short life. Despite increasing traffic from Lakeview, the line simply had too much track and too little revenue to support independent shortline operations, problems compounded by unreliable locomotives and other issues. In May 2009 UP and Lake County cancelled their leases.

LAKE RAILWAY

As MN's impending collapse became apparent, Lake County went searching for a new operator, as they did not wish to restart LCR. The county located Frontier Rail, who assumed the lease

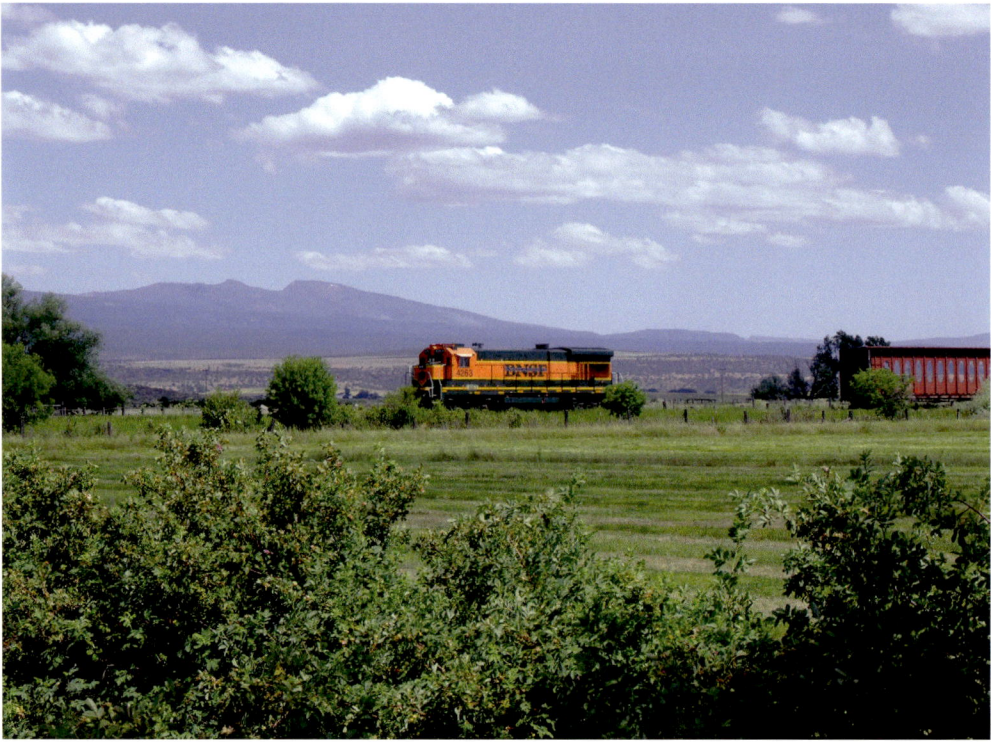

Leased NREX No. 4263 in Alturas in the early days of the Lake Railway. *Lee F. Hower*

immediately after MN vacated the property. Frontier incorporated Lake Railway (LRY) to operate the railroad. LRY immediately set out to rebuild both the physical plant and take care of the traffic base. In December 2009, LRY expanded when it leased from UP its line from Alturas to Perez, where the two railroads established a new interchange. LRY received a major boost in the summer of 2010 when the railroad handled into Lakeview many carloads of pipe for use in a natural gas pipeline then being built from Wyoming to Oregon.

As of this writing, LRY continues operations of the Perez–Alturas–Lakeview trackage. The company continues to invest heavily in improving the property and to this end spent the summer of 2014 replacing a lot of ties, dumping ballast, and performing a lot of surfacing and alignment work. At this point the railroad is far more dependent upon perlite traffic for its continued survival, but Collins' Fremont mill remains a substantial customer, shipping out lumber and woodchips. LRY operates two to three round trips a week and is experiencing some difficulty keeping up with the traffic offered to it. Big things may be on the horizon; in 2014, Red Rock Biofuels received $70 million in government and military grants to construct in Lakeview a plant capable of converting 140,000 tons of woody biomass into 12 million gallons of jet, diesel, and other fuels. Initial reports do not indicate if rail service is being considered as part of these plans, but the potential is there for the LRY to haul the next generation of forest products.

GREAT WESTERN/LAKE COUNTY/MODOC NORTHERN/LAKE RAILWAY

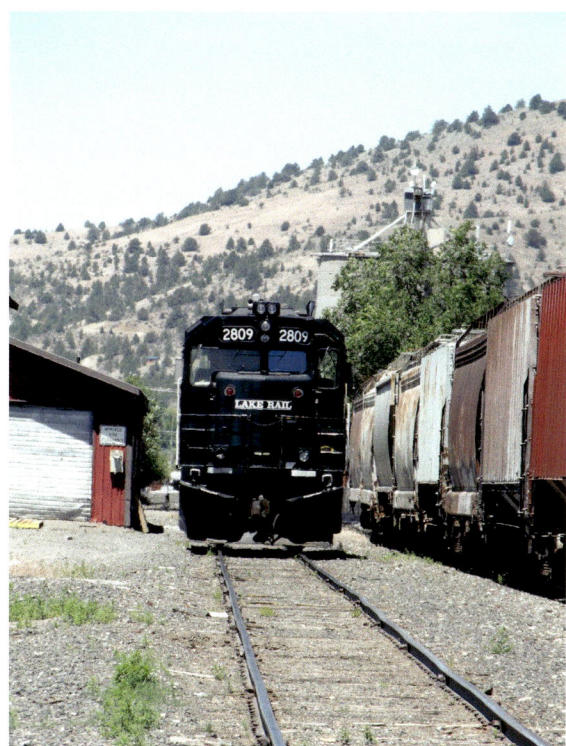

LRY No. 2809 in Alturas in June 2014.
Jeff Moore

LOCOMOTIVE ROSTER

N-C-O Division-Great Western Railway

1589—EMD GP-7, c/n 14697, Built 1951. Originally Chicago, Burlington & Quincy #233; to Burlington Northern #1589; to Great Western Railroad #1589. Transferred to N-C-O division 1986. Disposition unknown, but likely off the roster early 1990s.

1617—EMD GP-7, c/n 18977, Built 1953. Originally Chicago, Burlington & Quincy #261; to Burlington Northern #1617; to Great Western. Transferred to N-C-O Division 1986; sold to Lake County Railroad 1996.

1621—EMD GP-7, c/n 19604, Built 1953. Originally Chicago, Burlington & Quincy #265; to Burlington Northern #1621; to Great Western Railroad #1621. Disposition unknown.

3416—EMD GP-9, c/n 21334, Built 1956. Originally Southern Pacific #5641, then SP #3474, then SP #3416; to Great Western Railroad #3416. Leased to Lake County Railroad for at least the first several months of their operations. Disposition unknown.

Lake County Railroad

700—EMD GP-7, c/n 18604, Built 1953. Originally Nickel Plate Road #436; to Norfolk & Western #2436; to Weyerhaeuser Timber Corp. #776; to Chehalis Western #776; to Columbia & Cowlitz #700; to Lake County Railroad #700; to Modoc Northern 2006.

1617—Acquired from GWR 1996. To Western Rail 2005.

1761—EMD GP-9, c/n 19110, Built 1954. Originally Union Pacific #261; to Morrison-Knudson for re-manufacturing 1980; to Kyle Railways #101; to San Diego & Arizona Eastern #101; to San Joaquin Valley Railroad #101; to Western Rail Incorporated (WRIX); to Lake County 2005; returned to Western Rail in late 2008.

Modoc Northern

During its short tenure, MN used the ex-LCR #700; two General Electric road switchers, a B23-7 and a B30-7; three EMD SD-9s, one of which never made it to the road; and an ex-Burlington Northern SW-1000.

Lake Railway

700—Suffered a severe mechanical failure while leased to Modoc Northern and was in storage at Tule Lake following the demise of that road. Returned to Lakeview 2009, where it has been repaired and is now in service.

4263—General Electric B23-7, Built 1985. Originally ATSF #6406; to BNSF #4263; to NREX #4263 2007. Leased to Cornerstone Industrial Minerals, Lakeview, Oregon, 2008; to LRY. Returned to NREX February 2010 and sent to Council Bluffs, Iowa.

2802, **2809**—EMD GP49, c/n 837049-2 and 84703-5, Built 1983 and 1985. Originally Alaska Railroad #2802 and #2809; to National Railway Equipment; to Frontier Rail; to LRY 2014 and 2009.

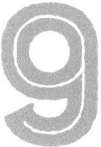

McCLOUD RIVER

BACKGROUND

In 1883, the Central Pacific pushed its railroad north from Redding, California, into the rugged Sacramento River canyon. The advancing rails met the southward building Oregon & California Railroad at Ashland, Oregon, on December 16, 1887. The line opened access to the vast pine forests of northeastern California, but further railroads would be required to harvest most of this timber. Nonetheless, the timber industry thrived along the new railroad, as many sawmills located along the line; however, geography limited available timber supplies.

The valley of the McCloud River presented a natural conduit for stage routes connecting the agricultural areas of the Fall River and Big valleys to the CP/SP mainline. Lack of transportation limited commercial development of the forests along the river, and as the 1800s waned a few pioneering companies tried establishing operations, using traction engines and bull teams to drag lumber to the SP. One started constructing a railroad east up Soda Creek, south of Dunsmuir, but only got four miles spiked down before the company failed.

BEGINNINGS

In mid-1892, lumberman Friday George moved a sawmill he owned from Soda Creek to a place he named Sugar Pine Park on the banks of Squaw Valley Creek at the western end of the McCloud River valley. George used a steam traction engine to move logs from the woods to the mill and then lumber from the mill towards the railroad, supplemented by locally hired teams. A high cost structure and volatile market caused George's operation to fail in 1894. A group of San Francisco based businessmen led by George Scott and William Van Arsdale purchased the property in the following liquidation auction, and by March 1896 they incorporated the McCloud River Lumber Company (McCRLCo) to take over operations. The new owners promptly renamed the community around the mill to Vandale.

Scott and Van Arsdale decided to solve the transportation problems by building a railroad from the mill to the SP at Upton. On January 21, 1897, the backers incorporated the McCloud River Railroad Company (McCRRR), who completed the planned line into Vandale on July 21, 1897. Within a month, the company changed the name of the town again, this time to McCloud. The railroad settled down to hauling mostly green lumber from McCloud to Upton, along with

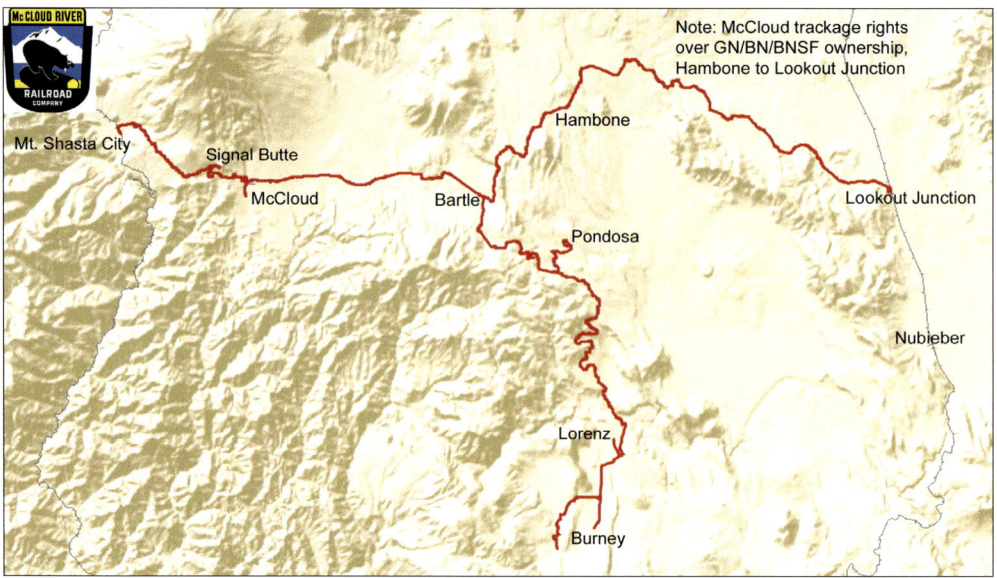

livestock, passengers and express, and any other freight offered to it.

McCRLCo quickly established itself as one of California's largest lumber operations. In 1902, a group of Minnesota timbermen purchased the companies; the new owners invested heavily in the properties, including a new sawmill complex, a planing mill, box factory, and sash and door factory. McCRRR built two lines east into the timber, the first to a second mill located northeast of McCloud the lumber company operated for a short time before a fire destroyed it, and the second east through the heart of the lumber company's vast holdings. The lumber company built a dense logging railroad network off of both lines to bring out the logs. By 1905, the railroad extended service to Bartle, where the rails turned north in a move widely seen as the start of an extension north to Klamath Falls, Oregon, where the ownership group held some timberlands; however, McCRRR rails halted their northward extension twenty-one miles north of Bartle, though the lumber company built its private road for a few miles north of there.

McCRRR existed primarily to move logs from the woods to McCloud and then lumber to the SP, first at Upton until a 1907 line changed moved the connection to Sisson (later renamed Mt. Shasta City). The railroad also handled a good deal of lumber for other smaller sawmills built at various points along the line. The railroad remained a subsidiary of the lumber company until the late teens, when the lumber company turned the railroad's stock directly over to its stockholders, making the railroad a nominally independent company; however, relationships between the two McCloud companies remained tight.

EASTWARD EXPANSION

The McCloud River companies continued their northward expansion until 1919, when the lumber company sold its holdings northeast of Mount Shasta to the Weed Lumber Company and instead purchased from the Red River Lumber Company the first of several timber sales located east of McCloud's cut over lands. McCloud's railroads, mostly the lumber company's private lines, spread east, though a few lines were built or otherwise incorporated into the common

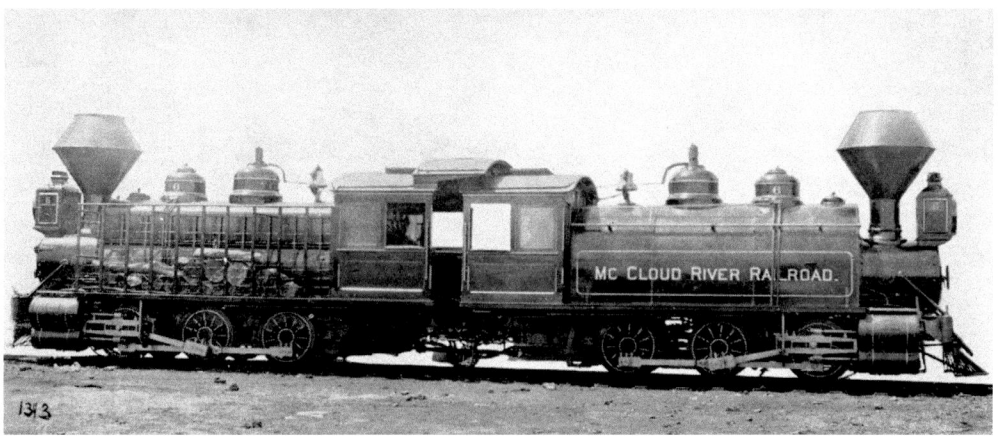

Builder's photograph of the No. 6. *Jeff Moore collection*

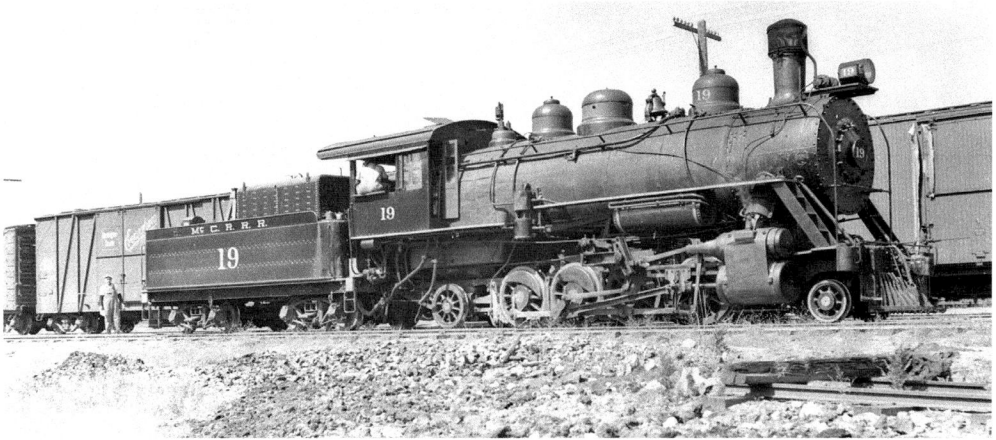

No. 19 switching in the McCloud yards. *Pennington photograph, Jeff Moore collection*

carrier railroad. In 1921, McCRRR collaborated with Pacific Gas & Electric to build the Pit River Railroad from Bartle southeast to a series of major hydroelectric projects then being built along the Pit River. Six years later, McCRLCo built a permanent logging community at Pondosa to serve as the base of its woods operations, and McCRRR extended its service to that community.

In 1928, one of the Red River sales conveyed to McCRLCo the harvesting rights to 80,000 acres located predominately in western Modoc County. The Great Northern (GN) and Western Pacific (WP) railroads at the time were planning their "Inside Gateway" across northeastern California, and this timber sale neatly bridged the eastern end of the existing McCloud operations to the planned GN-WP route. GN quickly struck an agreement to provide McCRLCo rails to build its main line through the sale to a connection with its planned route, along with an option to purchase this main line. Both McCloud companies, GN, and WP struck further agreements under which the McCRRR extended its ownership to Hambone, with the GN owning the line east of there; GN in turn hired McCRRR to operate the line, and on September 15, 1931, the first McCRRR freight operated through to Lookout Junction.

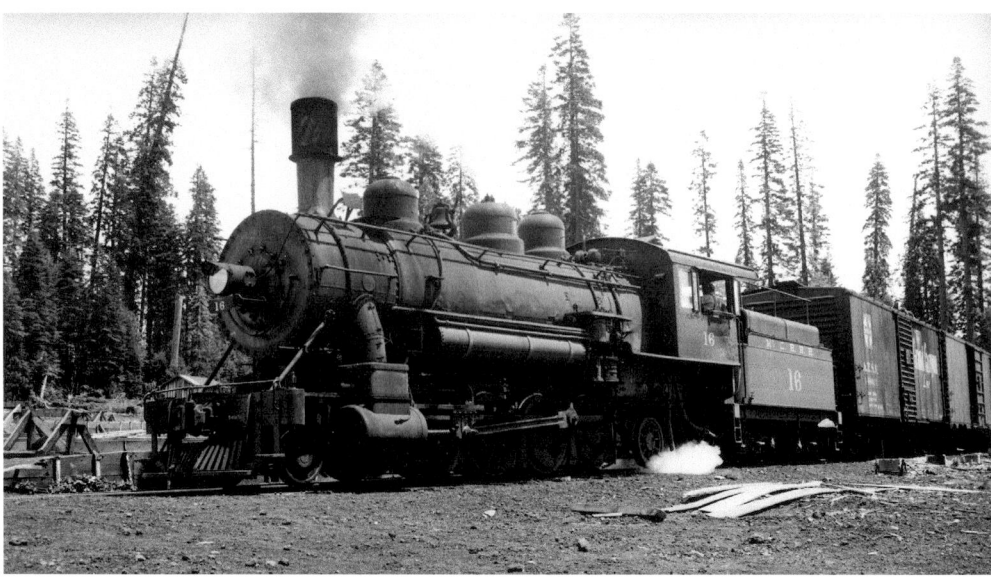

Second No. 16 switching boxcars near Pondosa. *Jeff Moore collection*

The McCloud companies managed continuous operations through the Depression years. McCRRR launched a bus service to augment and then replace its passenger trains. The railroad continued handling substantial traffic for other parties, including other sawmills, livestock, and several carloads a year of wine grapes for the large local Italian population. In the late 1930s, Red River made some of its timber around Burney, California, available, resulting in the construction of three new independent sawmills in the town, two of which promptly started shipping lumber over McCRRR from a reload established near Pondosa.

PROSPERITY

McCloud boomed from the late 1940s into the early 1960s. In the early 1950s, Jack Wagner wrote in his classic *Short Line Junction*:

> The McCloud River Railroad is a paradox and an optical illusion. It's large and yet it's small. You know full well that this is a short line, but the shops, yards and offices give the appearance of a much larger road. You begin to feel that this was once one of the trunk lines that somehow or other has been compressed to fit into a miniature empire of its own. And when you look up and see the towering magnificence and brilliant whiteness of Mount Shasta, looking for all the world like an exaggerated backdrop, you begin to feel that the whole thing is unreal and somehow you have been reduced to Lilliputian proportions and the scene is the window of some department store and the time is Christmas. But this is only a passing thought. When a train of logs clatters past, you put aside all visions of toy trains and department store displays and return to the realities of the present. The scale in miles may be small, but the operation here is fast moving, efficient, and plenty big time.

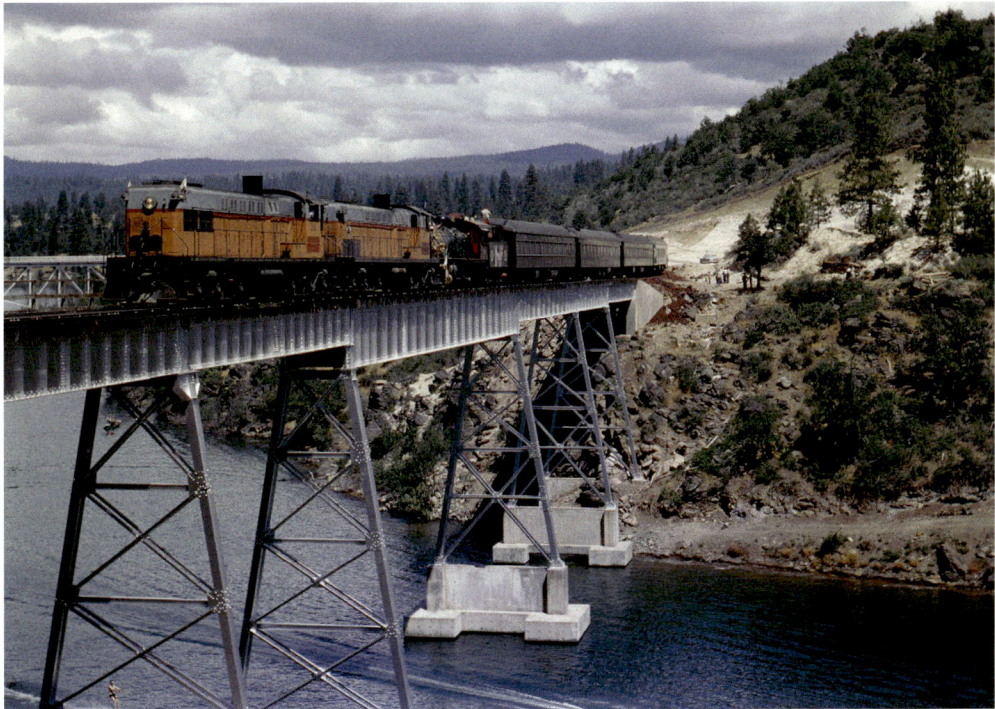

Nos. 29, 28, and 25 leading a special train celebrating completing the Burney extension across the Lake Britton bridge on 7/3/1955. *Jeff Moore collection*

Jack did not understate the railroad as it was; fourteen steam locomotives graced the roster, most of them heavily modernized by the efficient McCloud shops. At least three and sometimes more long trains departed McCloud each day, taking loaded boxcars and empty log flats out and bringing back loaded log flats and empty cars for tomorrow's lumber loads. Additional McCRLCo crews, using mostly equipment leased from McCRRR, worked the logging railroad lines snaking back into the woods from various log camps. A dozen and a half men worked in the shops, and several dozen more lived in the various section camps strung along the line.

A quartet of Baldwin diesels replaced steam power on the railroad by 1953. In 1954, McCRLCo purchased harvesting rights to 80,000 acres of Fruit Growers Supply Company land south of Burney, and the lumber company financed a thirty-two mile extension of the McCRRR to Burney. Two more Baldwin diesels and a 70-ton General Electric switcher the lumber company purchased put all steam to bed by the end of 1955; however, the railroad's president talked the board of directors into storing one of the steam locomotives as a token of the glory years.

McCRRR handled its first railfan excursion in 1948, followed by several more between 1950 and 1955. In 1962, the railroad dragged its old #25 out of storage and brought it back to operation. Weekend railfan trips became commonplace on the railroad.

By 1963, McCRLCo was one of the last large independent lumber companies remaining in California. U.S. Plywood Corporation (USP) made an offer the stockholders could not refuse, and soon reunited the lumber and railroad companies under their control. USP made many changes early in its tenure, including shifting all log movements to trucks, closing the woods camps, and ending McCloud's status as a company town.

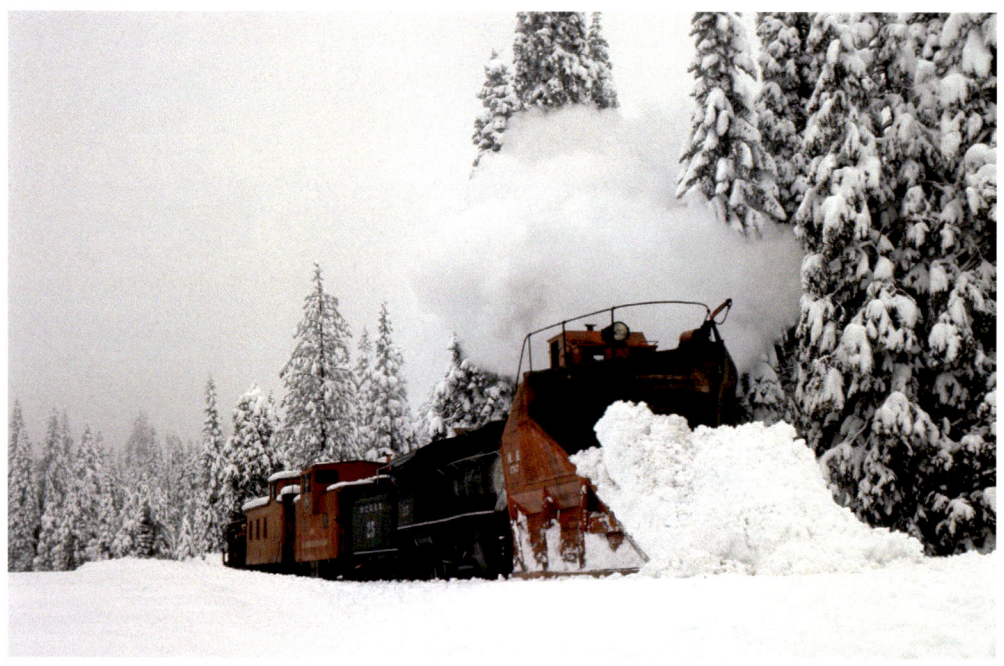

No. 25 pushing one of McCloud's large bucker plows on a railfan trip. *C. G. Heimerdinger Jr.*

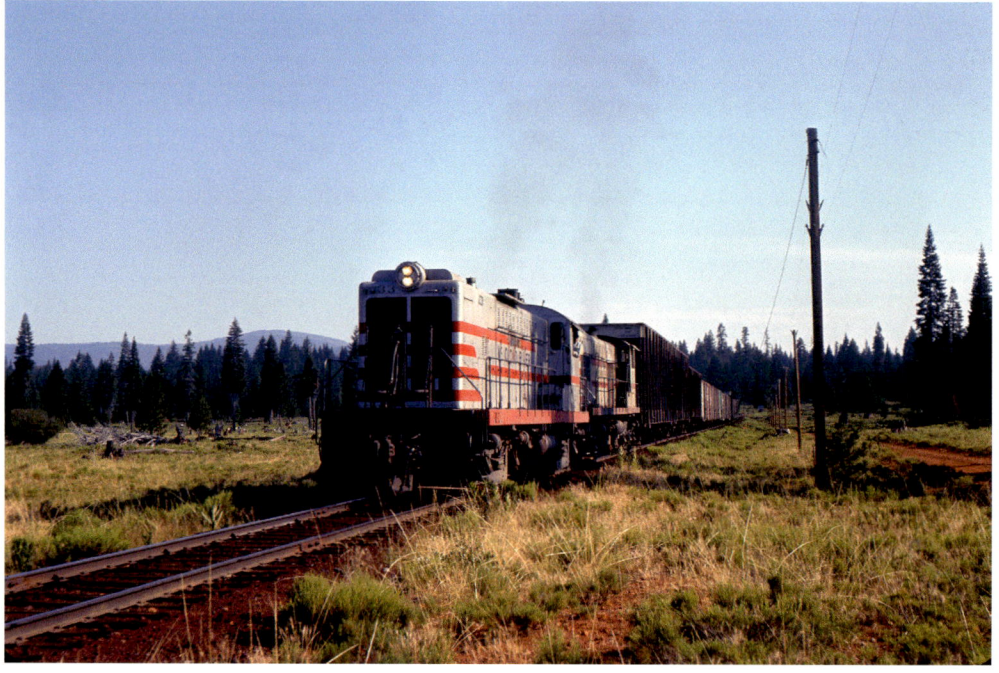

No. 33 and 29 rolling a Burney-bound freight through Bartle. *C. G. Heimerdinger Jr.*

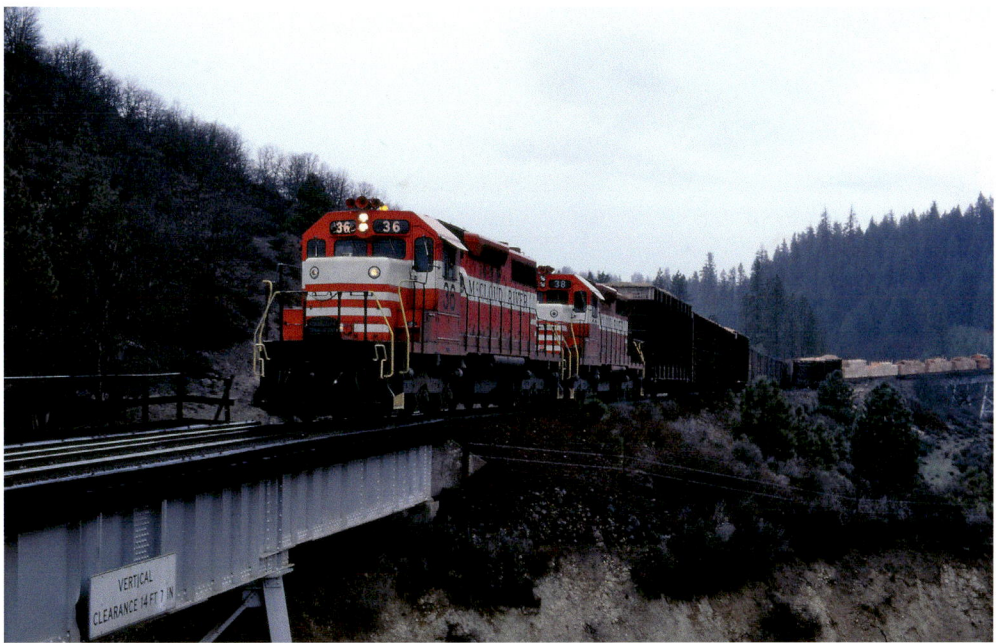

Nos. 36 and 38 at Lake Britton in January 1978. *Lee F. Hower*

Despite the loss of the log traffic, the railroad remained healthy. Daily trains still departed for Mt. Shasta City, Lookout, and Burney. Six sawmills and a plywood plant provided most of the traffic, supplemented by inbound carloads of fuel oil and propane, sporadic agricultural traffic, and occasional deliveries of supplies and equipment for more PG & E hydroelectric projects. The railfan excursion program remained strong, with a couple private companies attempting regularly schedule tourist railroad operations. The railroad's corporate parent changed through mergers, first to U.S. Plywood-Champion Papers, Inc., and then to Champion International Corporation. The steam excursion program lasted until 1975, when gasoline shortages cut into patronage and rising insurance rates sidelined the steam locomotive.

THE STRUGGLE TO SURVIVE

In December 1976, Champion International sold the McCloud River Railroad to Itel Corporation, one of the principle companies cashing in on the Incentive Per Diem boxcar boom. The McCloud shop became home to large numbers of boxcars Itel leased to other shortline railroads around the west, and Itel leased McCRRR its own fleet of 405 new boxcars, later supplemented with 94 former U.S. Plywood all-door cars rebuilt to standard boxcars.

Unfortunately, California's timber industry crashed at the end of the 1970s. By the early 1980s a series of sawmill closures, cumulating with Champion International shuttering the McCloud mill, reduced McCRRR's customer base to one plywood plant near Burney, plus two sporadically operating sawmills. As the incentive *per diem* boxcar market imploded, Itel sent many cars returned to it to McCloud for storage, and most of these ended up on McCloud's roster.

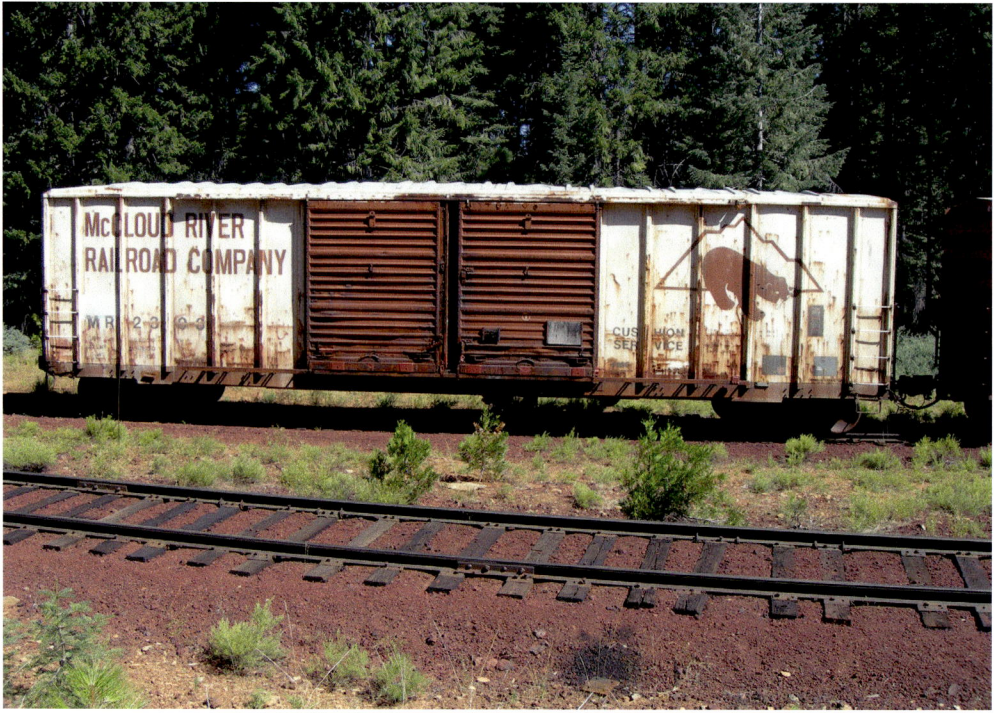

One of McCloud's incentive *per diem* boxcars. *Jeff Moore*

Despite the dark times, the railroad collaborated with the Great Western Railroad Museum to restore its steam locomotive to operation in 1982, sparking a revival of the steam excursion program. Perhaps the highlight of this occurred in 1985, when Columbia Pictures used the railroad as the set for a climactic scene in the movie *Stand By Me*, in which the locomotive chased the four main characters across the Lake Britton bridge. The last of these excursions operated in 1986.

McCRRR grimly hung on through the early 1980s. Traffic declined substantially, from 7,820 loads in 1976 to 801 loads in 1986. Both sawmills in Burney resuming full operations stabilized the company, aided substantially by a Federally-funded track rehabilitation grant the railroad received in 1982. The railroad launched an aggressive marketing campaign to attract new business, focusing heavily on the potential of an old warehouse building U.S. Plywood built in McCloud as a reload center. In 1983 and 1984 McCRRR originated many carloads of redwood from Simpson Timber's mill at Korbel (see Chapter 3). Then, in the later part of the 1980s the railroad landed three new substantial customers: Dicalite, a diatomaceous earth mining company, commenced loading bulk and bagged minerals at Cayton; a Burney co-generation plant received carloads of hog fuel; and, most importantly, a printing firm near Reno, Nevada started receiving paper through the McCloud reload, with trucks making the final delivery. Traffic handled in 1991 rebounded to 1,780 loads. However, by this point Itel had decided to rename itself Anixter and refocus exclusively into the telecommunications infrastructure industry, resulting in the sale of all other businesses the company owned. GE Capital purchased Itel's fleet of railcars, and various parties stepped forward to purchase various railroads.

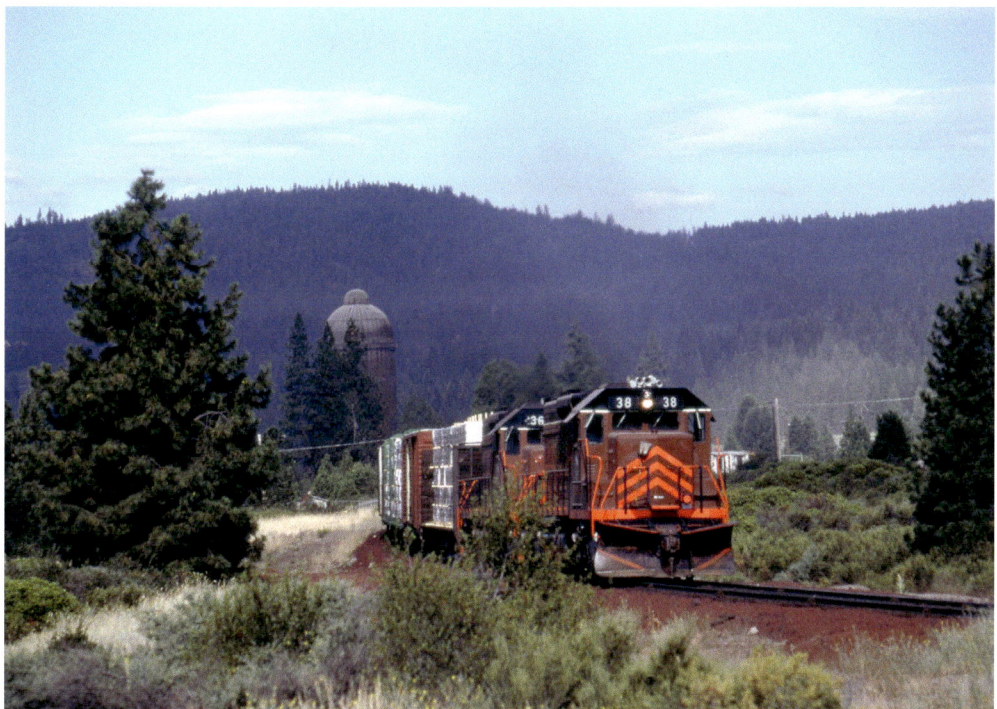

The McCloud sawmill's iconic sawdust burner awaits it fate as Nos. 38 and 36 depart for Lookout Junction in the early 1980s. *Wayne I. Monger*

A NEW START

In the early months of 1992 Itel signed an agreement selling McCRRR's assets to 4-Rails, Inc., set up by McCRRR's last president and his family. The affiliated McCloud Railway Company (MCR) commenced operations on July 1, 1992. By this point the railroad served only three steady shippers, namely the paper reload, a Sierra Pacific Industries sawmill in Burney, and Dicalite. Operations continued on much as they had before. The new company launched aggressive efforts to increase business, resulting in three new traffic sources from Burney by the fall of 1993, specifically woodchips SPI shipped to the Blue Herron Paper Mill in Oregon, outbound wheat from Goose Valley Ranch, and sugar beets.

In 1994, MCR hosted a chartered passenger excursion powered in part by a surviving ex-McCloud steam locomotive rented from the neighboring Yreka Western. The excursion graphically demonstrated the allure the railroad still held for railfans, prompting MCR to launch back into the passenger business. Excursions sponsored by the railroad or local groups operated out of McCloud and Burney starting in 1995, then, on June 1, 1996, the new Shasta Sunset Dinner Train made its first run. The McCloud community had been trying to reinvent itself, eventually settling on an upscale tourist destination centered around several bed and breakfast operations, and the dinner train complemented these other operations. Then, in 1997 the railroad returned its steam locomotive to service. A year later the railroad purchased a second former McCloud River steam locomotive, returning it to service in February 2001.

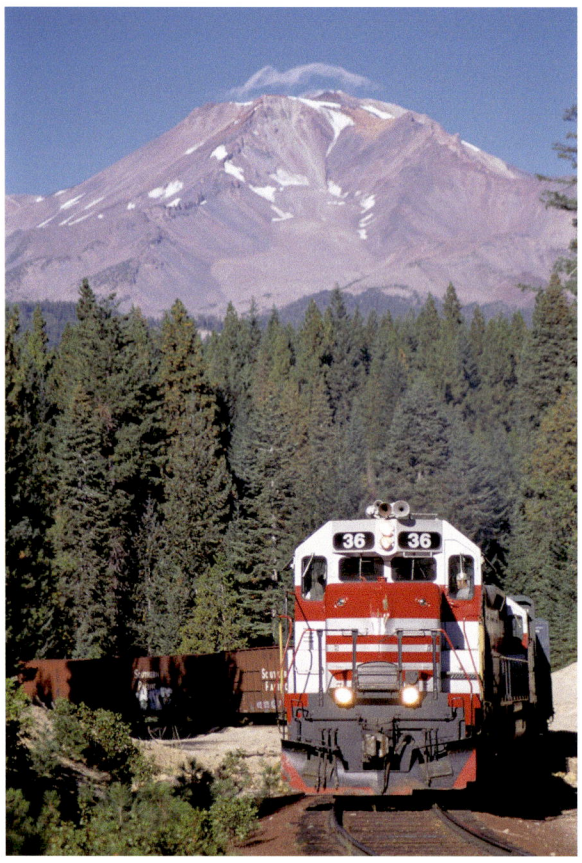

Left: Nos. 36 and 37 at Big Canyon on 11/25/1999. *Travis Berryman*

Below: No. 18 with a railfan excursion on 10/10/2004. *Travis Berryman*

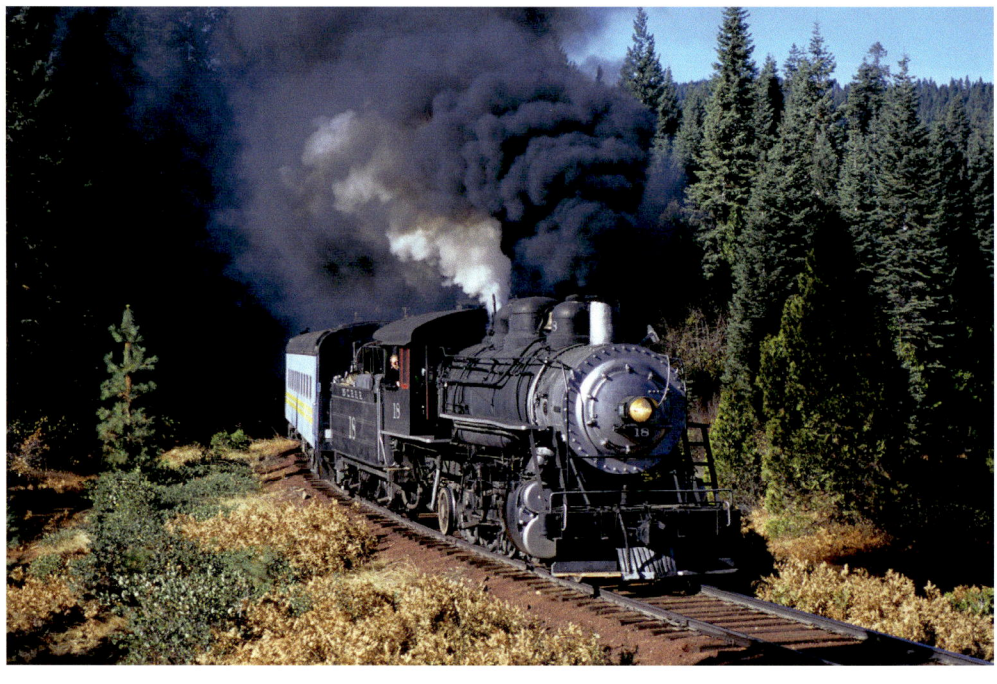

As the passenger traffic grew, the freight business suffered a major setback after BNSF received trackage rights directly into Reno as a condition of the UP-SP merger. MCR immediately lost the paper reload business, then representing approximately half of its freight revenues. The wheat and sugar beet traffic also ended, leaving the railroad with only Sierra Pacific and Dicalite as shippers. The passenger business remained strong, partially compensating for the loss of the freight revenue; however, the railroad still had to drastically cut expenses.

RETRENCHMENT

MCR arrived at a crossroads in 2003 and 2004. The passenger operations remained robust, anchored by the dinner train and a dozen or more steam excursions per year. The freight business continued to be slow, especially affecting the Bartle to Lookout line which saw at best one train a week. MCR interchanged less than six loads a week to BNSF; the paucity of traffic did not warrant continued operations of the line to Lookout, and by the end of 2003 BNSF struck a haulage agreement with UP under which the latter road moved MCR–BNSF traffic between MCR at Mt. Shasta City and BNSF at Klamath Falls, Oregon. MCR ran its last train to Lookout on December 16, 2003, and BNSF received permission to abandon the Hambone-Lookout trackage the following year.

More problems soon compounded the loss of the Lookout line. Sierra Pacific Industries opened a new reload for the Burney mill on the BNSF at Nubieber, cutting deeply into MCR's remaining traffic base. Years of deferred maintenance caught up with both tracks and equipment, and the railroad soon suffered mightily from derailments and equipment failures. Financial losses the freight business incurred averaged a half million dollars per year in 2002–2004. These factors, plus a lack of any real prospects for improved conditions, finally forced MCR's hand. On June 27, 2005, MCR submitted an application for authority to abandon its railroad, and the last freights to Burney operated on the last day of June 2006.

The next several years were trying ones for the railroad. Nestle proposed a mammoth water bottling plant for the old McCloud sawmill site, prompting the railroad to retain its common carrier status for the McCloud–Mt. Shasta line. However, the project encountered stiff local and regional opposition, eventually causing Nestle to cancel the plans. MCR at the same time had to deal with attempts by a couple parties to force a sale of the line east of McCloud, costing the company substantial time and money, only to have those efforts fail as well. Then came the recession of 2008, cutting deeply into the dinner train patronage. The last obstacles to MCR's abandonment of the line east of McCloud were removed by mid-2008, allowing the railroad to salvage the track materials. The dinner train and a little bit of car storage supported the remaining operation until January 2010, when the railroad suspended operations.

In mid-October 2011, the Mike Williams Group, owner of a railroad salvage firm and a small family of other shortlines spread from Missouri to Washington purchased the operating companies and assets. The new owner sent the dinner train cars to another operation in Idaho and has scrapped much of the equipment still in McCloud. The Williams Group has indicated possible plans for car repair and storage; passenger operations of some form may yet return; and a new owner of the McCloud sawmill site has launched a redevelopment of the site that might attract a new rail shipper. As of this writing, MCR remains in a state of suspended animation, waiting for whatever comes next.

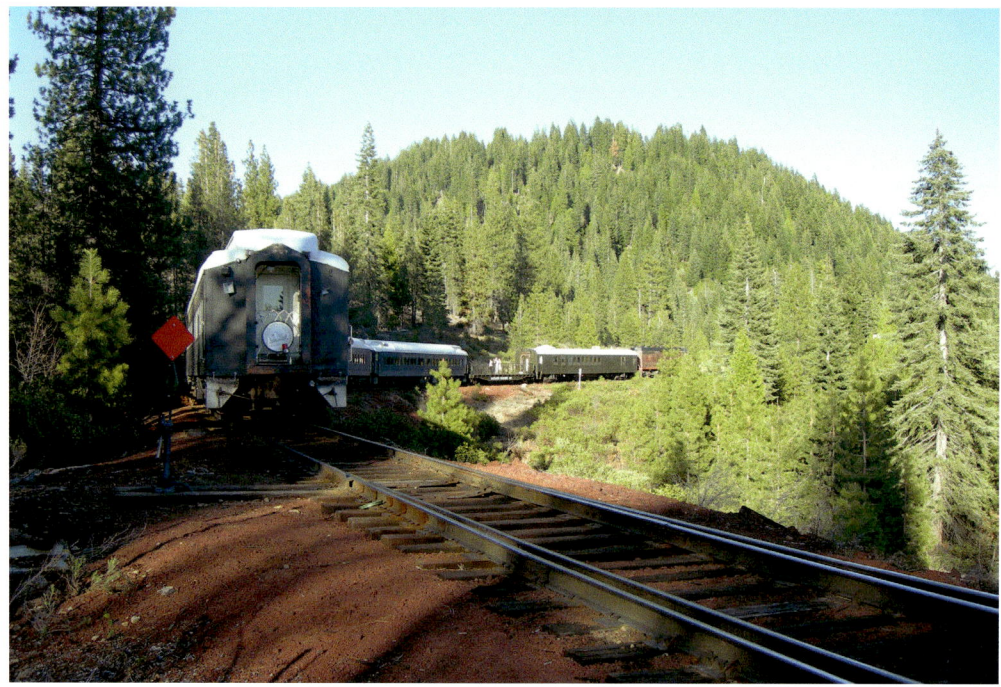

The Shasta Sunset Dinner Train at Signal Butte. *Jeff Moore*

LOCOMOTIVE ROSTER

1—Baldwin 2-6-0, c/n 11627, Built 1891. Originally California Railway #2, Oakland, California; to McCRRR #1 *circa* 1897. Re-numbered #12 6/1906.

2—Stearns 3-truck Heisler, c/n unknown, Built 1897/1898. Named *Van Arsdale*. Acquired new. Off roster *circa* 1900. Disposition unrecorded, but likely returned to manufacturer and scrapped.

3—Stearns 2-truck Heisler, c/n 1004, Built 1896. Originally Port Blakely Mill Company #3, named "Maggie"; Returned to Stearns; to McCRRR *circa* 1898; to Weed Lumber Company #2 by 1904; to Nevada County Narrow Gauge; to Willamette Valley Lumber Company #6 1914. Scrapped 1930.

4—Baldwin 2-6-2, c/n 16239, Built 1898. Acquired new. Retired 1934. Scrapped 1939.

6 (5)—Baldwin 0-6-0T+0-6-0T, c/n 17684 and 17685, Built 1900. Acquired new, but separated into two locomotives shortly after arrival, with one half renumbered #5. #5 to Weed Lumber Company 1917; to Lystul–Lawson Logging Company #5 1927. Scrapped. #6 to Atkinson Construction Company #6 1928; to A. D. Schader #6; to Permanente Metals Company #2515. Scrapped 1949.

7—Baldwin 4-6-0, c/n 7935, Built 1886. Originally St. Louis & San Francisco #300-series (possibly #302?); to Atlantic & Pacific #52 *circa* 1890; probably disposed of prior to consolidation of A

& P into the Santa Fe Pacific in 1897; to McCRRR by late 1900. To F. Rolandi (Hetch Hetcy Dam Contractor) 1917. Final disposition unrecorded.

8, 9—Baldwin 2-6-2, c/n 18595 and 18596, Built 1901. Acquired new. #8 to Amador Central #7 1939, then placed on display in Ione, CA, where it remains today; #9 to Yreka Western Railroad #9 1939; to Amador Central #9 1942; to Nezperce & Idaho Railroad #9 1945; to private party 1967; moved to Mid-Continental Railroad Museum, North Freedom, Wisconsin, for restoration, then to Kettle Moraine Scenic Railroad, North Lake, Wisconsin, 1972. Operated on Kettle Moraine until it closed in 2002. To Age of Steam Roundhouse, Sugarcreek, Ohio, 2015.

10—Baldwin 2-6-2, c/n 18674, Built 1901. Acquired new. To Yreka Western Railroad #10 1925. Scrapped 1944 at Yreka.

11—Baldwin 2-6-2, c/n 23875, Built 1904. Acquired new. To W. S. Zimmerman (dealer/scrapper in Portland, OR) 1926; leased by Consolidated Timber for use in Tillamook Fire salvage logging efforts. Scrapped 1939.

12—Baldwin 2-6-0, c/n 11627, blt. 1891. R-numbered from #1 6/1906. Retired 1925 and scrapped 1932.

14, 15—Baldwin 2-8-2, c/n 30850 and 30851, Built 1907. Acquired new. #14 retired 1950 and sold for scrap. #15 sold 12/1949 for scrap.

16:1, 17:1—Lima 3-truck Shays, c/n 2401 and 2402, Built 1911. Acquired new. Both sold to Fruit Growers Supply Company #4 and #5, Susanville, CA, in 1924 and 1925. Both scrapped 1953.

16:2—Baldwin 2-8-2, c/n 39394, Built 1913. Originally Silver Falls Timber Company #101; to McCRRR 1939. Sold 1955 to Purdy Company for scrap.

17:2—Baldwin 2-8-2, c/n 42912, Built 1916. Originally Pacific Portland Cement Co. #102; to Hyman-Michaels (dealer); to McCRRR 1942. Sold 1950 for scrap.

18—Baldwin 2-8-2, c/n 41709, Built 1914. Originally ordered by an Arkansas lumber company, but sold new to McCRRR after the original order fell through. Displayed through 1915 at Panama-Pacific Exposition in San Francisco. To Yreka Western Railroad #18 1956; to MCR 1998; to Nevada Commission for the Reconstruction of the V & T Railroad 2005. Leased to Sierra Railroad, Oakdale, CA, 2007, then moved 2009 to Virginia & Truckee, Virginia City, Nevada, where it is in service. Reportedly slated to eventually be re-numbered V & T #31.

19—Baldwin 2-8-2, c/n 42000, Built 1915. Originally Caddo & Choctaw Railroad #4; to Choctaw River Lumber Company; to Cia de Real del Monte y Pachuca #105, Pachuca, Hidalgo, Mexico; reported also to have been United Mining & Smelting Company #2069 while in Mexico; to McCRRR 1923. To Yreka Western Railroad #19 1953; to Oregon Pacific & Eastern Railroad #19 1970; to Yreka Western Railroad #19 1988. As of January 2015, locomotive is stored in close to operable condition in Yreka; legal possession of locomotive rests with Siskiyou County Sheriff's Office while courts sort out numerous liens and ownership claims surrounding locomotive.

20, 21—Baldwin 2-6-2, c/n 57617 and 57618, Built 1924. Acquired new. Both sold 11/23/1955 to Purdy Company for scrap. While en route to scrap yard the Stockton, Terminal & Eastern Railroad arranged to swap the #21's tender with their Baldwin 2-6-2 #3. The tender has remained with the #3 since, first to the California State Railroad Museum, Sacramento, California, then to Timber Heritage Association, Samoa, California.

22, 23—Alco 2-6-2, c/n 66316 and 66317, Built 1925. Acquired new. #23 sold 11/16/1955 to South San Francisco Scrap Metals Company for scrap. #23 to Arcata & Mad River Railroad #11, Korbel, CA, 1953, and scrapped 1956.

24, 25—Alco 2-6-2, c/n 66434 and 66435, Built 1925. Acquired new. #24 sold 11/16/1955 to South San Francisco Scrap Metals Company for scrap. #25 retired 1955, restored to operation 1962-1975 and then 1982-1986 in conjunction with Great Western Railroad Museum. To Great Western Railroad Museum 1988; to MCR 1996. Restored to service, operated 1997–2001, then 2007–2008. Sold 2/8/2011 to Oregon Coast Scenic Railroad, Garibaldi, OR.

26, 27—Alco 2-8-2, c/n 55492 and 57291, Built 1915 and 1917. Originally Copper River & Northwestern #72 and #73; to McCRRR 1938. #26 Sold 11/1955 through Luria Brothers (dealer) for scrap. #27 sold summer 1953 to Sixth Street Auto Wrecking Company for scrap.

28—Baldwin DRS-6-6-1500, c/n 73653, Built 1948. Acquired new. Retired from active service *circa* 1964 and cannibalized for parts until scrapped 1970.

29—Baldwin DRS-6-6-1500, c/n 74812, Built 1950. Acquired new. To Magma Arizona Railroad #10, Superior, AZ, 1969; donated 7/1994 to Arizona Railway Museum, Chandler, AZ.

30, 31—Baldwin S-12, c/n 75912 and 75913, Built 1953. Though designated a S-12, the #31 was not equipped with a turbocharger, developed 800 horsepower, and due to this is listed as a S-8 on most rosters. Acquired new. #30 To Rayonier, Inc. #203, Clallam, WA, 1963; to U.S. Steel #16, Pittsburg, CA; to Feather River Rail Society, Portola, CA, *circa* 1993; to MCR 1995. Stored out of service in McCloud in 2016. #31 to Chrome Crankshaft 1969; to Magma Arizona Railroad #9, Superior, AZ, 6/10/1969. Stored in the engine house at Superior.

32, 33—Baldwin RS-12, c/n 76024 and 76105, Built 1955. Acquired new. Both to Chrome Crankshaft 1969; to California Western Railroad #55 #56, Fort Bragg, CA, 1970. #55 scrapped *circa* 1992 in Fort Bragg. #56 to Traveltown Museum, Los Angeles, CA, *circa* 1992.

34- Baldwin AS-616, c/n 75449, Built 1952. Originally Southern Pacific #5253; to McCRRR 1963. To Oregon & Northwestern Railroad #4, Hines, OR 1969; to Feather River Rail Society (Western Pacific Railroad Museum), Portola, CA, 1992.

35, 36:1—Baldwin DRS-6-6-1500, c/n 74261 and 74258, Built 1949. Originally Southern Pacific #5207 and #5204; Both to General Electric 1962/1963; to Chrome Crankshaft (Dealer); to McCRRR 1964. #35 to U.S. Steel #39, Geneva, UT 1969, and scrapped early 1980s. #36:1 never painted by McCloud and seldom, if ever, operated. Cannibalized for parts until scrapped 1970.

36:2, **37**, **38**—EMD SD38, c/n 34880, 34881, 34882, Built 1969. #36/#37 to Itel Rail 1992, to MCR 1993; #38 to MCR 1992. All three remain in McCloud in 2016.

39—EMD SD38-2, c/n 74623-1, Built 1974. Acquired new. To McCloud Railway 1992; to Mid America Equipment Company, Mesa, Arizona, 1997; to Union Pacific #2824 1997, then UPY #824. In service on Union Pacific at its West Colton yard in 2016.

101, **103**—Plymouth DLC-6, c/n 2101 and 2766, Built 1925 and 1927. Originally McCRLCo #101 and #103; to McCRR 1964; to Great Western Railroad Museum 1983. Moved to Merrill, OR, #103 in pieces, where both are stored in 2016.

1804, **1810**—EMD GP-7u, c/n 15704 and 15691, Built 1951. Originally U.S. Army #1834 and #1821; to Alaska Railroad #1834 and #1821, then #1804 and #1810; Both to FSA Rebuilding, Pico Rivera, CA; stored partially dismantled in a scrap yard at Klamath Falls, OR; to McCRRR 1988. #1804 to Itel Rail 1992; to MCR 1993; to Nevada Industrial Switch, Exeter, CA 1993. #1810 to MCR 1992; to Nevada Industrial Switch, Exeter, CA 1992, but remained stored in McCloud until summer 1993. Both painted as "Grand Continental" #1804 and #1810 for movie *Under Siege 2*. #1804 leased to Corn Products, Stockton, CA; to Santa Clarita Railroad #1804, Newhall, CA, 1997; appeared in movie *Lethal Weapon 4*, then leased to Pacific Harbor Lines; sold 12/2002 to Gold Coast Railroad Museum, Miami, Florida, where it is in operation painted as Atlantic Coast Line #1804. #1810 to Oregon Pacific Railroad, Milwaukee, OR, 1999, named *Eileen Samuels*; to Archers–Daniels–Midland, Hugoton, Kansas, 2007.

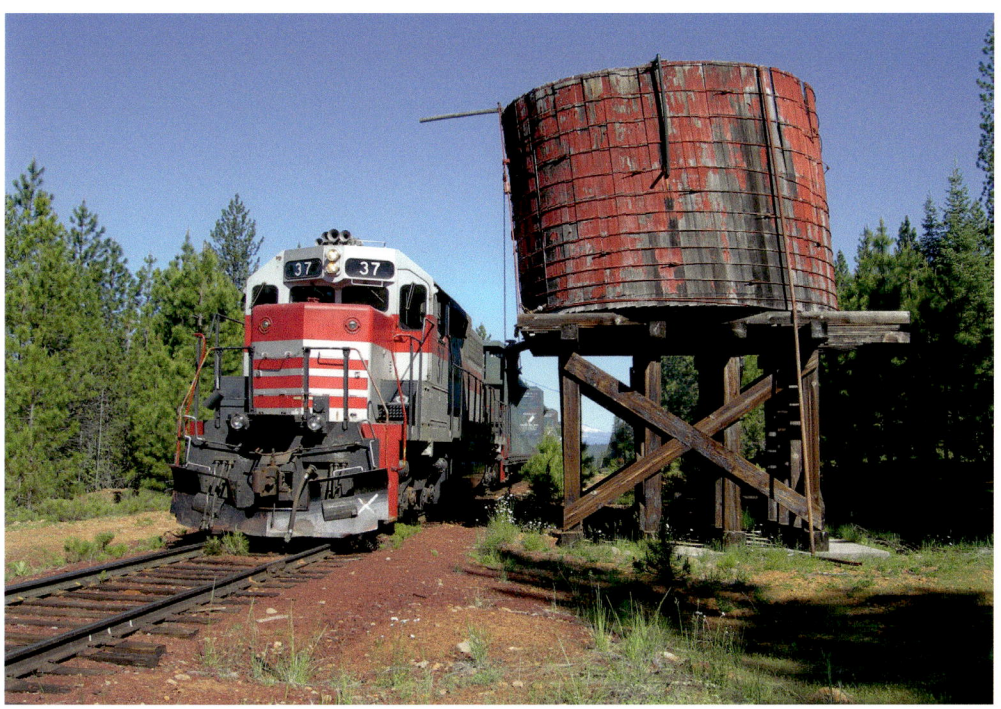

No. 37 rolling past the old Bartle water tank in June 2006. *Jeff Moore*

10

QUINCY

BACKGROUND

In 1852, prospectors looking for gold up the Feather River established Elizabethtown. Over the next six years the town shifted a mile to a new location named Quincy, named by one H. J. Bradley for his hometown in Illinois. Quincy remained a quiet community for many years, eventually becoming the Plumas County seat. The citizens felt sure a railroad would one day be built through town, but despite numerous surveys no construction occurred.

The situation changed in the early 1900s when the Western Pacific (WP) chose to run its new Salt Lake City-Oakland main line along the Feather River. Any joy Quincy felt soon turned to disappointment when it became apparent WP's engineering standards would force the railroad to be built on a grade hacked into the mountainside opposite the town. Quincy recognized it needed a railroad line to remain on the map, and set out to build one themselves.

THE QUINCY WESTERN

In 1908, several promoters incorporated the Quincy and Eastern Railroad and commenced securing the required charters, right-of-ways, and financing to build a rail line connecting Quincy with Hartwell, a station on the WP named after the family from which that road secured a right-of-way. In 1909, another new company, the Quincy Western Railroad (QW), took over the project. Local stock subscriptions came in strong, allowing the railroad to break ground in December 1909. The route chosen left Hartwell—subsequently renamed Marston, and then Quincy Junction—and descended down the mountainside on up to 2.77 percent grades for the first mile down to the valley floor, where the line ran across comparatively flat ground to reach Quincy. The company purchased a new passenger coach and locomotive. Construction progressed as labor availability and natural events allowed, and the first train steamed the full 5.389 miles of the new railroad on June 2, 1910.

The QW settled down to a quiet life, operating mixed freight and passenger trains to and from Quincy Junction. A small railbus provided service on days when only passengers would be handled. Carload freight business remained minimal until 1913, when Frank S. Murphy and associates built a sawmill, later incorporated as the Quincy Lumber Company. On the negative side, an increasing number of unregulated private automobiles undercut the railroad's

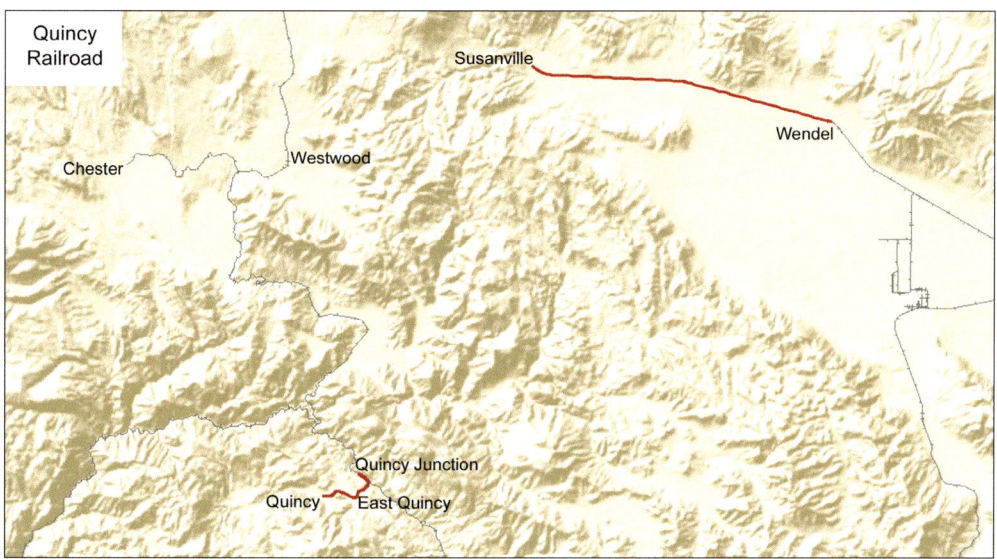

passenger business. Deficits became more prevalent than profits, especially as the railroad had to meet payments on debts the company assumed during its organization and construction. QW struggled against several monumental snowstorms, occasionally shutting the line down for days and sometimes weeks at a time. Railroad management also periodically discussed several extensions, but no money was available to finance any, and so the railroad continued its downward spiral.

QUINCY RAILROAD COMPANY

The QW continued struggling on through the 1910s, but experienced perpetual operating losses, periodically compounded by expenses incurred leasing locomotives when its own locomotive was unavailable. By the fall of 1917 the situation had become hopeless, and on September 17 the QW filed for permission to abandon operations and liquidate its assets. At the time, the railroad had cost $81,000 to build and equip, but had a cumulative loss of $26,000 on its operations to date. On top of that, it also had $40,000 of debt hanging over its head that could not be serviced given present or anticipated business levels.

The Quincy Lumber Company protested against the abandonment, as it needed the railroad to continue its operations. The easiest solution was for the lumber company to buy the railroad, and on November 10, 1917, a group of local businessmen led by lumber company officials incorporated the Quincy Railroad Company (QRR). The new company purchased the line for $25,000, and then invested additional money into improving the property, including a larger railbus. The railroad continued losing money, but this time had owners willing to tolerate losses, as the company was now part of a larger operation. The situation improved as the 1920s dawned and the railroad built spurs to new shippers, including a molding plant and an oil distributor. The Quincy Lumber Company constructed several logging railroads out into the woods from Quincy. In 1926 the railroad handled a good deal of supplies and equipment used in the Bucks Lake hydroelectric project, allowing the railroad to effect many improvements to its property, including a new locomotive.

The QRR survived the Depression, even with the closure of the sawmill that by now had become the principle reason for the railroad's continued existence. Good times arrived when the mill reopened in 1937, followed by other lumber companies locating mills in East Quincy. By the middle 1950s the QRR served five forest product plants operated by the Quincy, Meadow Valley, Essex, Calvada, and Mason & Hager lumber companies. Two freights a day transported their output to the WP connection. Passenger service eventually ended, with a company sedan providing the service in the last years. A new 44-ton General Electric diesel arrived in 1945, though the railroad retained its second steam locomotive for several decades afterwards. The railfan community discovered the railroad, and the Quincy took joy in hosting a series of popular excursions in the 1940s and 1950s. When the nearby Feather River Lumber Company closed its logging railroad down, it sent 2-6-2 #8 to Quincy for display; however, the locomotive often found its way onto the QRR for runs until state and federal railroad regulators got wind of what was happening and ordered the locomotive be placed on a disconnected siding so as to prevent future unapproved operations.

The Meadow Valley Lumber Company played an increasingly important role on the QRR. Meadow Valley's association with the railroad started in 1941, when the company built a planing mill, kilns, and box factory at East Quincy to process lumber trucked from a sawmill located back up in the mountains. In 1955, Meadow Valley purchased the Quincy Lumber Company, followed by purchasing control of the QRR on February 16, 1956. In 1964, Meadow Valley closed its various sawmills, replacing them with a new sawmill constructed adjacent to their other East Quincy facilities.

The Di Giorgio Corporation purchased Meadow Valley and the QRR in 1968. By this point, the QRR had one full time employee who served as the engineer, mechanic, and section foreman, helped out by three part time trainmen and four seasonal track maintenance laborers. The Meadow Valley/Di Giorgio mill provided the bulk of the traffic, supplemented by two other mills in East Quincy. Traffic to and from Quincy trailed off to periodic fuel oil loads for two dealers and occasional cars for the U.S. Forest Service and state highway department, which

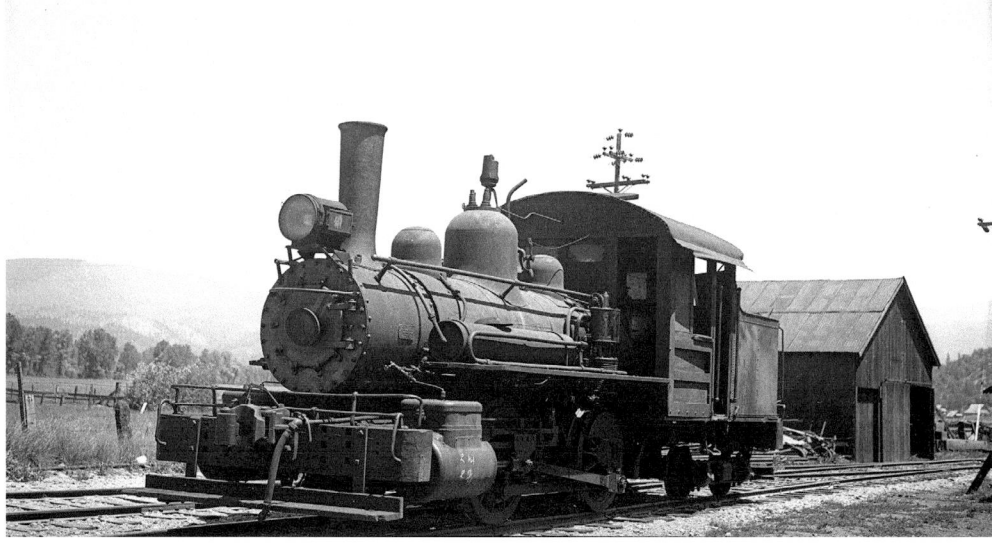

No. 1 in 1938. *Martin E. Hansen collection*

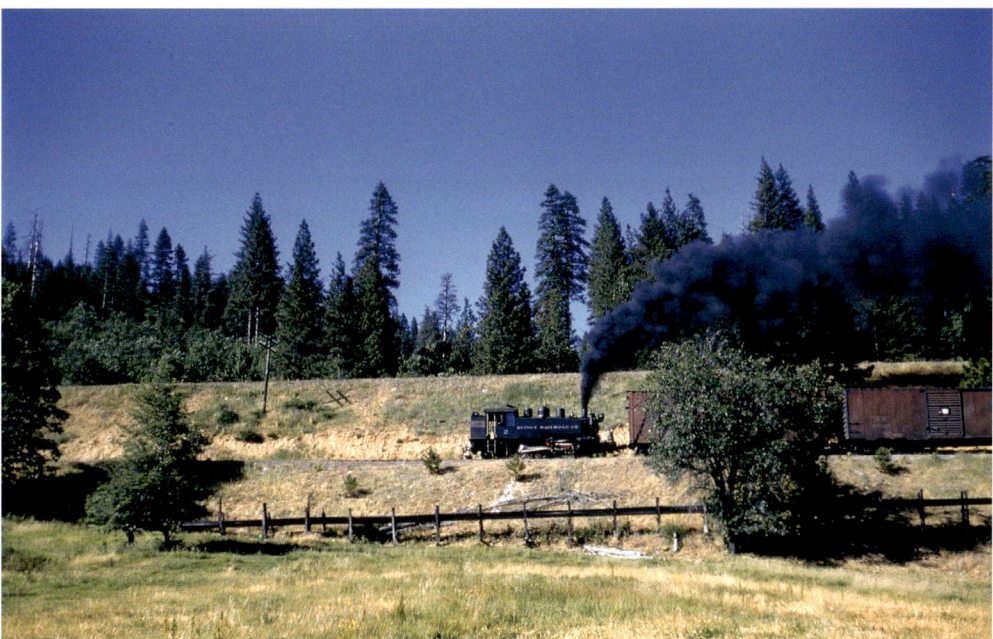

No. 2 lugging lumber loads towards Quincy Junction. *Bob Hanft photograph, Tom Moungovan collection*

was insufficient to justify continued operations past East Quincy. QRR operated its last train into its namesake town on December 15, 1969, and scrapped the line in early 1970.

QRR sold its standby steam locomotive to a railfan group in 1970. The small GE operated alone until 1973, when a larger second-hand diesel purchased from the WP arrived. A track upgrade program preceded the new power. By 1976, Sierra Pacific Industries owned the sawmill and the railroad. Woodchip traffic also moved out over the railroad for a while, but ended as SPI started burning the waste in a local co-generation plant instead of selling them on the open market. The railroad's connecting carrier changed after the UP acquired the WP.

Today's Quincy Railroad is about as simple of an operation as one can get. Two EMD switchers SPI transferred north from the Amador Central provide the power, and an old SP ballast hopper is the only other piece of equipment. Outside of Quincy Junction, the railroad only has four switches to its name—one double ended siding and a stub end spur outside the sawmill, and one spur into the loading dock. The mainline terminates inside the end of a sawmill building that doubles as the engine house. Operations are simple—the loading dock has a four-car capacity, and throughout each day the railroad will switch out loads, spot empties, and make runs to and from Quincy Junction to deliver loads and get more empties as needed.

The future of the railroad appears secure—SPI operates both large and small log mills at Quincy, and in 2014 the company extensively rebuilt the large log mill, indicating a level of potential operational security. On the other hand, the economic recession caused the small log mill to close between 2009 and 2010, and even with the recent rebuild of the large log mill a substantial change in lumber markets could force the mill's closure.

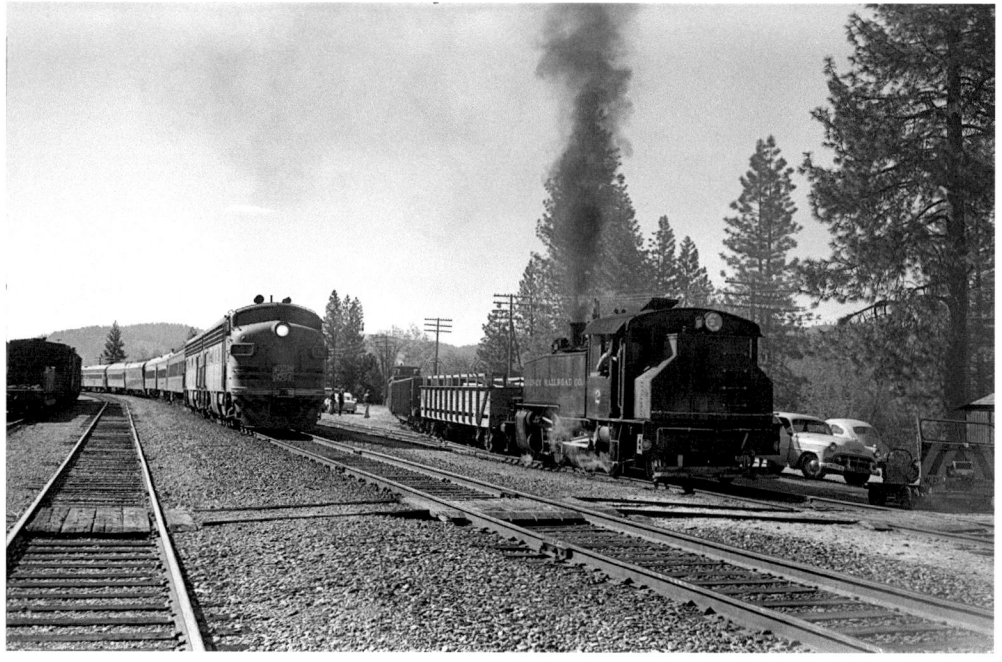

No. 2 meeting a WP passenger train on a railfan trip on 5/20/1962. *Don Hansen*

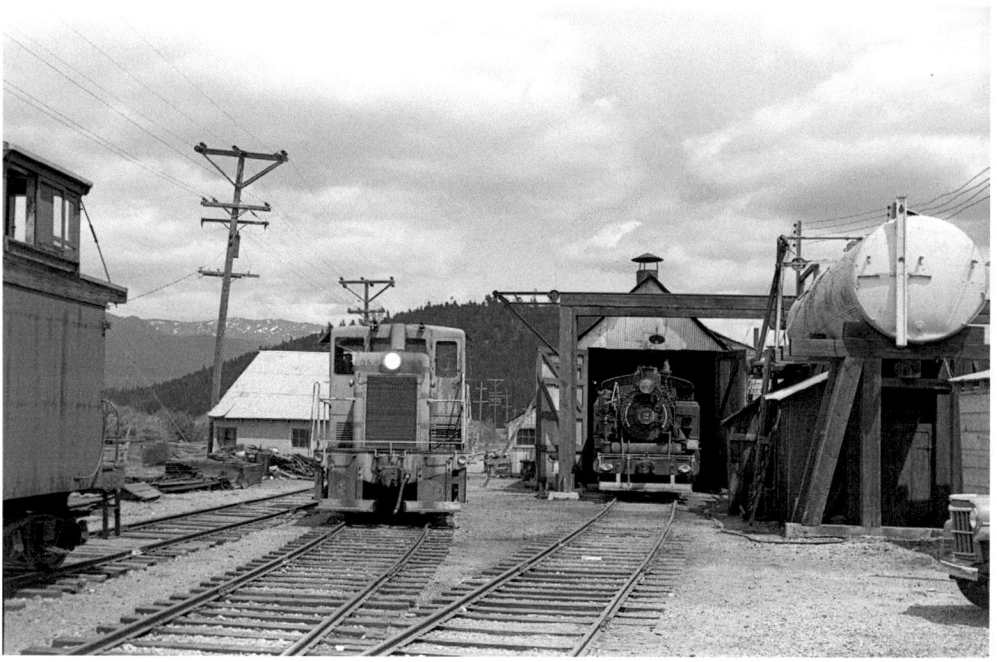

Nos. 2 and 3 in Quincy on 5/20/1962. *Don Hansen*

SUSANVILLE DIVISION

Between 1912 and 1914, Southern Pacific subsidiary Fernley and Lassen Railroad built a line from a connection with SP's mainline at Fernley, Nevada, to Westwood, California, to serve a sawmill The Red River Lumber Company built. The railroad passed through Susanville, which in time boasted several large sawmills, one of them built in 1920/1921 by the Fruit Growers Supply Company. Until 1953, FGS operated an extensive logging railroad network north from a connection with the F & L at Susanville Junction, between Susanville and Westwood. FGS purchased Red River's Westwood operations in 1944, only to close that sawmill in 1956. The company continued operating the Susanville mill until 1963, when they sold it to the Eagle Lake Lumber Company, a forerunner to Sierra Pacific Industries.

The Eagle Lake mill operations kept SP trains rolling into Susanville several times a week. Extensive flooding closed the Susanville-Westwood line in 1955, and the closure of the Westwood mill the following year kept SP from effecting repairs. SP finally asked for permission to abandon the line in 1966; however, they almost immediately hit a snag when the Eagle Lake Lumber Company initiated proceedings attempting to force SP to sell the line to it for continued operations. Purchasing the line would allow Eagle Lake to establish a long-coveted interchange with the WP, both for the increased shipping options and as a way to expedite woodchip deliveries to the Fibreboard paper plant at Antioch. SP was not thrilled with the application, as it preferred to keep Eagle Lake's traffic on its own rails, and in March 1967 SP withdrew the application so as to prevent the forced sale from occurring. By the time SP reinitiated abandonment proceedings in the late 1970s, Eagle Lake's desire to own the railroad had diminished.

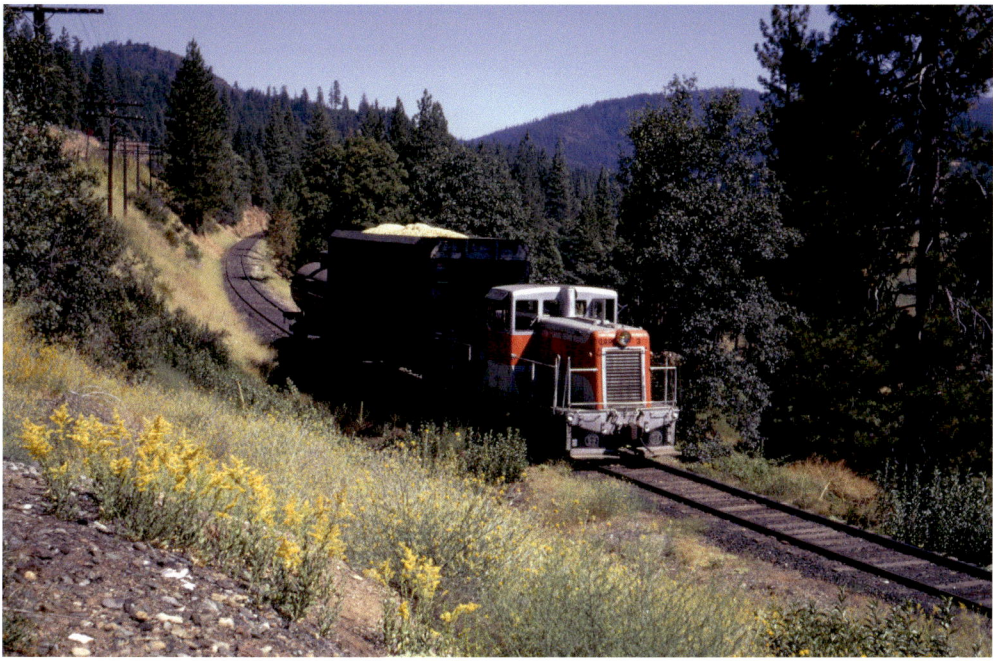

No. 3, wearing WP-inspired orange and silver paint, grinds up the hill towards Quincy Junction on 8/3/1969. *Henry Brueckman photograph, Tom Moungovan collection*

Sierra Pacific Industries eventually absorbed Eagle Lake Lumber, and they continued operations of the Susanville mill. However, the mill did not produce sufficient traffic to keep the branch viable, and in 1986 SP received permission to abandon the line. SP operated its last train into Susanville in February and officially placed the line out of service on April 18. The move opened the door for Sierra Pacific to take the line over as a private carrier. On May 7, SPI took possession of the 23.3 miles from Susanville to a connection with SP's Modoc Line at Wendel. Operations began with a leased SP locomotive until October, when SPI's own locomotive arrived.

Despite being a private carrier, SPI included the operation under the Quincy Railroad umbrella. The railroad settled down to a mostly unremarkable existence, running several trains a week over the line. The SPI mill provided almost all of the traffic, occasionally supplemented by a few cars handled under a private transportation agreement for a small millworks facility. The only exception to the outbound lumber and woodchip traffic came in 2003, when SPI purchased vast quantities of burned timber from the 2002 fires on the White Mountain Apache Reservation in Arizona and decided to ship some of it to Susanville. The railroad became the busiest it had ever been as long log trains arrived in Wendel, where the QRR crews broke them down into 15-car trains to take into Susanville for unloading.

Unfortunately, the log trains would be the last hurrah. In December 2003, SPI announced the imminent closure of the Susanville mill due to a lack of any further log supply. The mill shut down in April 2004, and the last train to Wendel operated on May 18. Scrapping the railroad required no further applications or permissions as the line had already been formally abandoned by SP back in 1986 and operated as a private carrier since, and the Jim Dobbas Company pulled the rails and ties in the spring and summer of 2006.

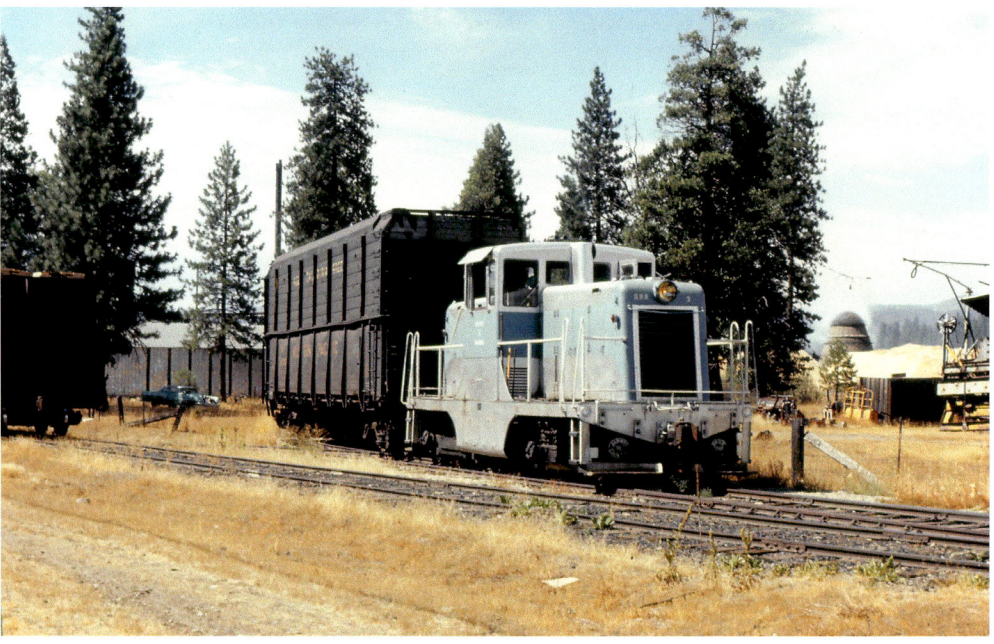

No. 3, now repainted blue and silver, switching at East Quincy in August 1971. *Lee F. Hower*

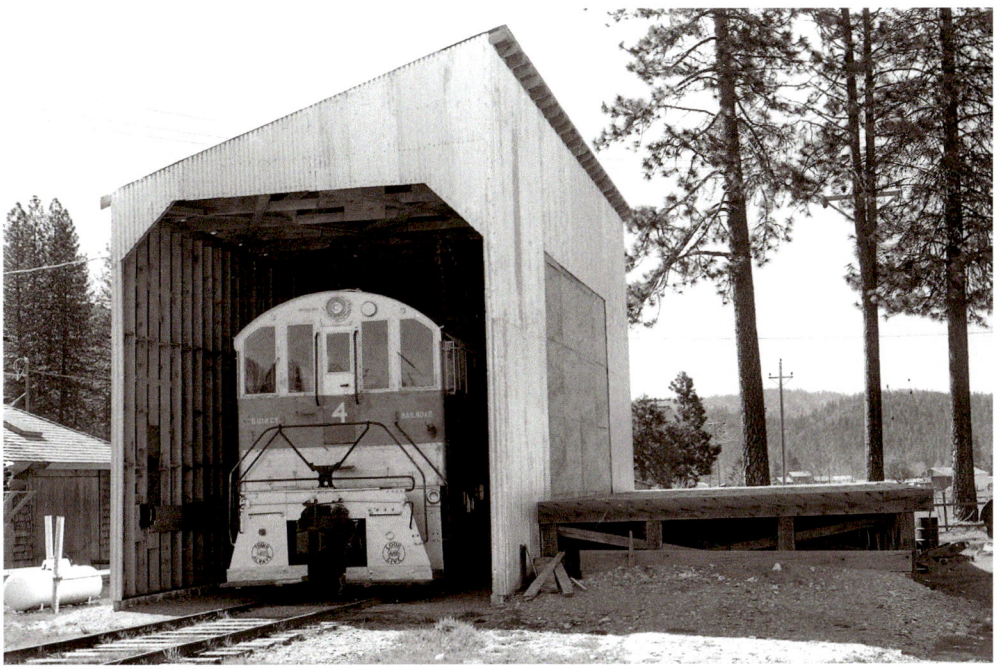

No. 4 in the East Quincy enginehouse. *E. O. Gibson*

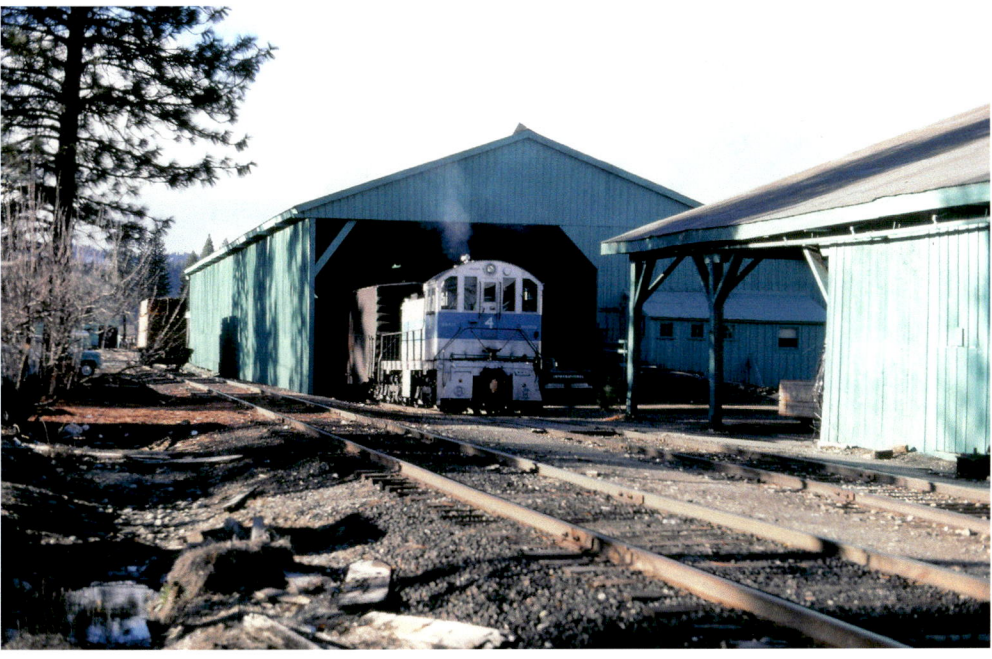

No. 4 switching at East Quincy in January 1978. *Lee F. Hower*

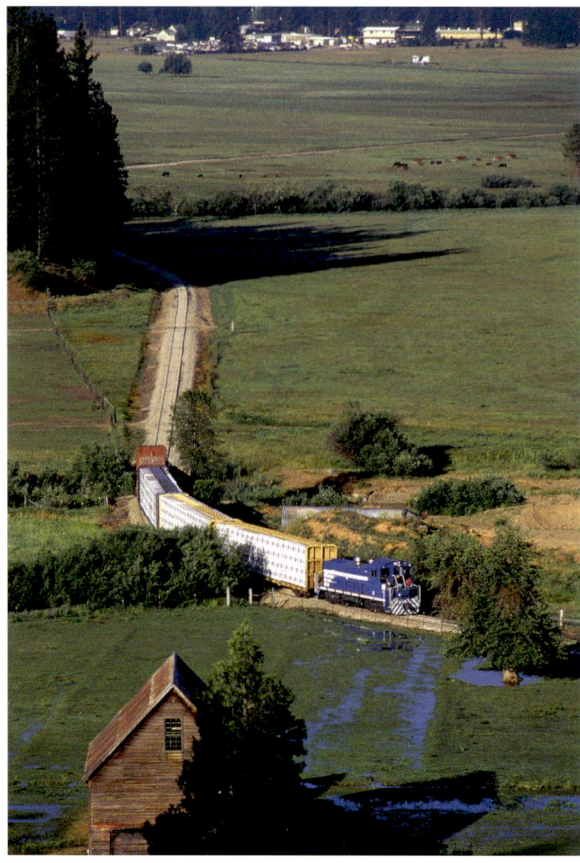

Left: No. 5 with lumber loads for Quincy Junction. *Sean Zwagerman*

Below: No. 4, now repainted yellow and black, leads a train across the valley floor. *Sean Zwagerman*

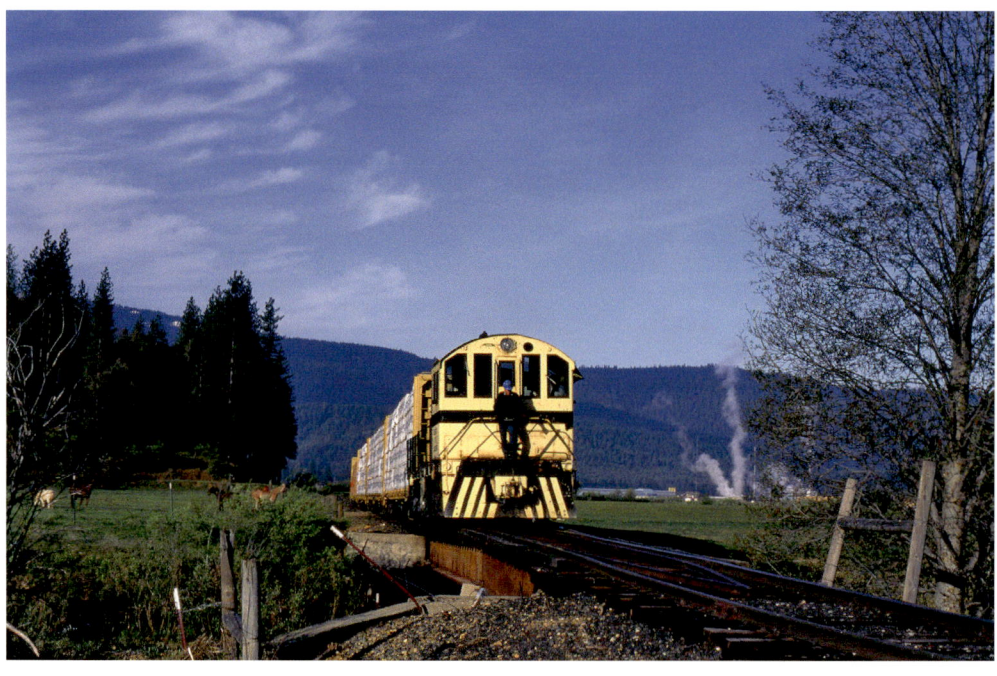

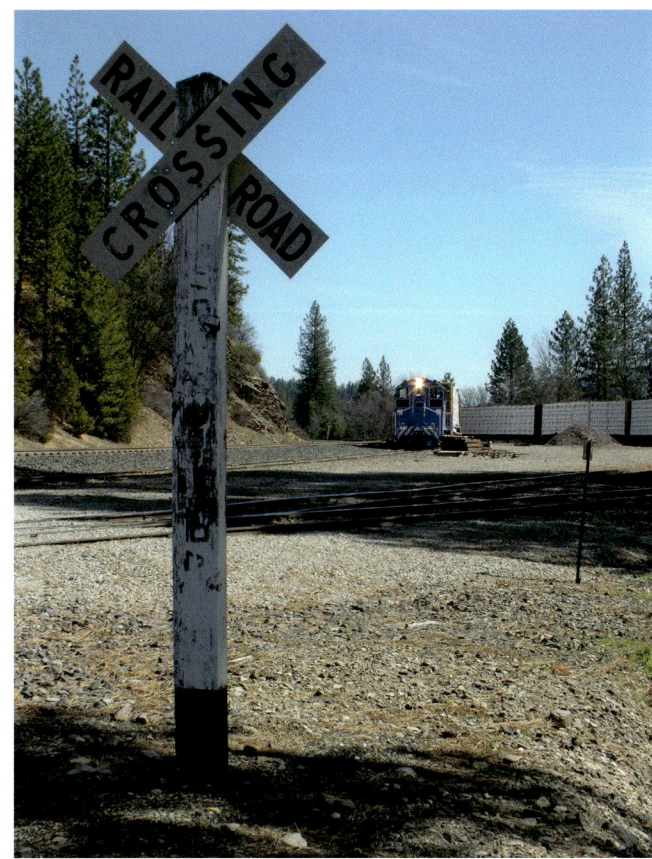

Right: No. 12 spotting loads at Quincy Junction in March 2015. *Jeff Moore*

Below: No. 1100 at Wendel in 1991. *E. O. Gibson*

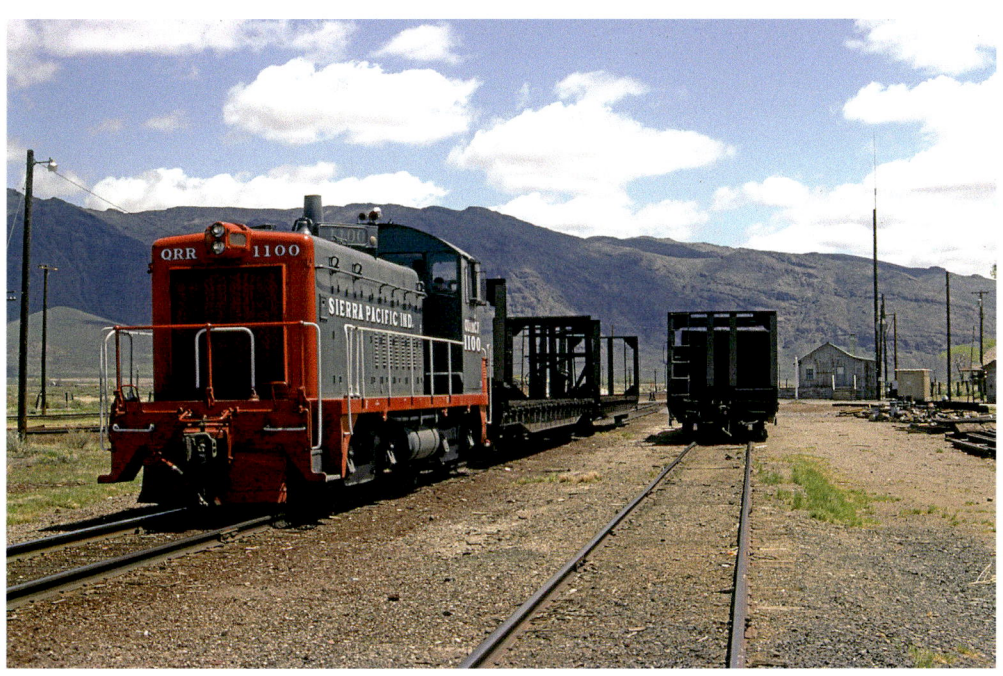

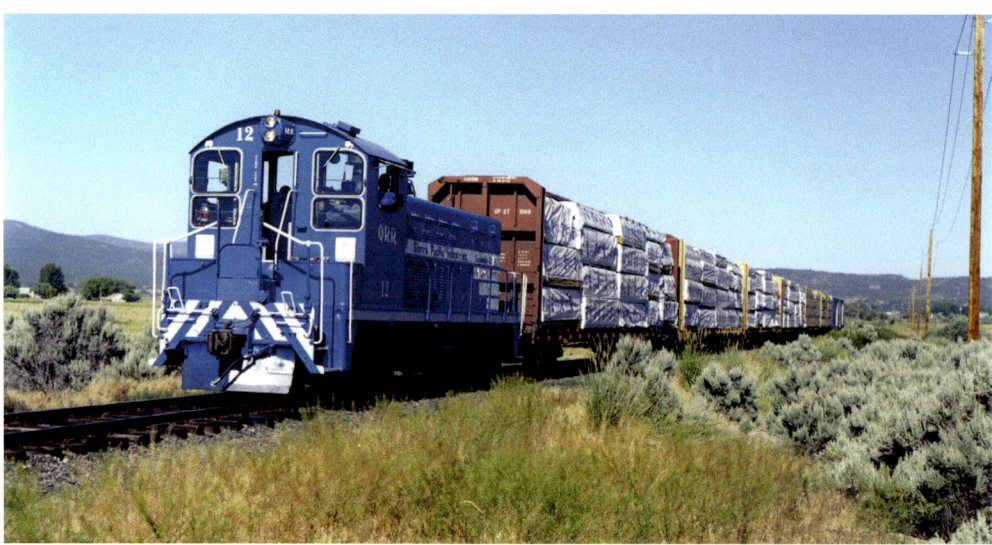

No. 12 on the road from Susanville to Wendel. *Jim Bryant*

LOCOMOTIVE ROSTER

1—Alco 0-4-4T, c/n 46915, Built 1909. Acquired new; sold 1947 to Essex Cedar Company for use as a stationary boiler.

2—Alco 2-6-2T, c/n 65032, Built 1924. Acquired new. To Iron Horse Railroads, Inc. 1970, then to Pacific Locomotive Association, first at Castro Point Railway, and now at Niles Canyon Railway, Sunol, CA.

3—General Electric 44-ton, c/n 27819, Built 1945. Acquired new; to Feather River Rail Society (Western Pacific Railroad Museum), Portola, CA.

4—Alco S-1, c/n 69685, Built 1942. Originally Western Pacific #504; to Sacramento Northern #405; to QRR 1973. To Feather River Rail Society (Western Pacific Railroad Museum), Portola, CA.

5—EMD SW-1200, c/n 28344, Built 1963. Originally Ashley, Drew & Northern #178, then #1208; to Amador Central 1995; to QRR #5 1997, Quincy, CA.

12—EMD SW-7, c/n 15636, Built 1952. Originally Arkansas & Louisiana Missouri #11; to Chattahoochee Industrial #11; to Amador Central #12 1996; to QRR #12 1997, Susanville, CA, then to Quincy, CA.

1100—EMD TR-6, c/n 13549, Built 1950. Named *Lil' Lulu*. Originally EMD demonstrator unit #1600, part of a cow/calf pair with a cabless unit; to SP #4600, then #1100; Optioned 1985 to John Bradley, Laytonville, CA, and stored and occasionally used on Eureka Southern until returned to SP 1986, then sold to QRR, Susanville; to Feather River Rail Society (Western Pacific Railroad Museum), Portola, CA.

In addition to its own power, QW and QRR leased locomotives as needed, including several from Boca & Loyalton and WP in the early years, former SP GP-9 #2873 from the Western Pacific Railroad Museum around 1998/1999, and SP SW-1200 #2268 to operate the Susanville line from May through October 1986.

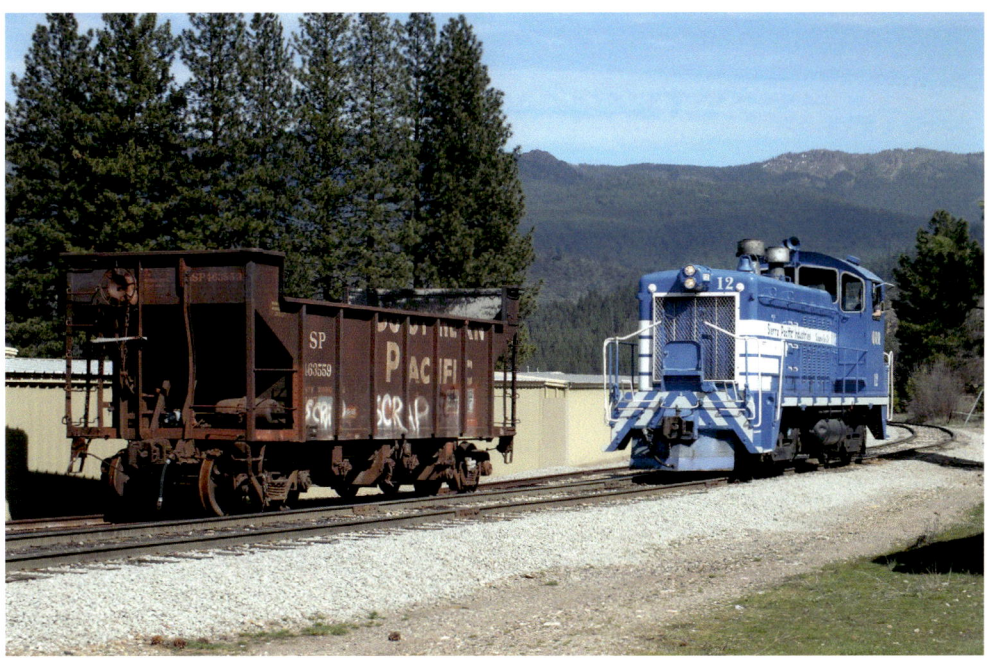

No. 12 passes the road's ballast hopper in East Quincy in March 2015. *Jeff Moore*

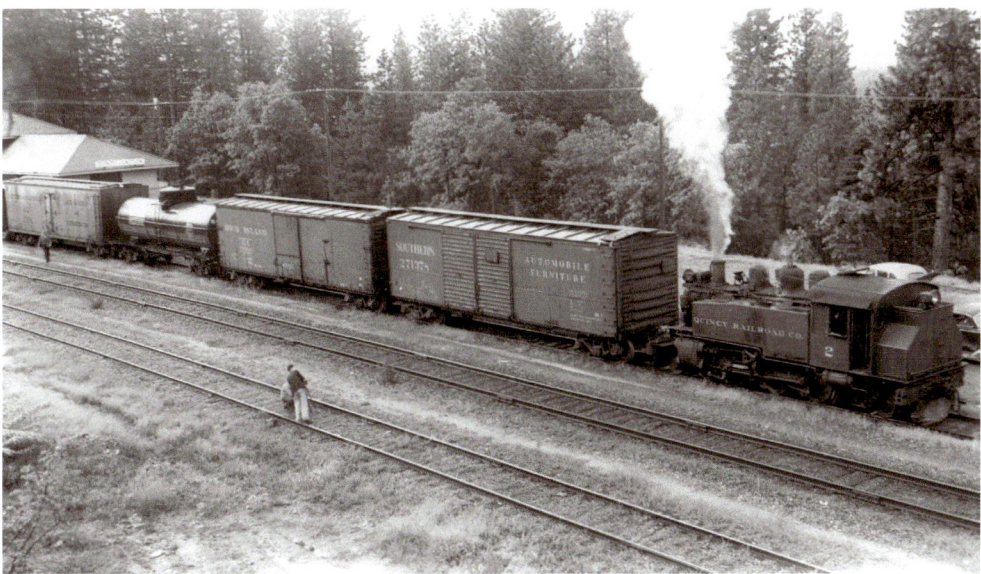

No. 2 switching at Quincy Junction in the 1940s. *Jeff Moore collection*

11

SIERRA

BACKGROUND

The Sierra is without doubt the most storied of California's lumber shortlines. The railroad's roots lay in the Arizona desert of 1893, where a flood and competing rail line forced the Prescott & Arizona Central Railroad out of business. A visionary named John Bullock built the P & AC, and after its failure he gathered up the remnants and headed for California, where he contemplated a wide open field of possibilities to fill empty holes in the state's railroad map. In 1896, Bullock ventured into the "Mother Lode" country of Tuolumne and Calaveras counties, and immediately decided his future railroad should be built here. Bullock made connections with banker William H. Crocker and Prince Andre Poniatowski, who had been dispatched from Paris to invest French capital in American businesses. Crocker and Poniatowski formed the California Exploration Company, which by the time of Bullock's arrival had accumulated substantial timber and mining holdings, and they quickly agreed to finance Bullock's railroad as means to further development of these ventures.

THE EARLY YEARS

Bullock, Crocker, and Poniatowski incorporated the Sierra Railway Company of California on February 1, 1897. Preliminary surveys had already been run from Oakdale east into the foothills, and grading began as soon as practical. Bullock brought rails, locomotives, and equipment north from Arizona, and by June the first passenger train operated over twenty miles of completed railroad. Construction progressed from there, reaching Jamestown on November 10, 1897; Sonora near the end of February 1899; and Tuolumne City on February 1, 1900.

The Sierra prospered from the start, reaping rich rewards from the variety of passenger and freight traffic the region provided. Bullock, Crocker, and Poniatowski were not content to let traffic come to them; in the end, they built the railroad in part to develop their other holdings, and as the railroad completed its line they proceeded to do just that. In addition to the gold mines, the backers also owned vast forested acres, and in 1899, they together and with others incorporated the West Side Flume & Lumber Company, followed two years later by the Standard Lumber Company. West Side built a substantial mill fed by a narrow gauge logging railroad at Tuolumne City, while Standard built or bought several mills in the mountains to the east and

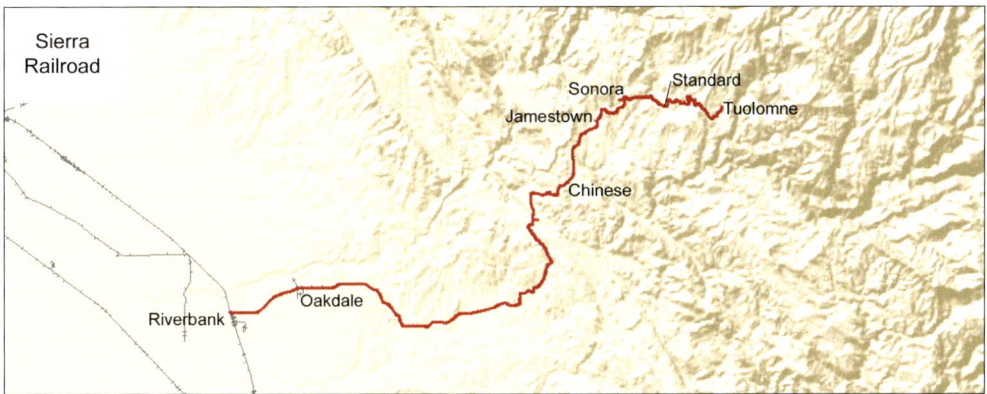

leased a planing mill and some factories in Sonora. Several other affiliated railroads existed as part of these ventures—West Side operated part of its logging railroads for several years as the Hetch Hethy & Yosemite Valley Railroad, and Standard used a combination of its 30-inch gauge Empire City Railway and the standard gauged Sugar Pine Railway to bring green lumber down to Standard, partially on trackage rights over the Sierra. In 1913, the Standard company built a new sawmill at Standard to replace both the mills to the east and the Sonora plants, and the Sugar Pine Railroad existed thereafter to bring logs down to the new mill. The founders eventually sold both lumber companies, the West Side company to a group of Michigan lumbermen in 1903 and the Standard company to the Pickering Lumber Company in 1920.

The Sierra's early success caused the owners to consider a broad range of expansion alternatives, the most ambitious of which contemplated a four mile long tunnel through the Sierras to connect with the Virginia & Truckee Railroad in Nevada. The ownership group did complete several more modest extensions, including building a branch to Angels Camp in 1902. In 1905, the ownership group incorporated the Yosemite Short Line Railroad to build a 30-inch gauge railroad from Jamestown to Yosemite Valley, both to haul tourists and to develop the forests through which the line would pass.

Sierra gained a second connection with the outside world in 1904, when the Atchison, Topeka & Santa Fe (ATSF) completed a branch line extending from their mainline at Riverbank east into Oakdale. In subsequent decades SP abandoned their line north and south of Oakdale, but continued operations to the town on trackage rights over the ATSF.

BOOM, BUST, THEN BOOM AGAIN

The great San Francisco earthquake and fire of April 1906 and the financial panic of 1907 wrecked the finances of Crocker and Poniatowski. Work on the Yosemite Short Line ceased immediately, after only eight miles of the line had been completed. Despite these setbacks, the Sierra prospered, due in large part to higher freight rates and increased lumber shipments destined for San Francisco's rebuilding. A series of major dam and hydroelectric projects in the late 1910s and 1920s drove revenues to new heights. The Sierra built several branches to dam projects, and became the connecting carrier to the Hetch Hetchy Railroad, which built a 67-mile line to the site of the dam inundating Hetch Hetchy Valley; in addition to dam construction traffic, this line also generated lumber loads from a California Peach Growers Association operation.

The end of the dam building and a sharp decline in lumber traffic coincided with substantial payments on both Sierra and YSL bonds coming due. Sierra entered receivership in 1932, but continued operations, though there were casualties, such as the abandonment of the Angels branch in 1935. The big mills in Standard and Tuolumne closed, and to help compensate Sierra won a contract to operate the Hetch Hetchy Railroad during an expansion of the dam. Just enough other business came the railroad's way to keep it in operation through the dark years.

Sierra's depression started to ease at the end of the 1930s, helped immensely by the reopening of the Tuolumne mill in 1935 and the Standard mill in 1938. The railroad exited receivership in 1937 with a new name, Sierra Railroad Company, and an ownership group led by Crocker Associates, organized by William Crocker and his family. Then came the war years, and the Sierra boomed again, this time almost exclusively on lumber traffic, supplemented with some passengers, mining products (especially lime), and fuel oil. A bus and trucks expanded the company's service.

The good times continued on into the post-war era. The steam power and close proximity to the San Francisco bay area made the railroad a Mecca for railfans. The old-time equipment led to another major revenue source as Hollywood fed America's near insatiable appetite for "Westerns". Sierra hosted its first film crew in 1919, and by the late 1940s set designers and movie producers routinely turned various points along the line into almost every state west of the Mississippi River for numerous epic Westerns and TV shows.

TOURISTS, MOVIES, AND LUMBER

The Sierra hosted trials of demonstrator diesels from both Baldwin and General Electric in the very early 1950s, but instead accepted delivery in 1952 of its #38, a large Baldwin 2-6-6-2. Steam power would last but three more years before the railroad gave into reality and ordered two Baldwin switchers. The #38 pulled a "Farewell to Steam" excursion on April 17, 1955, hauled its last freight train the following day, and then the diesels took over. Sierra built a new

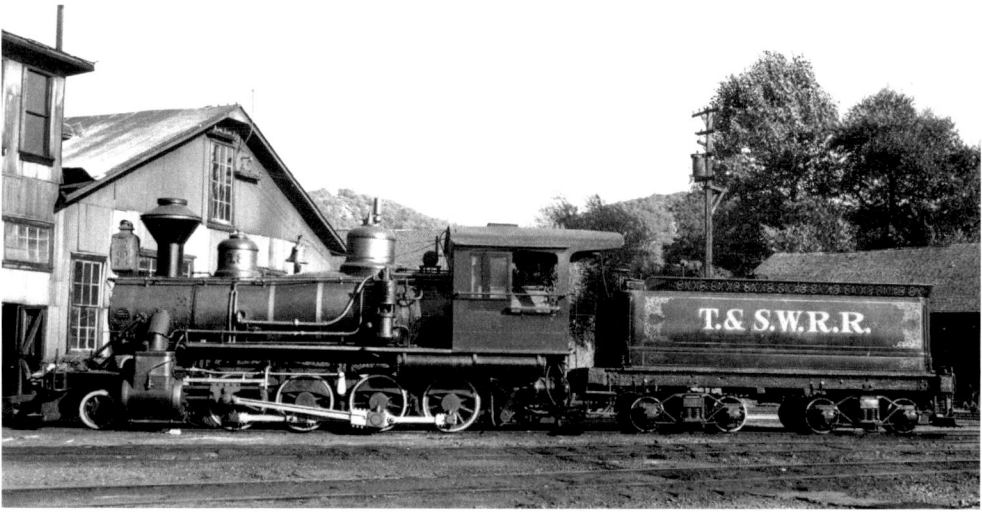

No. 18 painted for a movie shoot in September 1946. *John A. Taubeneck collection*

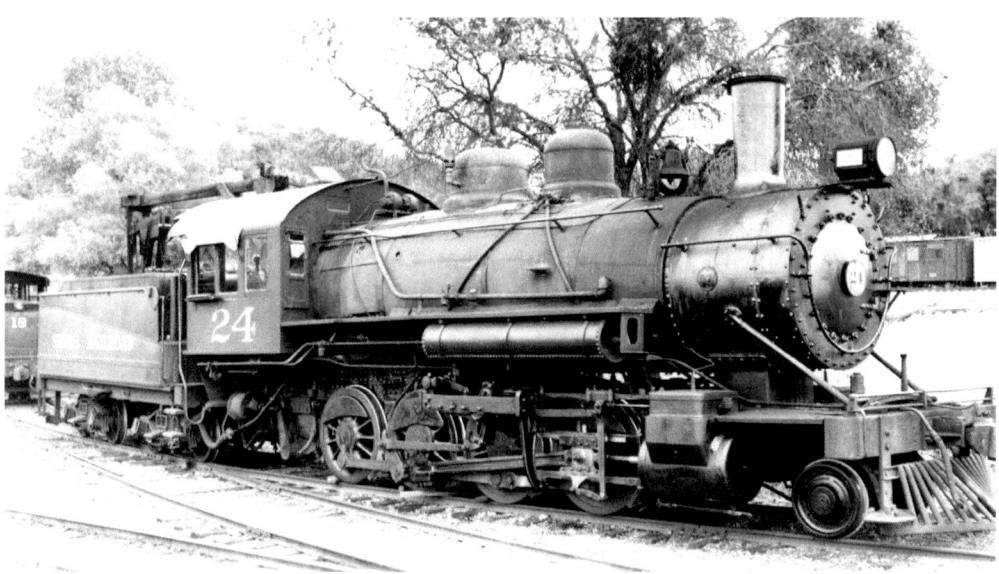

No. 24 in Jamestown. *John A. Taubeneck collection*

shop building for the diesels in Oakdale, but decided enough movie work existed to retain the steam era roundhouse and shop facilities at Jamestown.

Steam would not stay down for long. On October 6, 1957, the railroad resumed operating trips for the public, using passenger cars from the SP. Steam whistles could be heard echoing amongst the foothills now for tourists and railfans alike in addition to the frequent movie work. This first excursion revival would prove to be short lived, however; on October 19, 1963, a steam locomotive derailed on a switch while pulling a train full of tourists, bringing an immediate end to the runs—but not the movie work.

Meanwhile, the freight business started to decline. The first hit came in 1962, when fire destroyed West Side's Tuolumne mill. Sierra operations thereafter truncated at Standard; however, Pickering continued running their log trains over the Sierra line from Ralph to Standard until 1963, when that railroad also closed, ending all operations beyond Standard, though the last of the Pickering railroad would not be removed until 1974. Fibreboard purchased Pickering's operations in 1965, resulting in a steady stream of woodchips destined for the Antioch paper mill but a significant decline in lumber carloads. Sierra trains still ran out of Oakdale five days a week, switching Snider Lumber at Chinese, Sequoia Pine Mills at Keystone, and Fibreboard at Standard, plus United States Lime Products at Sonora.

In 1970, Crocker Associates decided to give tourist railroads another try, capitalizing on the facilities at Jamestown and remaining steam power. On May 1, 1971, Railtown 1897 opened its doors to the public, proving to be an immediate success. Regularly scheduled steam excursions with names like *Mother Lode Cannonball*, *Wine and Cheese Zephyr*, and *Twilight Limited* operated out of Jamestown to all parts of the system. On the negative side, movie and filming work dropped off significantly as the Western genre fell out of favor with the American movie going public.

Sierra also jumped into the incentive *per diem* boxcar game, leasing several groups of new boxcars mostly from Itel between 1975 and 1977, supplemented by an additional 100 cars subleased from the McCloud River in 1980.

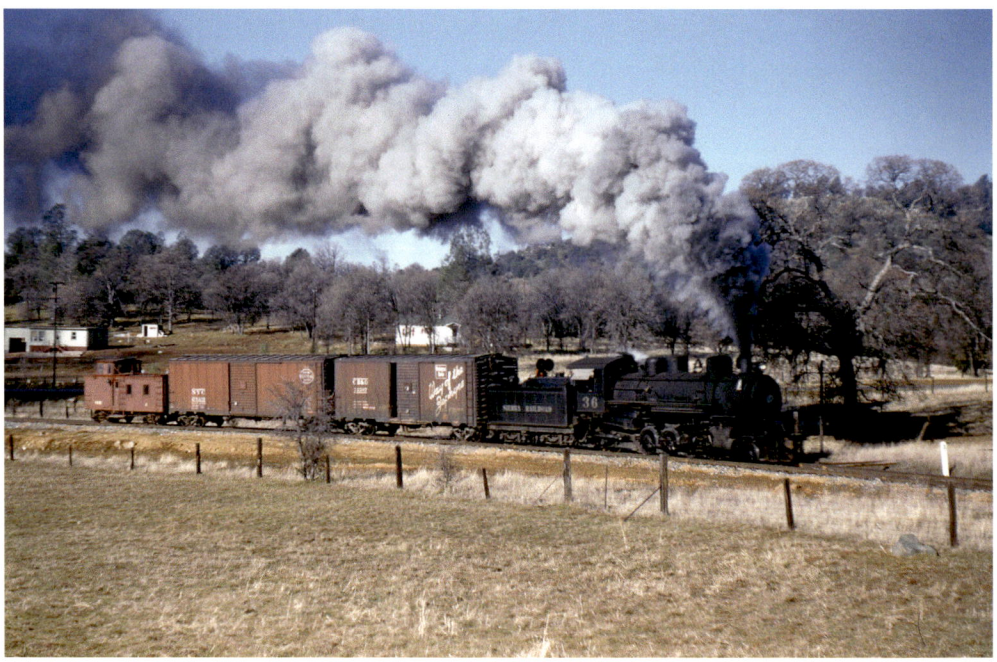

No. 36 with a short freight on 1/8/1955. *John Hungerford photograph, Tom Moungovan collection*

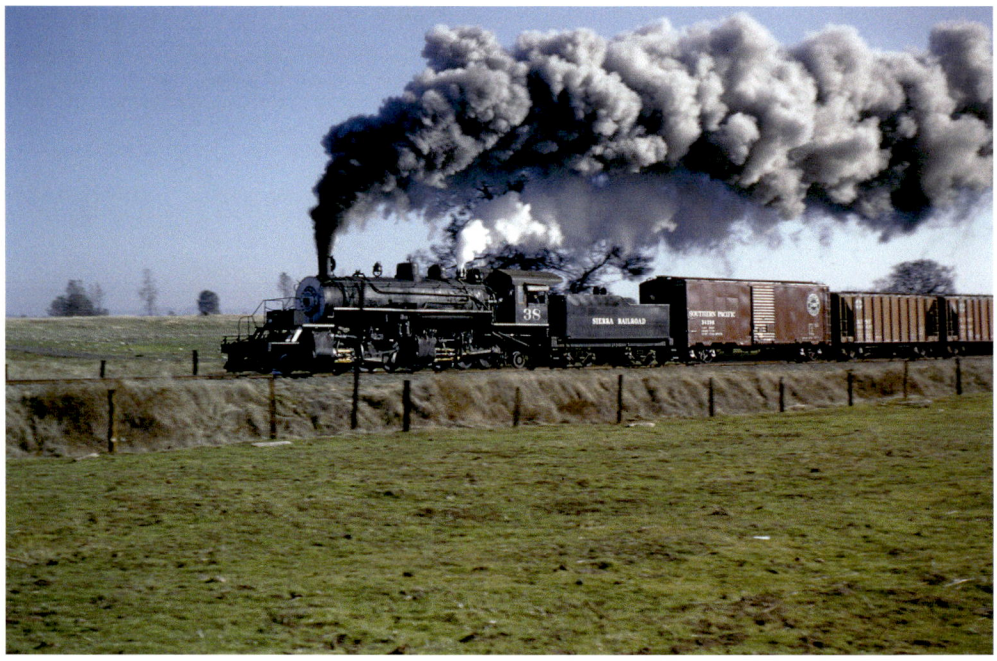

No. 38 loping through the plains east of Oakdale. *John Hungerford photograph, Tom Moungovan collection*

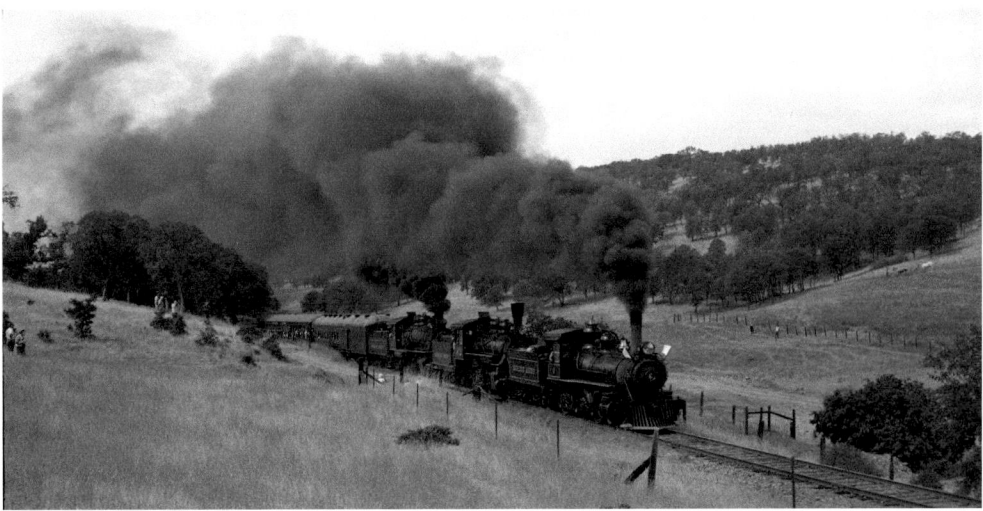

Nos. 3, 28, and 34 lead a fan trip on 9/5/1971. *Don Hansen*

SEPARATION

By 1979, freight shippers had been reduced to the mills at Chinese and Standard and asbestos shipments from Chinese, and gas shortages and spiraling inflation cut deeply into the tourist business. Crocker Associates reluctantly concluded the time had come to sell the railroad, and the last steam excursions operated by the end of the year. On May 1, 1981, Crocker conveyed the freight assets—including the mainline and diesel locomotives—to Silverfoot Associates of Chicago, organized by James Foster. Silverfoot applied a new coat of green paint to the diesels but otherwise operated the property much as they found it.

Charles Crocker III had a grander vision for the 26 acres surrounding the Jamestown shops and the equipment residing thereon. The State of California Department of Parks and Recreation opened the California State Railroad Museum (CSRM) in 1981, and had little interest in taking another railroad project; however, local officials, railfan organizations, and other groups bypassed the Department and went straight to the state legislature, who allocated funds. Crocker Associates received $750,000 for the property and donated another $1.2 million worth of equipment. On June 19, 1982, the state dedicated Railtown 1897 State Historic Park. Excursion trains returned to the railroad on July 1, 1983.

The Sierra settled into the form it would hold for the rest of the 1980s and early 1990s. A series of concessionaires operated sporadic excursions, supplemented by occasional movie and television work, most notably *Back to the Future III*. Meanwhile, on the freight side, Fibreboard merged into Louisiana-Pacific Corporation, only to be spun off again in 1988, mostly to insulate L-P against numerous asbestos liability claims piling up against the old Fibreboard operations. Fibreboard controlled both the Chinese and Standard mills by this point, and shipped little more than woodchips over the railroad. Carloadings fell two-thirds between 1981 and 1995, and derailments and equipment failures plagued the railroad. Sierra terminated its boxcar leases in 1986 and briefly offered piggyback service, but could not compete with ramps on the mainline railroads.

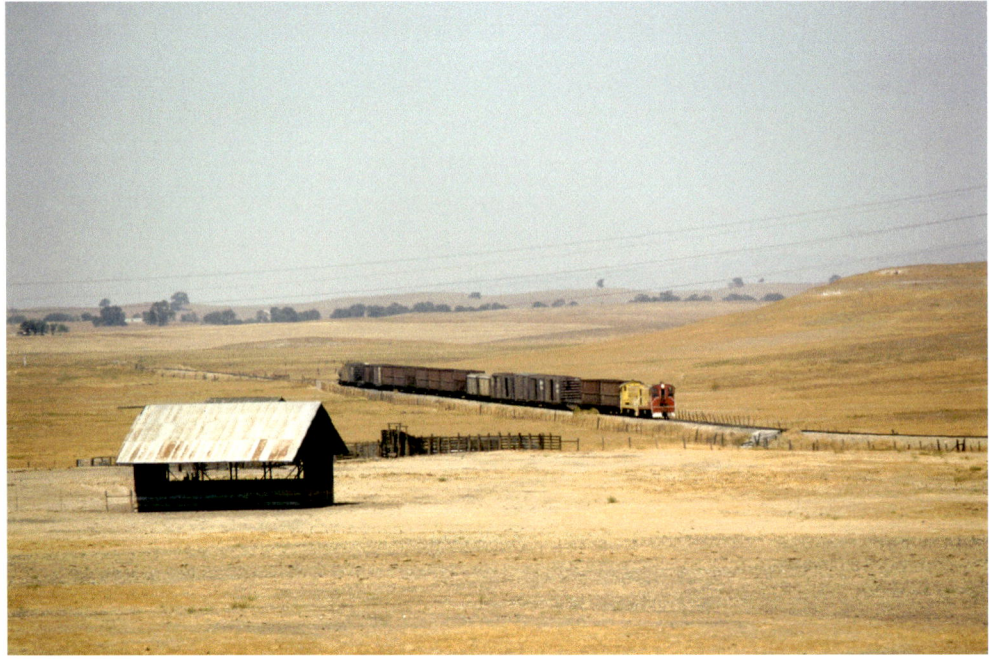

A typical Sierra freight of the early 1970s east of Oakdale on 9/1/1972. *Dave Stanley*

REVITALIZATION

In the early 1990s, a group of visionaries based in the Santa Cruz, California, area incorporated the Sierra Pacific Coast Railroad (SPCR). The new company focused initially on attempting to establish freight service over the Santa Cruz, Big Trees & Pacific Railroad, from Santa Cruz to the sand mines located above Felton, but had grand plans to rebuild the old South Pacific Coast line over the mountains to San Jose. The focus of the company quickly expanded to the Sierra, and on March 21, 1995, the new Sierra Railroad Division of SPCR operated its first train. However, by this point SPCR was experiencing substantial financial difficulties and had badly overextended itself. By July 1995, SPCR faced immediate insolvency, and on August 24, 1995, control of the Sierra passed to one of its major backers, Coast Enterprises Corporation, controlled and led by Mike Hart.

Fortunately for the railroad, this second ownership change coincided closely with Sierra Pacific Industries purchasing Fibreboard, including both mills Sierra served. SPI and Sierra soon signed a 30-year agreement under which SPI agreed to pay the railroad to haul at least 1,896 loads per year, regardless of actual carloadings. With that guarantee in hand, Sierra could commence rebuilding the roadbed, with both its own funds and state grant money. The railroad also upgraded its locomotive fleet, replacing the aging Baldwins with more reliable power.

Meanwhile, Railtown 1897 underwent a transition of its own. In 1992, the state placed Railtown under the umbrella of the CSRM, and then in 1996, the state transferred operations to the CSRM Foundation. Excursion trains continued operating, running 5-mile long round trips out of Jamestown.

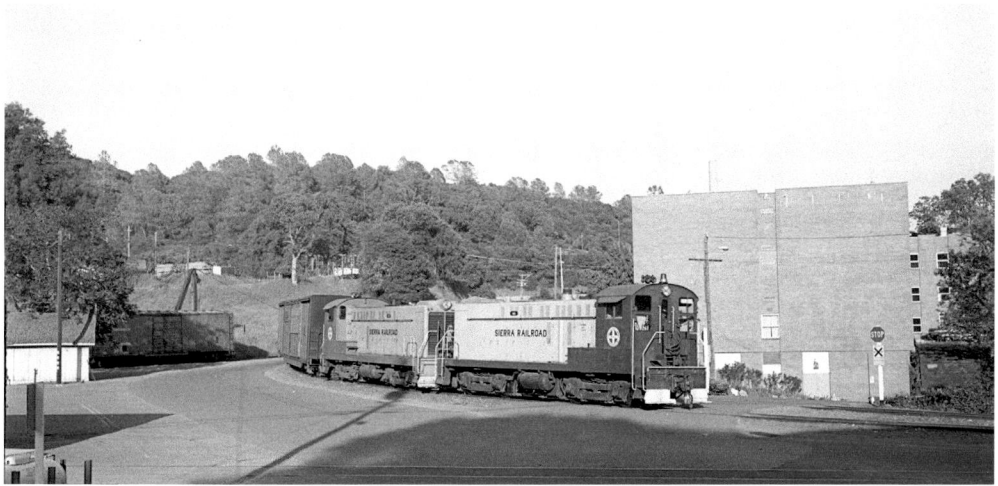

Nos. 44 and 40 disrupting traffic in Sonora on 5/5/1972. *Don Hansen*

EXPANSIONS AND THE FUTURE

Since 1997, the Sierra has worked hard to expand its business base. In 2000, the company launched the *Golden Sunset* dinner train out of Oakdale. Sierra got another name change in 2003, when the ownership group merged the railroad with the recently acquired Yolo Shortline (operating West Sacramento to Woodland, California) into the Sierra Northern Railroad. Other railroads currently operated by the Sierra Northern management include switching the port facilities at West Sacramento and the California Western Railroad.

The Sierra and then Sierra Northern had been in negotiations with both UP and BNSF about the shortline taking over the Oakdale operations of both roads since at least 1996. BNSF finally agreed to sell their Riverbank-Oakdale line to Sierra Northern in 2008, expanding the shortline's operations to Riverbank, including a substantial industrial park. However, Sierra Northern has been unable to strike a similar agreement with Union Pacific, who as of this writing continues to send their trains into Oakdale on trackage rights over the shortline to switch the Sierra Northern interchange and their other customers in town.

Lumber traffic from the SPI mills at Chinese and Standard continue to dominate the traffic base on the Sierra's original line. Traffic moved is all lumber, with no woodchips shipped for several years now. The railroad did handle large inbound movements of burned raw logs SPI imported from Arizona in 2003. SPI closed the Standard mill in 2009; however, the company decided to rebuild the mill so as to handle smaller logs, and the mill reopened in November 2011. Sierra continues pursuing other business; to date, seasonal propane shipments to a dealer in Sonora starting around 2008 has been the largest new traffic source. Perhaps the biggest potential source of new traffic is a large proposed limestone quarry that has been in various planning stages since at least 1997 that could—should it be built—provide a significant boost for the railroad. Sierra Northern has also periodically explored other possible sources of revenue, including generating electricity from old diesel locomotives during a recent power crunch in the state. Lastly, the Sierra Northern has taken the unusual step of rebuilding some of its older power into "Genset" hybrid locomotives in the Oakdale shops, using kits purchased from an outside source.

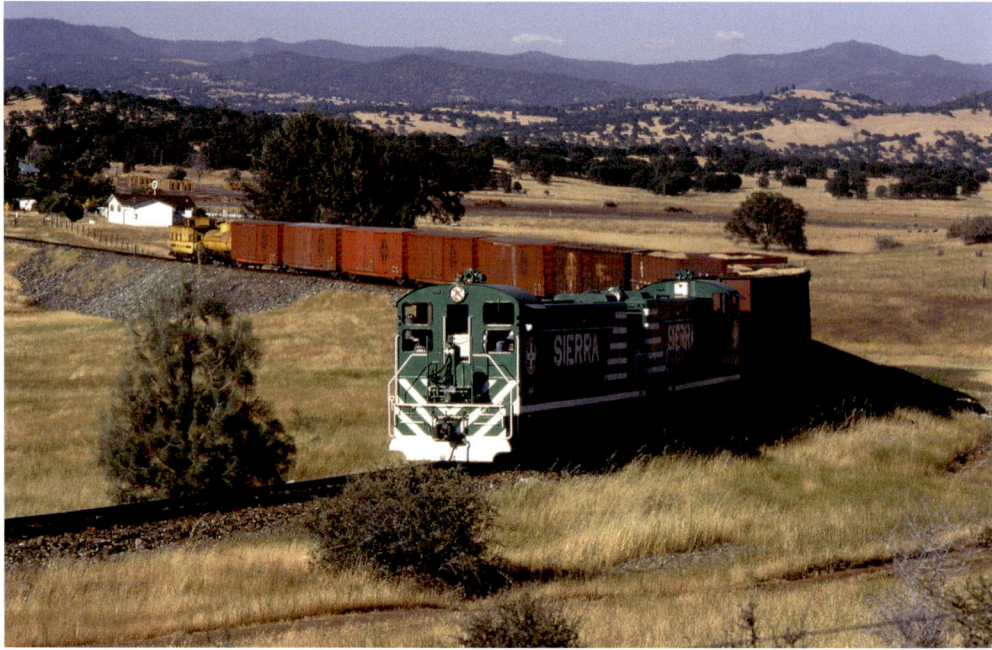

Several Sierra incentive *per diem* boxcars are part of the train powered by Nos. 44 and 42 in June 1981. *Dave Stanley*

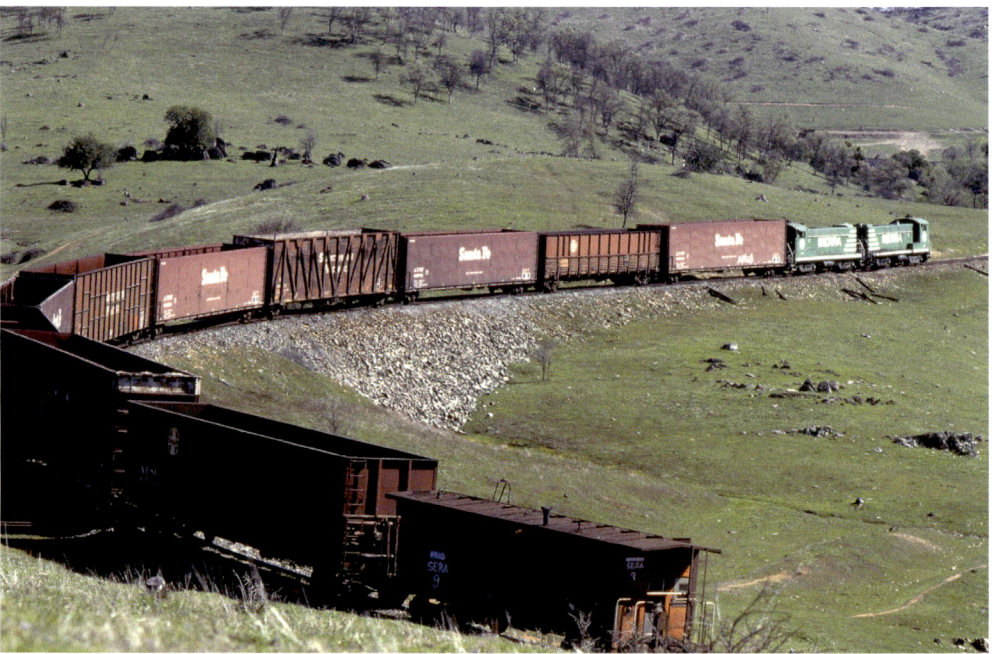

Ten woodchip hoppers and a caboose follow Nos. 44 and 40 through Hetch Hetchy Junction on 3/27/1987. *Dave Stanley*

Unlike most other operations covered in this book, the future of this railroad appears secure. SPI has been expanding its workforce at the Chinese and Standard mills, and the rebuild of the Standard mill speaks especially well for the future of that operation. Other substantial freight traffic sources may be on the horizon. Railtown 1897 continues to maintain its operations, alternating diesel powered trips with steam on the weekends, and the involvement of the Foundation has provided some cushion against the often volatile state parks budget. These operations appear well poised to continue Bullock, Crocker, and Poniatowski's dreams.

LOCOMOTIVE ROSTER

A—Plymouth DLC-6, c/n 1958, Built 1925. Originally HC Collins; to Key Machinery; to Sierra. Used as Jamestown shop switcher.

1, 2:1—Unknown 4-4-0s, purchased for construction of road and sold afterwards. No other information.

2:2—New York 0-6-0, c/n 506, Built 1889. Originally Montana Union #109; to Northern Pacific #529; to Sierra; to Lassen Lumber & Box #23, Susanville, CA, 1918; to Red River Lumber Company #23 1929. Scrapped 1940.

2:3—Lima 3-Truck Shay, c/n 3177, Built 1922. Originally Hutchinson Lumber Co. #2; to Feather River Pine Mills #2; to FRRY #2. Retired 8/1966 and sold to State of California for display at Oroville Dam, then moved to Railtown 1897 State Historic Park, Jamestown, CA, where it is in service.

3—Rogers 4-6-0, c/n 4493, Built 1891. Originally Prescott & Arizona Central #3; to Sierra 1897. Retired 1932, then restored for movie work. Reboilered and returned to service.

4—Baldwin 4-4-0, c/n 5851, Built 1882. Originally Northern Pacific #99, then #652; to Sierra 1899; to Pickering Lumber #14 1917. Scrapped 1938.

5—Schenectady 0-6-0, c/n 5177, Built 1899. Acquired new; to Hawaii Consolidated Railroad 1903.

6—Baldwin 4-4-0, c/n 6113, Built 1883. Originally Northern Pacific #114, then #653; to Sierra; to Atlas-Olympia Company, Oakdale. Scrapped 1937.

7—Baldwin 4-4-0. c/n 5674, Built 1882. Originally Northern Pacific #93; to Sierra 1899. No further information.

9—Stearns 2-truck Heisler, c/n 1036, Built 1899. Acquired new; to Sugar Pine Railway #8; to West Side Lumber #1 1937; Scrapped 1947.

10—Lima 2-truck Shay, c/n 718, Built 1902. Acquired new; to Diamond Match Company 1917.

11—Lima 2-truck Shay, c/n 788, Built 1903. Acquired new; to Pickering Lumber 1918; to Verdi Lumber Company; to Clover Valley Lumber Company. Scrapped 1952.

12—Lima 3-truck Shay, c/n 789, Built 1903. Acquired new; to Pickering Lumber Company #12 1924; to Connel Motor Truck, Stockton; to Pacific Locomotive Association (Niles Canyon Railway), Sunol, California.

18—Baldwin 2-8-0, c/n 29790, Built 1906. Acquired new. Retired 1953, tender sold to Tidewater Southern for their #132; to West Coast Trailer Sales lot, Sacramento, to Great Western Railroad Museum 1984. Stored in McCloud, California, and now Merrill, Oregon.

20—Baldwin 2-8-0, c/n 43344, Built 1916. Acquired new; to U.S. Army #6814 1942; to Kurth Lumber Company #20, Jasper, Texas.

21—Climax 2-Truck, c/n 746, Built 1906. Acquired new; to Sugar Pine Railway #1 1908; to Grant Rock & Gravel; to Railway Equipment Company; to Sillwater Lumber; to Zimmerman, Wells & Brown; to Sigardson & Bartholomew Logging; to Jamestown–Oregon Lumber.

22—Baldwin 2-8-0, c/n 53205, Built 1920. Acquired new; to California Western #41 1940. Scrapped.

24—Baldwin 2-8-0, c/n 39577, Built 1912. Originally Nevada Copper Belt #3; to Sierra 1923; Scrapped 1955.

26—Baldwin 2-6-0, c/n 32646, Built 1908. Originally Ocean Shore #6; to Sierra 1921; to Davies-Johnson Lumber Company 1924. Scrapped 1939.

28—Baldwin 2-8-0, c/n 55246, Built 1922. Acquired new; to Railtown 1897. In service.

30—Baldwin 2-6-2, c/n 55412, Built 1922. Acquired new; to Howard Terminal Railway, Oakland, CA, 1937; to Pacific Locomotive Association (Niles Canyon Railway), Sunol, California. Currently under restoration.

32—Baldwin 2-6-2, c/n 57018, Built 1923. Acquired new; to Tidewater Southern #132 1940. Scrapped, with boiler sold to a sulfur mine west of Winnemucca, Nevada.

34—Baldwin 2-8-2, c/n 58679, Built 1925. Acquired new; to White Mountain Scenic Railroad, Arizona, then to Heber Creeper Railroad, then to Great Western Railroad Museum, but never removed from Jamestown where it remains stored.

36—Alco 2-8-2, c/n 68278, Built 1930. Acquired new; to White Mountain Scenic Railroad, Arizona; to Heber Creeper, Heber City, Utah; to Great Western Railroad Museum, Merrill, Oregon.

38—Baldwin 2-6-6-2, c/n 61781, Built 1934. Originally Weyerhaeuser Timber Company #4, Klamath Falls, Oregon; to Sierra 1952; to Rayonier #38, Crane Creek, Washington; to Great Western Railroad Museum. Stored at McCloud, California, then Merrill, Oregon.

SIERRA

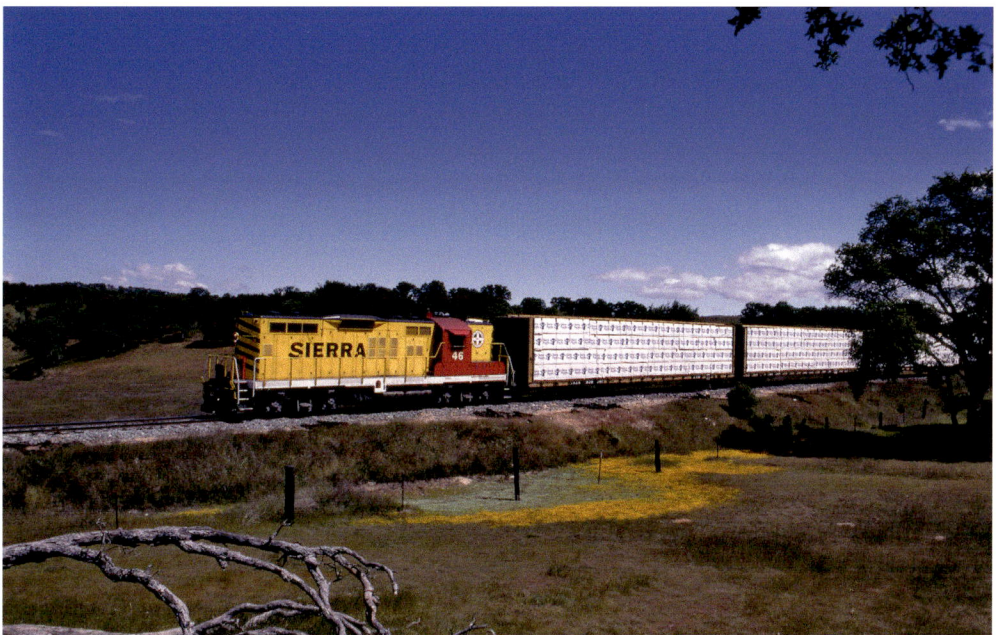

No. 46 with westbound lumber loads. *Sean Zwagerman*

40, 42—Baldwin S-12, c/n 76092 and 76093, Built 1955. Acquired new. #40 scrapped 2008; #42 remains in occasional service, though it has been for sale.

44—Baldwin S-12, c/n 75140, Built 1951. Originally Sharon Steel #10, then #2; to Sierra 1966. Scrapped 2008.

45—EMD GP-9, c/n 19352, Built 1954. Originally Great Northern #667; to Burlington Northern #1819; to BNSF #1612; to Sierra. Seldom if ever used, may have been parted out.

46—EMD GP-9E, c/n 22913, Built 1957. Originally Southern Pacific #5731, then #3572, then #3773; to Sierra 1996. To JL Consulting; to Specialty Locomotive.

47—EMD GP-7, c/n 16906, Built 1952. Originally Reading #607; to Central California Traction #60; to Sierra. Transferred to other Sierra Northern operations.

48—EMD GP-20, c/n 26868, Built 1961. Originally ATSF #1162, then #3162, then #3062; to BNSF #2044; to Sierra.

50—EMD GP-20, c/n 26836, Built 1961. Originally ATSF #1130, then #3130, then #3030; to BNSF #2020; to Sierra.

52—Railpower Genset RP20BD, rebuilt 2014 by Sierra from EMD GP7, c/n 17449, Built 1952. Originally ATSF #2794, then 2115; to BNSF #1324; to Yolo Shortline #135; to Sierra #135, then rebuilt.

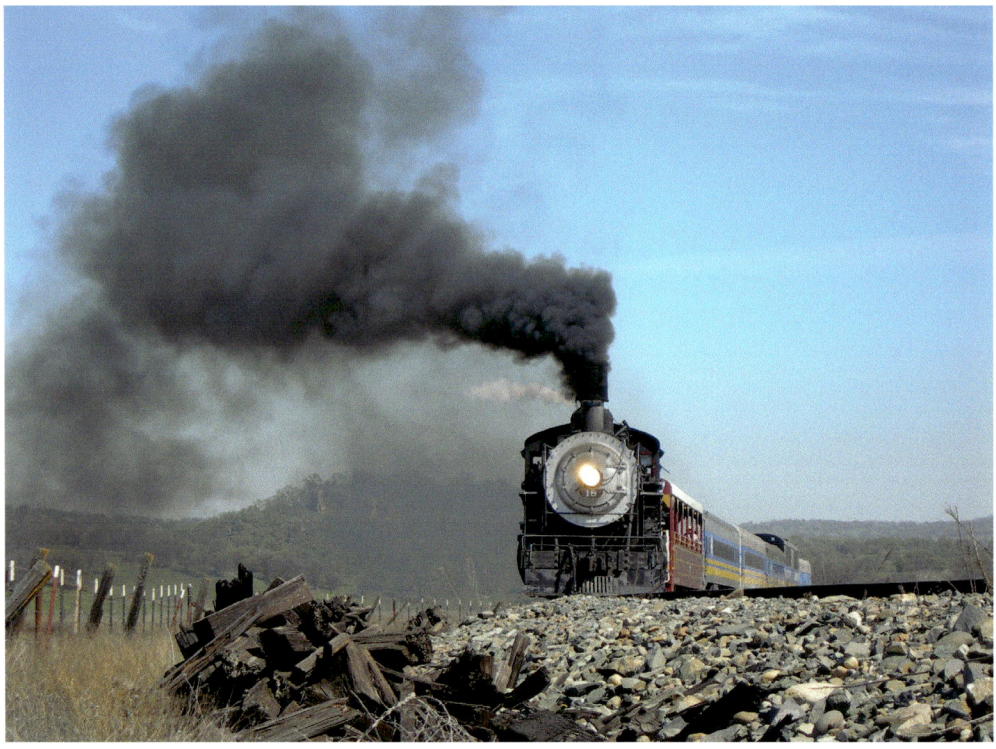

Leased former McCloud River No. 18 powering a railfan trip in March 2008. *Jeff Moore*

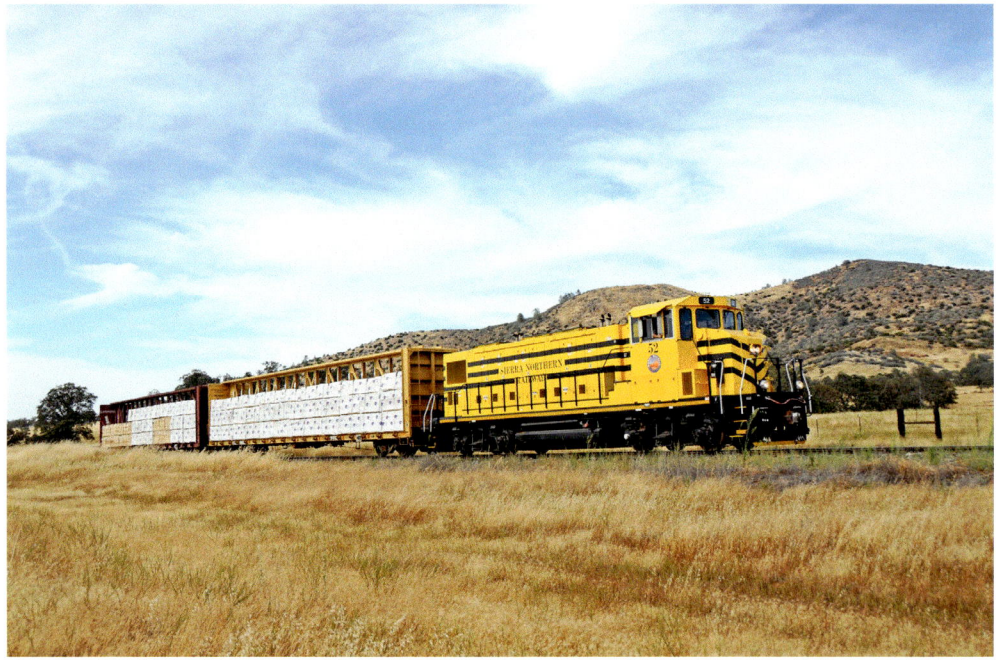

Genset No. 52 leads two loads from Standard. *Drew Jacksich*

107—EMD F-7B. Originally Milwaukee Road #110B, then converted to slug SE2. To Dakota Rail SE2; to Washington Central #107 and converted to a HEP car for *Spirit of Washington* dinner train; to Sierra, who removed HEP equipment.

131—EMD GP-9, c/n 22941, Built 1957. Originally SP #5759, then #3600, then #3803; to Yolo Shortline #131. Moved to Oakdale for conversion to Genset and is being used primarily on the dinner train until the planned conversion.

1227—Lima 0-6-0, c/n 1494, Built 1914. Originally SP #1227; to display in Alameda; to Golden Gate Railroad Museum, San Francisco; to Sierra for possible restoration.

In addition to the above, Sierra also leased two former ATSF/Amtrak CF-7 locomotives (#593 and #594) around 1995 and owned five ex-Burlington Northern General Electric B30-7AB (#4000, #4001, #4006, #4025, and #4046), all sold to NREX. The Oakdale shop converted another ex-SP GP-9 to a Genset (Sierra Northern #133) in 2012 that saw limited service on the Sierra before being transferred to another operation. Short Line Enterprises #8 (Cooke 4-4-0. c/n 1861, Built 1888) spent several years in the late 1970s on the railroad. Railtown 1897 has three ex-military locomotives, two Alco MRS-1 diesels #546 and #613 that have also been used by Sierra on short term leases and Whitcomb RS4TC #1265.

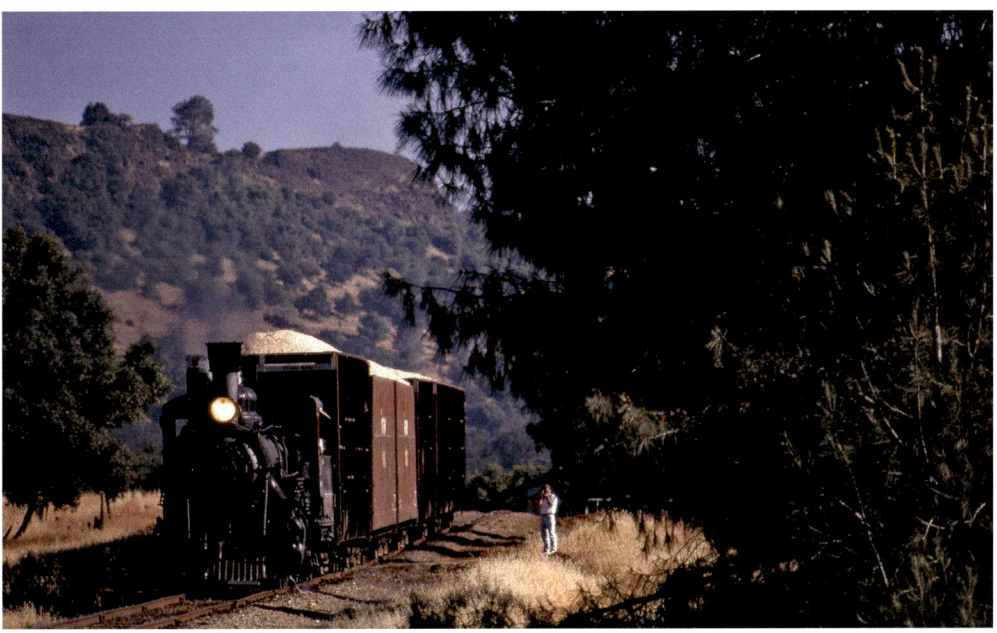

No. 28 filling in on a regular freight after the diesel suffered a mechanical failure on 6/7/1991. *Dave Stanley*

12

YREKA WESTERN

BACKGROUND

In 1851, a prospector named Abraham Thompson found gold nuggets in a narrow valley forty miles northwest of Mt. Shasta. The new town of Thompson's Dry Diggings had a population of 2,000 people by the time it was six weeks old. The name changed to Shasta Butte City, and then in 1852 to Yreka. The sudden influx of population caused California to create Siskiyou County, also in 1852, with Yreka promptly named the county seat.

Yreka prospered on the back of its gold mines and then as an important stop on the wagon roads spreading out to other mine camps and agricultural areas in the surrounding mountains. When the Central Pacific pushed its line north of Redding in 1883, the initial surveys routed the future line through Yreka; however, after again evaluating the rough topography north of town, the CP changed its route so as to follow the Shasta River. Adding insult to injury, the CP laid out a new town named Montague on its line, honoring the original engineer who surveyed the route passing through Yreka. This was a bitter pill for Yreka; to see what happened to towns left off the railroad map the citizens needed to look only as far south as Shasta, which had been the commercial and economic center of northern California until the CP bypassed it in favor of the newly established town named Redding. In a scant ten years Shasta declined to near ghost town status while Redding flourished. Yreka needed a railroad to remain relevant.

YREKA RAILROAD COMPANY

The citizens of Yreka initially attempted to change CP's mind, but were rebuffed, as running the mainline through the town would add substantially to the construction and operating costs. By 1887, Yreka decided to build its own railroad. Initial plans called for the line to be built ten miles south to the CP; however, the mainline road had no stations in that area and the shortline would be forced to build their own. Instead, on May 28, 1888, the citizens organized the Yreka Railroad Company to build a line running east to Montague. Stock subscriptions, bond sales, and borrowing raised sufficient cash to start construction. Rails connected Yreka to Montague by the end of the year, and operations commenced on January 9, 1889.

The Yreka Railroad settled down to a quiet existence, handling mostly passengers and limited freight traffic. Various propositions to either extend the railroad or build a new railroad

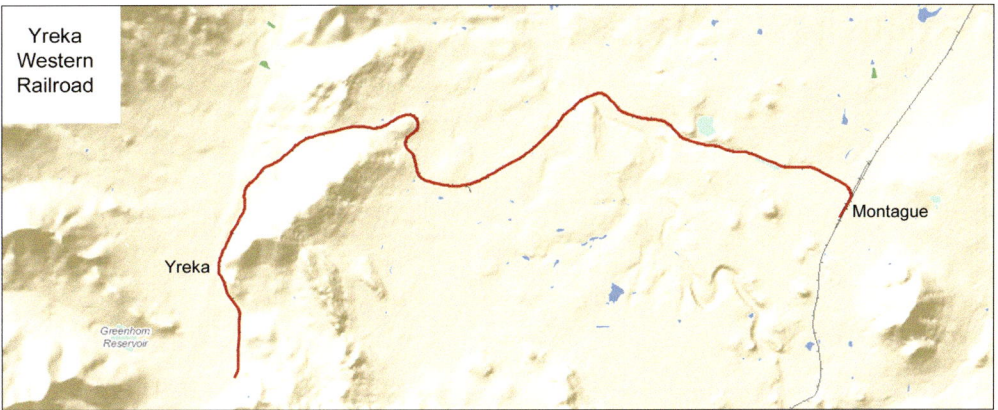

connecting Yreka with Scott Valley to the west came and went. In 1906, San Francisco based firm Scott & Van Arsdale—flush with cash from their recent sale of the McCloud River companies—purchased the Yreka Railroad and revamped the westward extension plans. Work began at Yreka on April 18, 1906, but immediately stopped when word that morning's San Francisco earthquake and fire reached the area. Like almost all other financial firms based in the city, Scott & Van Arsdale suffered extensive losses and could not continue construction.

Despite the natural disaster, Scott & Van Arsdale continued running the Yreka Railroad for the next several years. A railbus capable of handling several loaded freight cars economized the operation and allowed the company to continue; however, the railroad still lost money, and by 1920 Scott & Van Arsdale gave up. A group of local investors raised sufficient cash to purchase the company and preserve railroad service. The local ownership lasted eight years, as in 1928 the Klamath River Holding Company purchased the company. The Klamath company intended to extend the Yreka Railroad 108 miles to the Gray Eagle copper mine near Happy Camp. Preparatory work continued into 1929, only to be stopped again by the stock market crash and an I.C.C. decision finding no economic basis for the planned extension and denying the railroad permission to build it. By January 1932 the railroad passed into receivership.

YREKA WESTERN RAILROAD

On July 12, 1933, the trustee representing Yreka Railroad's bondholders purchased the company at a courthouse steps auction. The trustee incorporated the new Yreka Western Railroad (YW) on August 24, and the ICC approved the sale on April 18, 1935. However, financial results did not improve, and by August 1935 the new company lapsed back into receivership under the care of Orlo G. Steele. The company was both a financial and physical wreck by this point—unpaid debts piled up, and the tracks had become so bad that a round trip to Montague routinely consumed several days. Perhaps the low point came when a train consisting of one carload of fuel oil consumed a full week making the Montague to Yreka run, with near constant derailments limiting forward progress to fifty feet on one of the days.

Despite the near hopeless situation, Steele refused to give up on the company. He found financing to upgrade tracks and purchased suitable locomotives. Most importantly, Steele cooperated with the city of Yreka to locate sites for new industrial development, and the mainline was extended several times to serve new sawmills built south of town. In addition to outbound

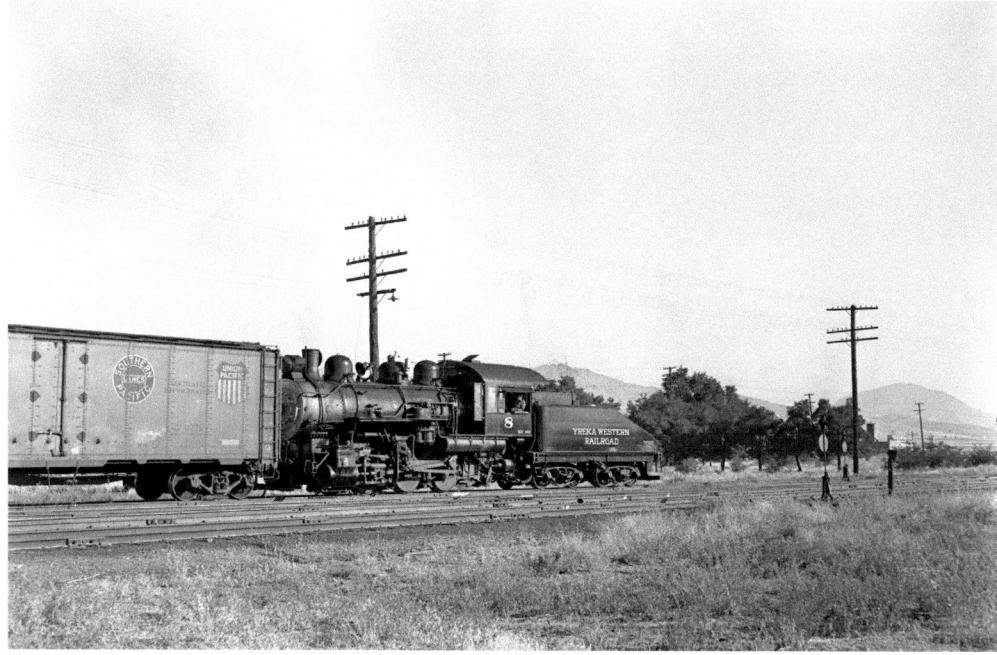

No. 8 switching in Montague on 8/1/1949. *Don Hansen collection*

lumber, the railroad also generated many carloads of raw logs harvested from nearby forests and destined for the Fruit Growers Supply Company mill in Hilt. The traffic base further expanded in the early years of the Second World War when the Gray Eagle copper mines reopened in 1941 and started reloading their products from trucks to railcars in Yreka. The YW also opened its own truck line, feeding traffic from Scott Valley and elsewhere to the railroad.

In 1942, railroad contractor A. D. Schader purchased the YW. Five decades into its existence, the railroad finally found the prosperity it always sought. Lumber traffic boomed, requiring the YW to purchase increasingly heavier locomotives. The entire railroad was rebuilt with heavier rail and ballasted.

KYLE RAILWAYS

A. D. Schader died in December 1954, and his will instructed the YW to be sold. Willis B. Kyle, then in the wholesale steel business, purchased the company in 1956. By this point the boom years of the war had passed, and the railroad slipped back into negative financial results. Kyle set out to change this, purchasing 600 acres near the midpoint of the line and offering it free of charge to prospective shippers. Lumber and other traffic rebounded.

The YW tested Baldwin diesel demonstrators in 1950; during the demonstration, a log truck attempted to beat a train to a crossing, resulting in a collision damaging one of the diesels and killing the truck driver. YW stuck with its steam power, making it a popular destination for the railfan community by the middle 1950s. A used diesel finally arrived in 1958; however, the railroad kept two steam locomotives on hand, and they continued to pitch in as backups

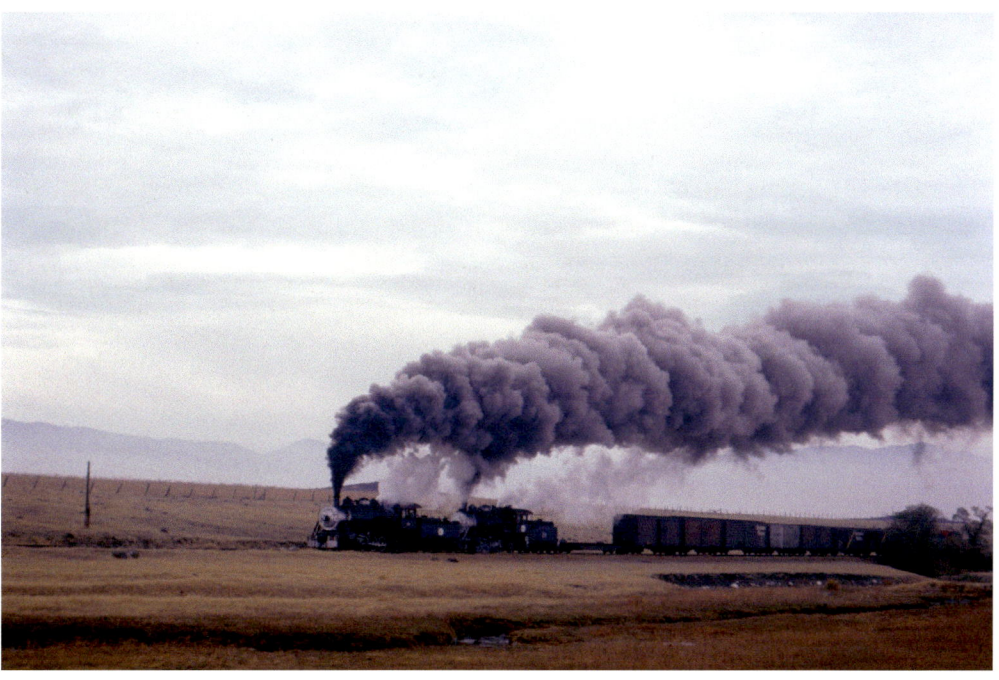

Nos. 18 and 19 powering a freight around 1964. *C. G. Heimerdinger Jr.*

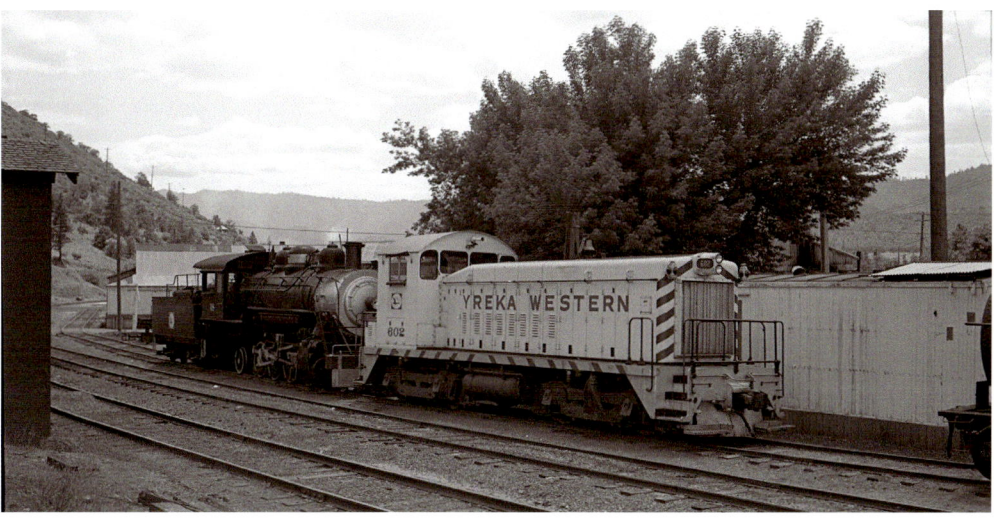

Nos. 602 and 18 in Yreka on 6/20/1964. *Don Hansen*

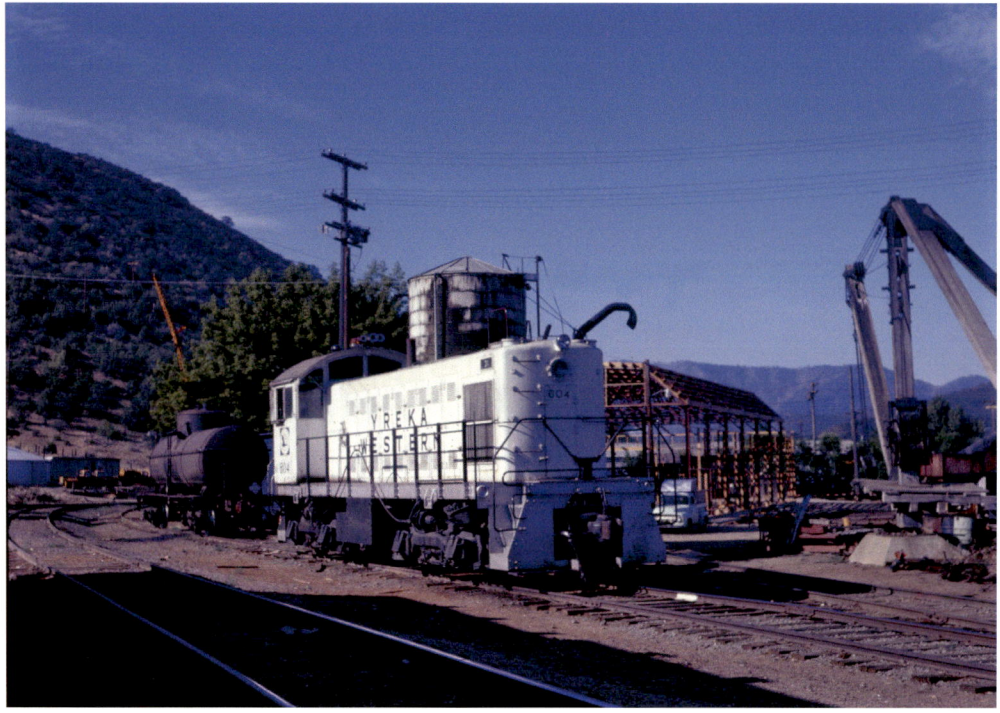

YW's new shop building is under construction behind the No. 604. *C.G. Heimerdinger Jr.*

and handle excursions through the 1960s. The railroad developed a logo featuring a profile of a flying goose, reportedly inspired by nearby Goosenest Mountain. As the 1970s dawned, Kyle started acquiring other railroads, and adopted the logo for all roads in his corporate empire. Unfortunately for the YW, this empire ended use of steam power on the road, as a mechanical failure sidelined one locomotive in 1964, and then in 1970 Kyle sent the other steamer off to another Kyle road in Oregon.

The YW prospered through the 1970s. Lumber and woodchip traffic remained strong, topping out at 2,500 loads a year in 1978. The railroad jumped into the incentive *per diem* market, first by reconditioning 47 boxcars purchased from the Western Pacific, followed by leasing 100 new cars from Brae in 1978.

THE BLUE GOOSE

The declines in the timber industry at the end of the 1970s hit the railroad hard. Sawmills closed, and trucks handled an increasing proportion of the lumber traffic, leaving the railroad with only low-value woodchip traffic. Carloadings plummeted, from 2,500 loads in 1978/1979 to 324 in 1986. YW got out of the boxcar business, scrapping its own cars in 1981 and turning the leased cars back to Brae. By the late 1980s and early 1990s the YW shippers were down to a handful—Hi-Ridge Lumber was the biggest, averaging six woodchip and one to three lumber loads each week. The adjacent Timber Products veneer plant chipped in 2–4 woodchip loads each week. Other traffic included a handful of inbound propane loads a month, very occasional

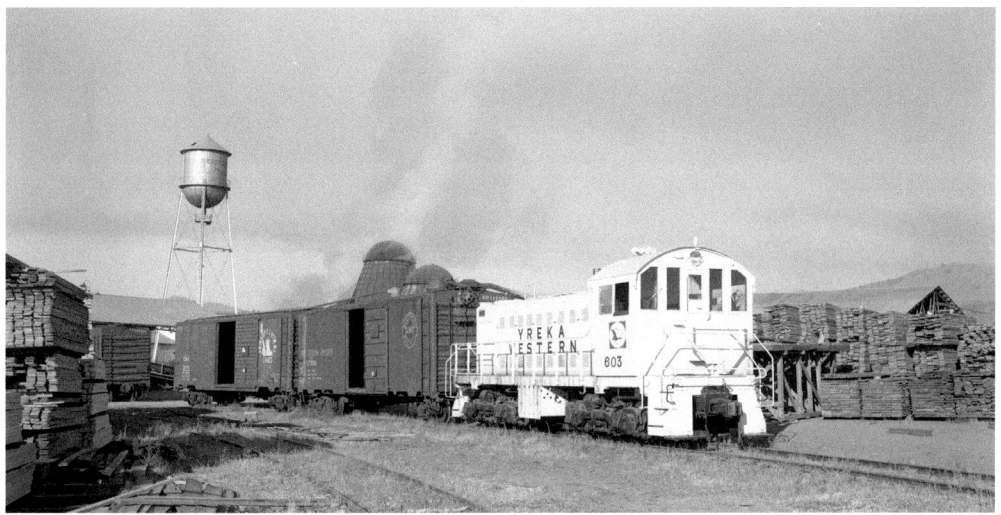

No. 603 switching a lumber mill in Yreka on 8/4/1964. *Don Hansen*

inbound lumber loads or outbound chips to or from Klamath River Moulding Company, and periodic outbound loads of copper concentrate trucked to Yreka from Happy Camp. Freights ran twice a week, on Tuesdays to the SP interchange at Montague and a switch job Friday afternoons.

The decline in freight business troubled Kyle. In 1985, the YW filed an abandonment application with the ICC; though eventually rejected on procedural grounds, the possibility of losing the railroad galvanized efforts to save it. In 1986, the City of Yreka signed an agreement with the YW to operate *Blue Goose* excursion trains over the line. The first trip ran on June 16, 1986. The 1986 season was a disappointment; however, 1987 was much better, helped by an extensive advertising campaign coupled with free publicity generated when the journey of the nation's Christmas Tree started on the road. The YW terminated the agreement with the city after the 1987 season and assumed operations itself. Ridership continued climbing, helped immeasurably by the return of the steam locomotive from Oregon in 1989. During the summer months, trains departed Yreka five days a week, making the trek to Montague in about an hour. Trains laid over in Montague, and several restaurants and gift shops catering to the excursion riders opened along the street facing the tracks.

DECLINE, REBIRTH, DECLINE

The YW rolled along through the 1990s with few changes. Willis Kyle died in 1991, though operations of his shortline empire continued on under the direction of Lynn Cecil, Kyle's business partner. Larry Bacon, a local attorney, capably managed the railroad's operations. Freight traffic remained static, with the only variations coming when Timber Products imported a few carloads of logs from New Zealand. The tourist train continued running, becoming one of the top tourist attractions in Siskiyou County.

The situation changed rapidly in 1999. Hi-Ridge Lumber, source of the majority of YW's freight traffic, closed down. By this point Kyle Railways had sold off almost all of its other railroads, most of them in 1997 to States Rail, another shortline holding company. The YW simply could

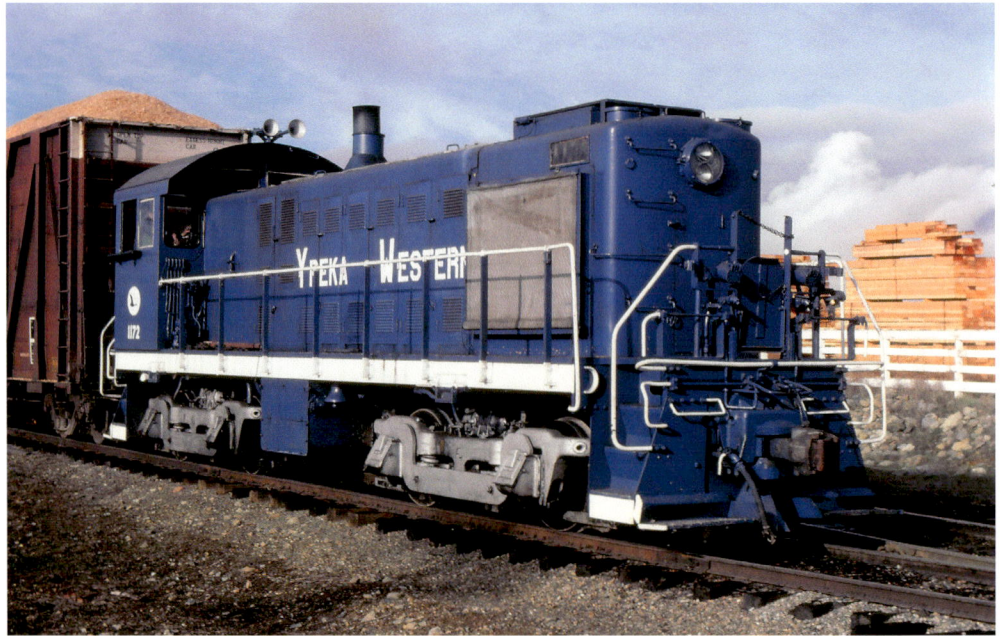

No. 1172 in January 1978. *Lee F. Hower*

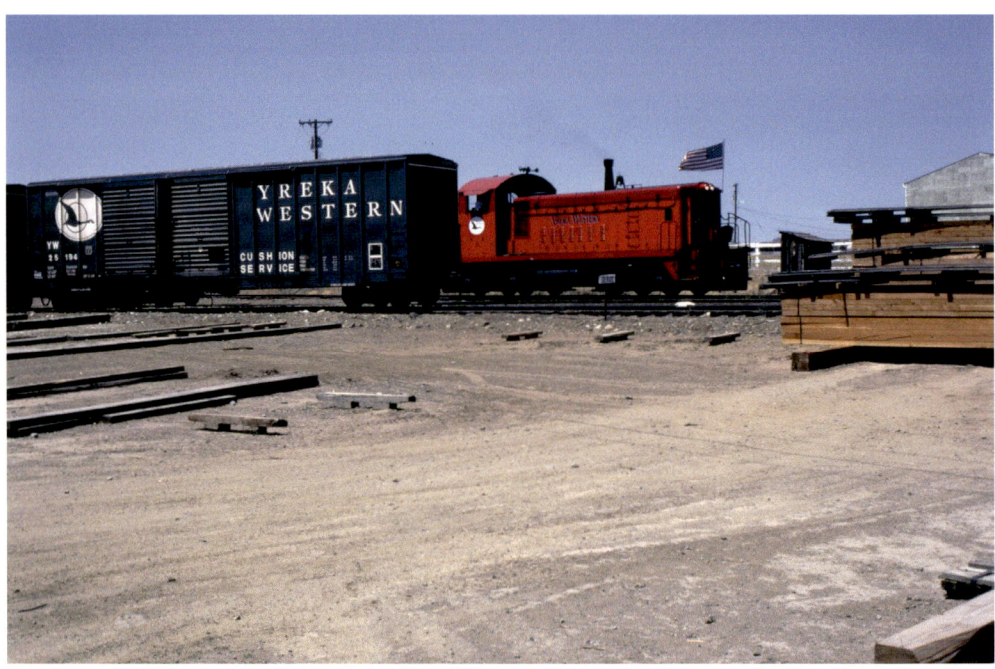

No. 21 rolling past one of the road's incentive *per diem* boxcars. *Wayne I. Monger*

not carry on viable operations without Hi-Ridge, and in 1999 the railroad received permission to abandon the railroad. However, once again local officials and groups came together, but instead of buying the railroad themselves the committee located the Rocky Mountain Mining and Railroad Museum, who purchased the YW on January 14, 2000.

The new owner inherited a property still on unstable financial ground; however, a savior soon appeared. Timber Products (TP) always had been a minor shipper, contributing only a few carloads of woodchips each week. The company produced veneer and peeler cores in its Yreka plant that moved north to other TP facilities in southern Oregon by truck. The Central Oregon & Pacific (CORP), operator of the former SP line over the Siskiyou Mountains since 1994, identified this as a commodity that could move by rail, and TP agreed to such a proposition based on a promise of "same day" rail service. The YW moved over 2,000 loads in 2000, the most traffic the railroad moved in any year since 1979.

Steam excursions continued on until new federal boiler regulations implemented before the 2002 season sidelined the steamer; however, a tunnel fire in the Siskiyous the next year closed the CORP line as a through route, shifting the TP traffic back to trucks. The YW effectively shut down for lack of revenue until the tunnel reopened in 2005, at which time the TP traffic came back to the rails. With the revenue stream again stabilized, the YW completed the work required to bring the steamer back to operation again.

Tourist and freight trains once again kept the railroad healthy through the next several years. Then, in 2008, the next turn in the bust-boom-bust cycle through which the YW always lived occurred. In the face of the recession-reduced traffic, CORP suspended all train service over the Siskiyous, once again forcing TP traffic back onto trucks. The YW had insufficient revenue to continue operations and again closed up shop.

SCRAPPINGS, CAR STORAGE, AND FUTURE PROSPECTS

The YW entered an economic tailspin after 2008. Without income the road could not pay its bills, and creditors fell upon the company. Lienholders seized several pieces of equipment and other properties, though the railroad successfully prevented some of the seizures pending a formal abandonment of the railroad. In the meantime, the company survived by scrapping all surplus trackage and almost all remaining equipment the road owned. A little bit of car storage also helped, though that too ended. As of this writing the property is in a moribund state; the steam locomotive, one diesel, an old ballast hopper, and an ex-SP baggage car are all that remain on the line, plus two passenger coaches owned by other parties, and a multitude of on-going legal issues surround everything.

The future of the YW is an open question. As of this writing, CORP has reopened the line over the Siskiyous, but to date TP has yet to resume shipping anything over the YW, and the company has been ambiguous as to whether or not it might start using rail again. If TP were to resume shipping it could give the portion of the line between their mill and Montegue some measure of potential security; however, any such revivals will require substantial up-front capital to satisfy liens against and rehabilitate the property. Resuming passenger operations would require rebuilding the scrapped trackage around the depot and acquiring new passenger equipment. Like the nearby McCloud Railway, the YW waits in a state of suspended animation for whatever comes next.

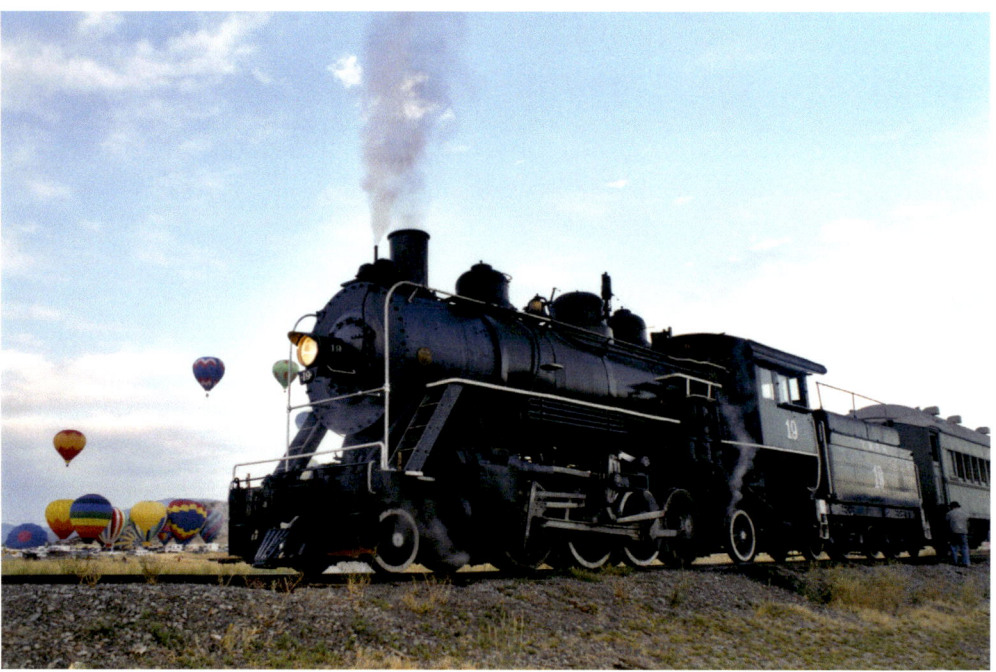

No. 19 with an excursion train during the Montague Hot Air Balloon Festival. *Roger Titus*

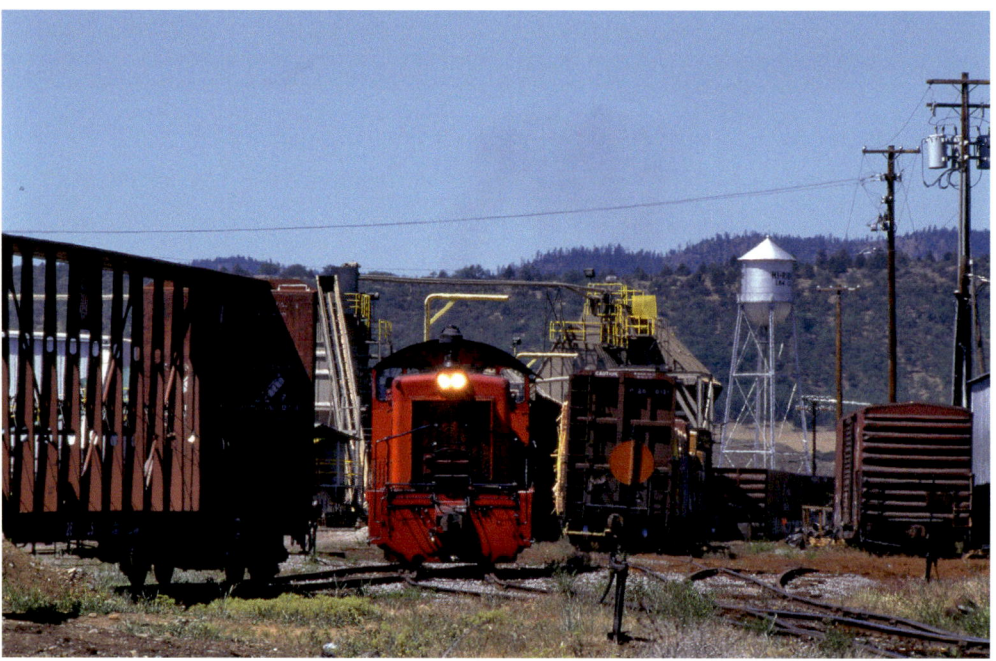

No. 21 switching carloads of veneer and woodchips in the Timber Products mill. *Sean Zwagerman*

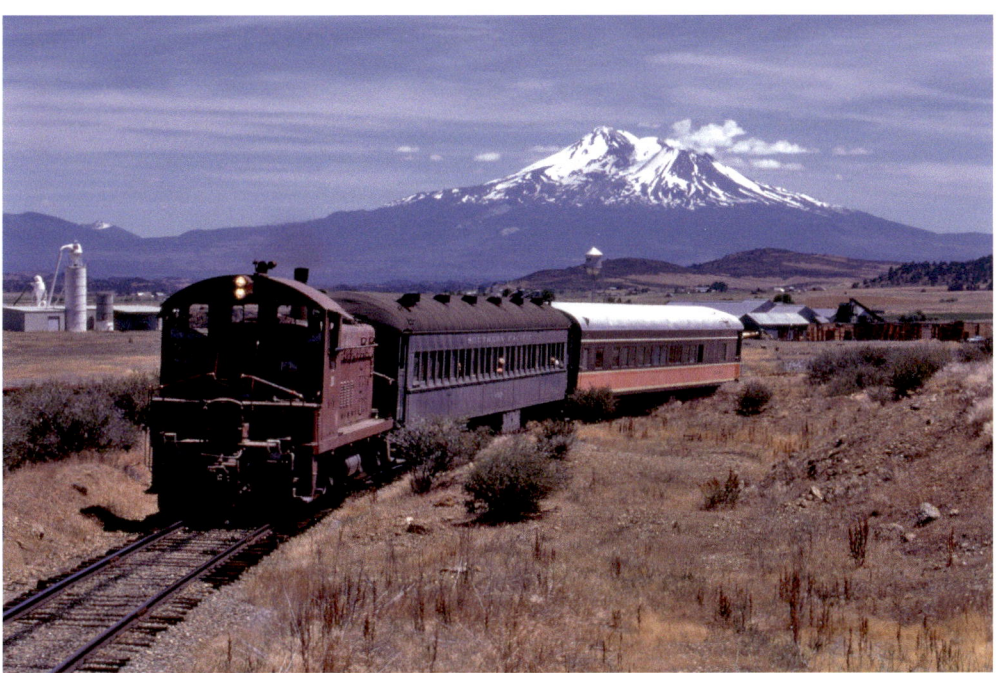

No. 20 leads an early *Blue Goose* excursion train heading for Yreka. *Wayne I. Monger*

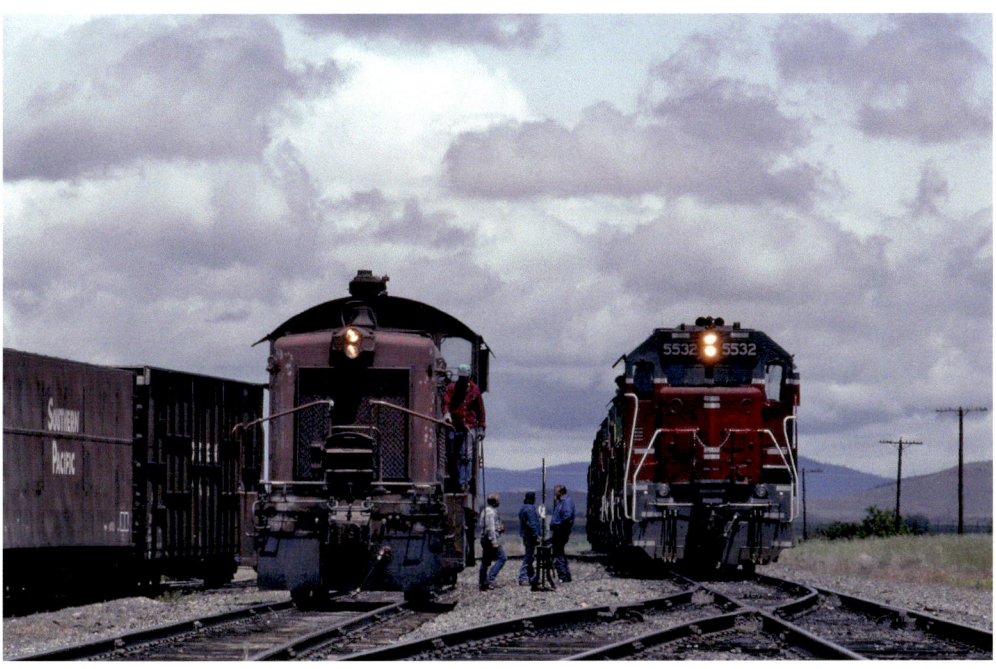

YW and Central Oregon & Pacific crews exchanging notes in the yards at Montague. *Sean Zwagerman*

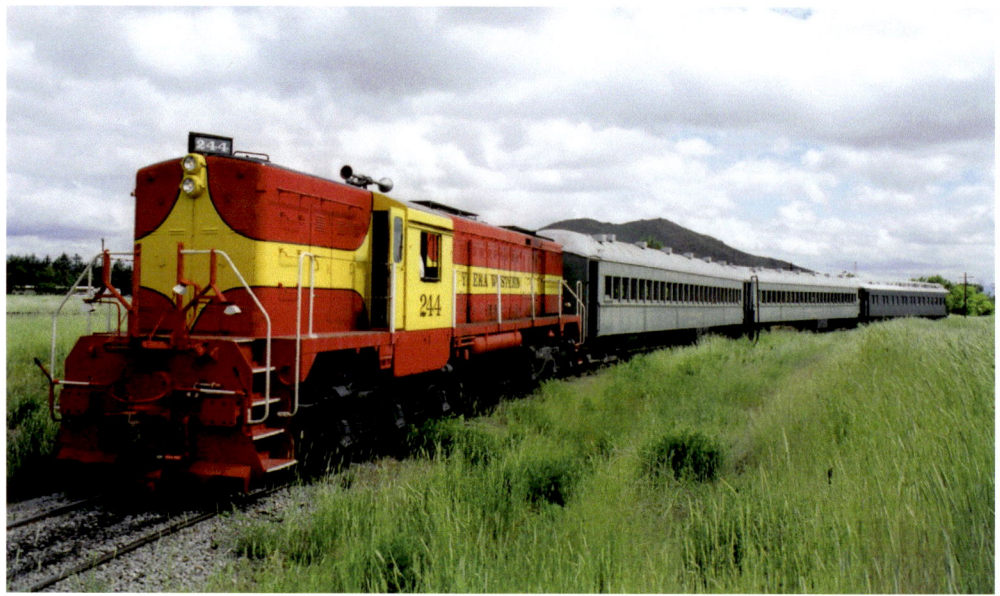

No. 244 leading a *Blue Goose* excursion train somewhere on the line. *Roger Titus*

LOCOMOTIVE ROSTER

No #—Plymouth HLB, c/n 3098, Built 1929. Originally Fischer, Ross, McDonald & Kahn, Azusa, CA; to Kaiser Paving Company; to YW 1936; to U.S. Army; to Berg Metals.

1—Baldwin 2-4-2T, c/n 9648, Built 1889. Acquired new; Scrapped 1930.

2—Cooke 4-4-0, c/n 1725, Built 1886. Originally Corvallis & Eastern #11; to Oregon Central & Eastern #11; to Oregon Pacific #11; to YW #2 1898. Scrapped 1918.

3—Schenectady 4-6-0, c/n 1639, Built 1882. Originally Southern Pacific of Mexico #48; to SP #207, then #1681, then #2093; to YW #3 1906; Scrapped 1932.

7—Brooks 0-6-0, c/n 54563, Built 1914. Originally State Belt #7; to YW 1944. Scrapped 1956.

8—Baldwin 0-6-0, c/n 43670, Built 1916. Originally State Belt #8; to YW 1944. Scrapped 1956.

9—Baldwin 2-6-2, c/n 18596, Built 1901. Originally McCloud River #9; to YW #9 1939; to Amador Central #9 1942; to Nezperce & Idaho Railroad #9 1945; to private party 1967; moved to Mid-Continental Railroad Museum, North Freedom, Wisconsin, for restoration, then to Kettle Moraine Scenic Railroad, North Lake, Wisconsin, 1972. Operated on Kettle Moraine until it closed in 2002. To Age of Steam Roundhouse, Sugarcreek, Ohio, 2015.

10—Baldwin 2-6-2, c/n 18674, Built 1901. Originally McCloud River #10; to YW #10 1925. Scrapped 1944 at Yreka.

18—Baldwin 2-8-2, c/n 41709, Built 1914. Originally McCloud River #18; to YW #18 1956; to McCloud Railway 1998; to Nevada Commission for the Reconstruction of the V & T Railroad 2005. Leased to Sierra Railroad, Oakdale, CA, 2007, then moved 2009 to Virginia & Truckee, Virginia City, Nevada, where it is in service. Reportedly slated to eventually be re-numbered V & T #31.

19—Baldwin 2-8-2, c/n 42000, Built 1915. Originally Caddo & Choctaw Railroad #4; to Choctaw River Lumber Company; to Cia de Real del Monte y Pachuca #105, Pachuca, Hidalgo, Mexico; reported also to have been United Mining & Smelting Company #2069 while in Mexico; to McCloud River 1923; to YW #19 1953; to Oregon Pacific & Eastern Railroad #19 1970; to YW #19 1988. As of January 2015, locomotive is stored in close to operable condition in Yreka; legal possession of locomotive rests with Siskiyou County Sheriff's Office while courts sort out numerous liens and ownership claims surrounding locomotive.

20, **21**—EMD SW-8, c/n 17335 and 17337, Built 1953. Originally SP #4608/#1113 and #4601/#1115; to Chrome Crankshaft 1978; to YW 1978. #20 scrapped 2011. #21 converted to a SW-900 and remains on railroad in 2016, though recently listed for sale in an equipment auction.

94— Lime 3-truck Shay, c/n 2943, Built 1917. Originally Longville Lumber #94; to DeRidder & Eastern #94; to Weed Lumber #94; to Long-Bell Lumber #94; to YW 1943. Scrapped 1946.

100—Alco (Brooks) 2-8-2, c/n 61857, Built 1920. Originally Portland Astoria & Pacific #100; to Weed Lumber #100; to Long Bell Lumber #100; to YW 1955; Scrapped 1955.

244—Alco/GE MRS-1, c/n 80352/#31674, Built 1953. Originally US Army #2119; to US Navy #65-00541; to Feather River Railroad Society (Western Pacific Railroad Museum); to Northern Nevada Railroad, but never delivered, and sold instead to YW *circa* 2002. Scrapped 2011.

439—EMD SD9, c/n 20214, Built 1955. Originally SP #5436, then #3914, then #4439; to Chrome Crankshaft; to Livingston Mountain Locomotive Works #439; leased to Tacoma Eastern, then stored on Battle Ground, Yacolt & Chelatchie Prairie, before going to YW. Sold to Modoc Northern but never delivered, then to Western Rail #439.

602—EMD SW-8, c/n 17230, Built 1952. Originally Bamberger #602; to YW 1958; to Oregon Pacific & Eastern 1978; to Molalla Western #602 1994, then Oregon Pacific #602; to Western Rail #602 2010.

603, **604**—Alco S-1, c/n 69199 and 69201, Built 1940. Originally Northern Pacific Terminal #30 and #31; to YW 1963. **#603** to Port of Tacoma #703 1970, then #5703; to Mt. Rainier Scenic Railroad #30; to Lake Whatcom Railway #30. **#604** to Port of Tacoma #704 1974, then #5704. Retired and scrapped.

1171, **1172**—Alco S4, c/n 81393 and 81394, Built 1955. Originally Union Pacific #1171 and #1172; to Chrome Crankshaft; to YW 1972. #1171 never operated by YW, but parted out until scrapped 1985-1988. #1172 to Pend Orielle Valley #101 1979; traded to Coast Engine & Equipment 1986, but returned to POVA. Scrapped 1987.

13

OTHER ROADS

ANDERSON & BELLA VISTA

Around 1891, the Shasta Lumber Company built the Anderson & Bella Vista Railroad, stretching 15.39 miles between the named communities. Shasta Lumber's operations consisted of a sawmill and narrow gauge logging railroad located near Round Mountain feeding rough cut lumber through a 32-mile long flume to a planing mill, box factory, and drying yards at Bella Vista. The A & BV replaced the wagons previously used to transport lumber from Bella Vista to the SP mainline. The Terry Lumber Company purchased the operations in 1897; however, by 1913, Terry sold the A & BV to the Afterthought Copper Company, operator of a copper mine at Ingot, who incorporated the railroad as the California, Shasta & Eastern (CS & E). Afterthought never acted on its plans to extend the CS & E east to Ingot.

Terry operations carried through until 1917, when the company succumbed to accumulated financial problems. The Red River Lumber Company purchased both the Terry and CS & E companies. Red River operated the Terry property for only 1920 before closing it down; however, CS & E operations staggered on until 1937, when Red River scrapped out the railroad, though the I.C.C. did not grant formal abandonment permission until 1946. Two principle remnants of the road remain, the first being Deschutes Road- built almost entirely upon the old A & BV grade—and one of the locomotives, which has been resting in the bed of the Sacramento River a few miles out of Anderson since running off a ferry in the late 1890s.

BOCA & LOYALTON

In 1900, lumbering interests started building the Boca & Loyalton Railroad, extending north from the Southern Pacific mainline at Boca. The railroad replaced steam traction engines, which had been dragging wagons of lumber to the SP for over a decade. The railroad reached Loyalton, a center of commercial lumber operations in the Sierra Valley, in 1901. Further extensions brought the line to Beckwourth and then Mormon (Portola), along with several branches.

The B & L boomed in 1907-1909 as the Western Pacific built its mainline across Sierra Valley; however, by 1910 the company entered a steep tailspin. By 1915, the B & L operated in receivership, and on December 1, 1916, the WP purchased the B & L. WP control brought abandonment of the Loyalton-Boca segment; but the WP and now UP still operate much of the rest of the road, the Portola to Hawley segment as its mainline and the Hawley to Loyalton section as a branchline. A Sierra Pacific Industries sawmill kept UP trains rolling into Loyalton until it closed in 2001; the branch remains today but has been used only for car storage. Much of the line south of Loyalton has been inundated by reservoirs, but substantial grades- some with ties still in place- and a few decaying trestles remain today.

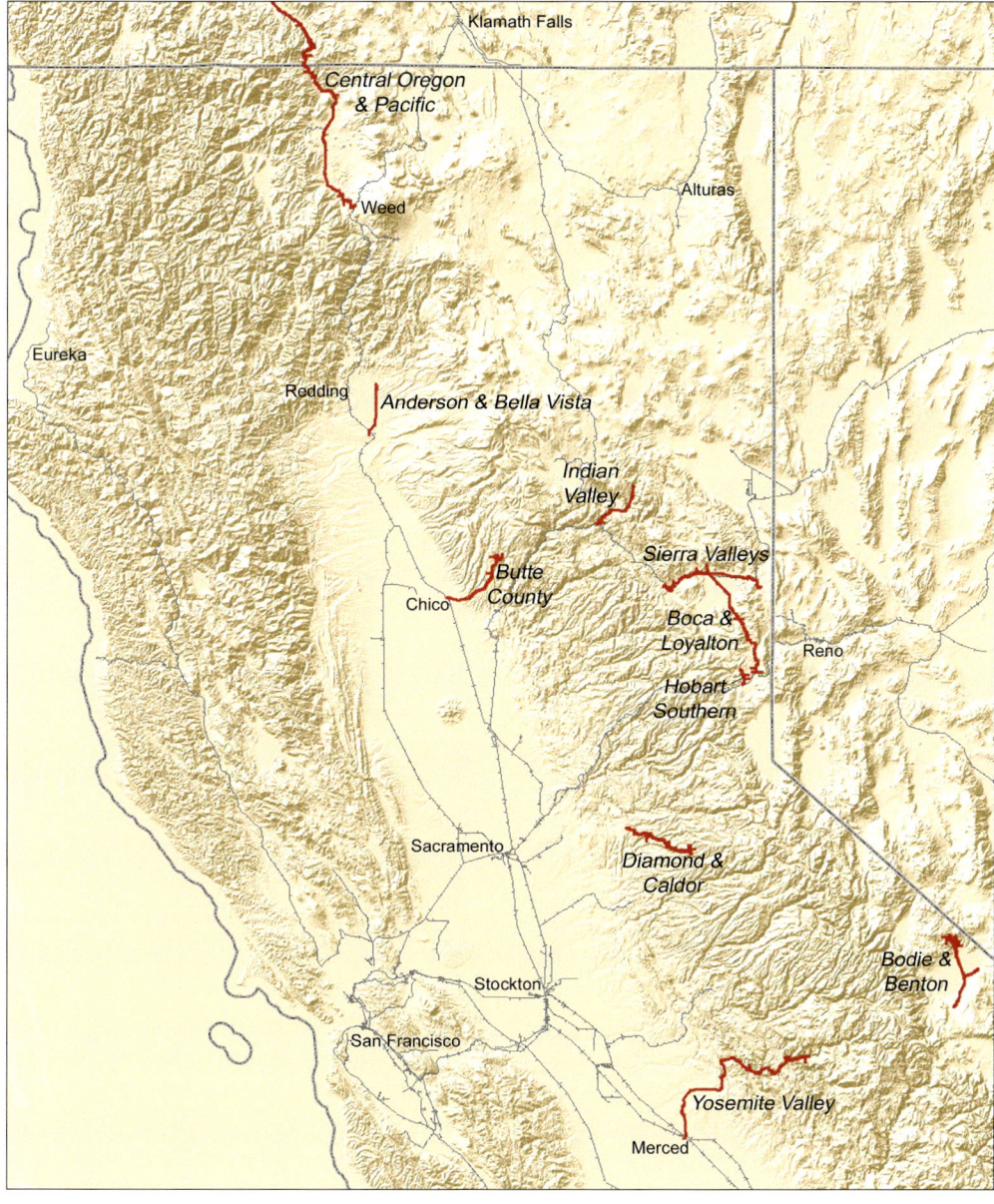

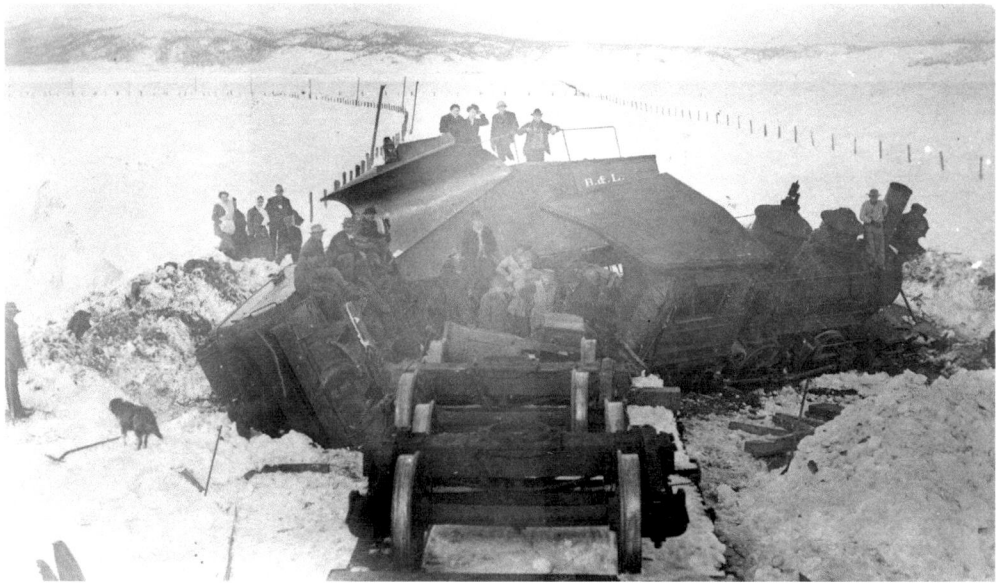

B & L's plow train wrecked while trying to open the line after a snowstorm. *Jeff Moore collection*

BODIE & BENTON

Bodie on the Sierra's eastern slope typified the mining industry's near insatiable demand for forest products used as fuel, in timbering shafts, and in general construction. In 1881, the Bodie Railway & Lumber Company built a 32-mile long narrow gauge railroad extending from Bodie south to Mono Mills, site of a sawmill erected in front of substantial pine timber. In 1882, the name changed to the Bodie & Benton Railway & Commercial Company, and work began on an eastward extension towards a proposed connection with the Carson & Colorado Railroad at Benton; however, the company abandoned this project with only nine miles of completed grade.

The Bodie & Benton settled down to its principle role of handling lumber and cordwood from the sawmill to Bodie. A series of log spurs built into the timber south of the mill brought logs to the mill. The name changed in 1893 back to Bodie Railway & Lumber Company, and then again in 1906 to the Mono Lake Railway & Lumber Company, and finally in 1908 to the Mono Railway Company.

By 1915, Bodie was well on its way towards its eventual ghost town status. The mill would require an extension of the logging railroad to remain in operation, and the sawmill and railroad required extensive rehabilitation, all unjustifiable expenses in the face of slacking lumber demand. The mill closed after 1915, and by 1917 the railroad ran out of things to haul. The railroad had been organized and run as a private road, but had still hauled whatever traffic offered to it; this policy landed the company in some trouble when it proposed abandoning the line. Some parties in Bodie protested the abandonment, resulting in a California Railroad Commission finding the company indeed had held itself as a common carrier; however, the Commission also saw no economic justification for continued operation and authorized the abandonment, and the railroad was no more by 1918. For more information on this story, see *Railroad in the Sky*, published in 2011 by the Friends of the Bodie Railway & Lumber Company.

BUTTE COUNTY

Shortly after 1900, the Diamond Match Company moved to develop their California holdings. Planned facilities included an expansive match factory at Barber, just south of Chico, and a sawmill at what would shortly be named Stirling City in the mountains to the east. In 1903 and 1904, the company built the Butte County Railroad (BC) connecting the two facilities. A private logging railroad extended into the timber beyond Stirling City.

Diamond sold BC to the Central Pacific (Southern Pacific) in October 1903, who promptly leased the road back to Diamond. BC thus maintained independent operations until December 1, 1915, when Diamond elected to not renew the operating lease. SP took over, operating the line as their Stirling City branch. Diamond closed the Stirling City mill in 1958, though raw log traffic and then a small stud mill kept SP trains running until 1974. SP abandoned and removed the entire BC line in the years thereafter.

CENTRAL OREGON & PACIFIC

In 1993, Southern Pacific launched an intensive effort to spin off branchlines and secondary mainlines to new shortline railroads. One of these sales conveyed SP's original mainline between Black Butte, California, and Eugene, Oregon, together with the Coos Bay branch west from Eugene—totaling 439 miles—to the new Central Oregon & Pacific Railroad (CORP) on December 1, 1994. The bulk of these lines lay in Oregon, with CORP's California footprint restricted to a couple dozen miles north of Black Butte.

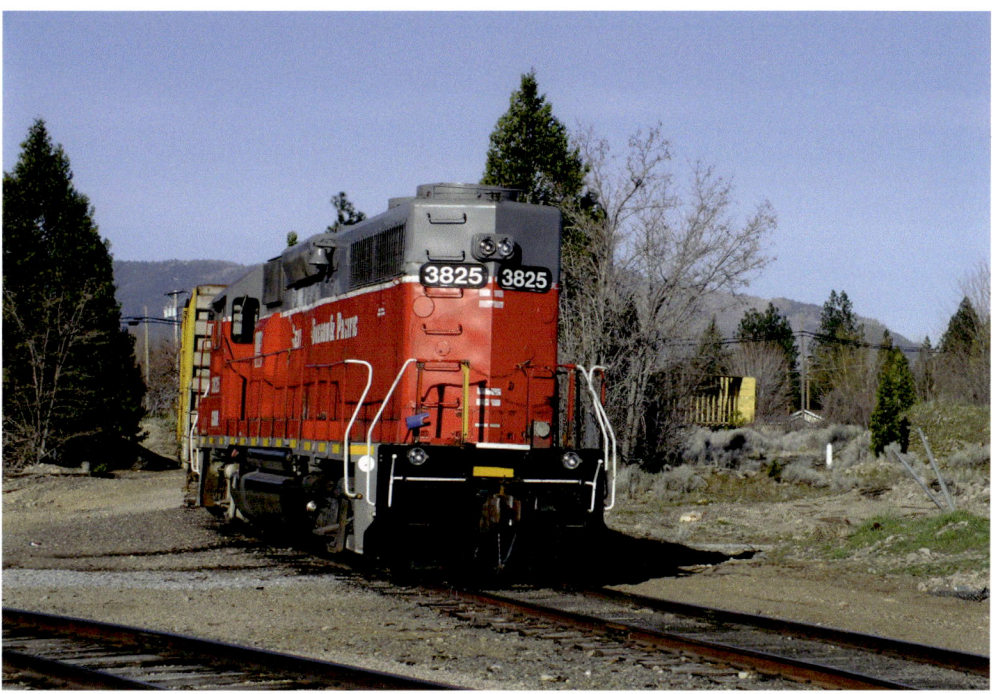

Central Oregon & Pacific No. 3825 laying over in Weed between runs in March 2015. *Jeff Moore*

CORP's California operations have always been based out of Weed. CORP operated a daily road freight north, usually meeting a corresponding freight coming south from Medford to swap cars, usually at Montague. In addition to through lumber traffic coming south from Oregon, CORP also developed substantial intraline movements, mostly raw log movements for Roseburg from their plant in Weed destined for their massive facilities in Dillard, Oregon, and the Timber Products veneer and peeler core traffic discussed in the Yreka Western chapter. In 2008, CORP consolidated all Oregon loads to the Union Pacific interchange at Eugene, ending operations over the line into California, including the intraline movements. CORP's California operations then consisted of a switch job working the Roseburg veneer mill, a water bottling plants, a handful of agricultural shippers around Grenada, and car storage. In late 2015, the road reopened the line over Siskiyou Summit, again expanding its California operations.

DIAMOND & CALDOR

In 1900, the California Door Company built a sawmill at Caldor and a planing mill and box factory at Diamond Springs, on Southern Pacific's Placerville branch, to supply its sash and door factory in Oakland. The company initially shipped lumber from Caldor to Diamond Springs on wagons drawn by animals or steam tractors; however, both proved inefficient, and by 1901 the company decided it needed a railroad. The narrow gauge Diamond & Caldor (D & C) completed its 34.69–mile line in 1904. As with other operations, a private logging railroad extended into the woods beyond Caldor.

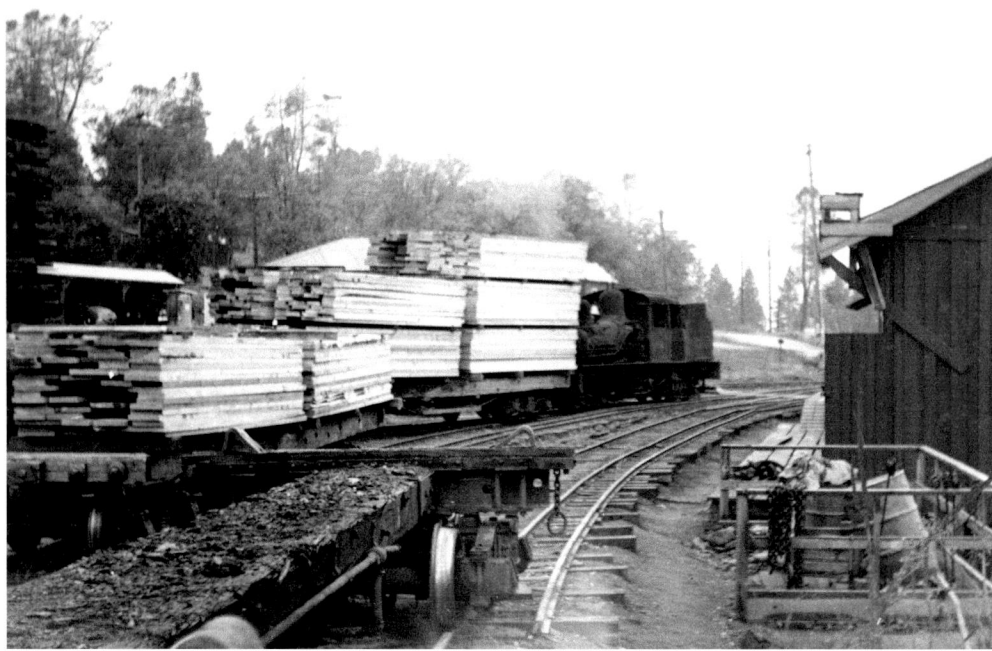

Diamond & Caldor Shay No. 4 switching in Diamond Springs in 1952. *J.R. Cummings photograph, John Taubeneck collection*

The D & C handled lumber until 1923, when a fire destroyed the Caldor mill. California Door decided to rebuild the mill at Diamond Springs, relegating the D & C to a log hauler only. Save for a few years of Depression-induced shutdown, railroad operations continued until 1952, when the California Railroad Commission ordered the company to switch from link-and-pin to automatic couplers. The end had come, and the railroad was abandoned in 1953.

INDIAN VALLEY

In 1916–1917, the Engels Copper Mining Company built the 21.5-mile long Indian Valley Railroad (IV) running from a connection with the Western Pacific mainline at Paxton north and east to their mine and smelter at Engelmine. A small amount of lumber and some log traffic supplemented the copper traffic.

In 1930, the Engle company suspended all operations at Englemine, leaving the IV with little more than a couple hundred carloads annually of mostly lumber. To make matters worse, WP's new Northern California Extension heading towards its eventual connection with the southward building Great Northern paralleled the IV main between Paxton and Crescent Mills. In 1937, the IV received permission to abandon its line south of Crescent Mills, with the grade promptly sold to the State for conversion into a highway. The rest of the railroad held on in hope the copper mines would reopen; however, a 1937 crash in mineral prices ended any reopening talks, and with its cash reserves almost gone the IV gave up. Approval for abandonment came quickly, with common carrier service ending by December 1938 and all operations ceasing in early 1939.

HOBART SOUTHERN

In 1896, the Sierra Nevada Wood & Lumber Company built a standard gauge railroad running 6.5 miles from Truckee north to Overton, later renamed Hobart Mills, as a private road to haul out lumber cut by a sawmill the company built. An extensive narrow gauge logging railroad brought logs out of the forests to the mill.

The line would have remained beyond the scope of this work but for a decision in 1930 to incorporate the Hobart Southern Railroad as a common carrier to take over operations of the standard gauge. Common carrier operations lasted only from 1932 until 1937, when the final closure of the Hobart Mills sawmill deprived the railroad of any further revenue. The Hobart Southern suspended operations after December 1 of that year and scrapped the railroad out shortly afterwards. The line was not yet done, though, as in the late 1940s Fibreboard built a new private railroad on the HS grade to haul raw logs destined for their Antioch paper mill. This line operated in 1952 and 1953, with the rails again removed in 1955.

SIERRA VALLEYS

In 1885, the Sierra Valley & Mohawk Railroad commenced construction of a narrow gauge line running west from a connection with the Nevada-California-Oregon Railroad at Plumas Junction. Work struggled on through financial difficulties and reorganizations as the Sierra

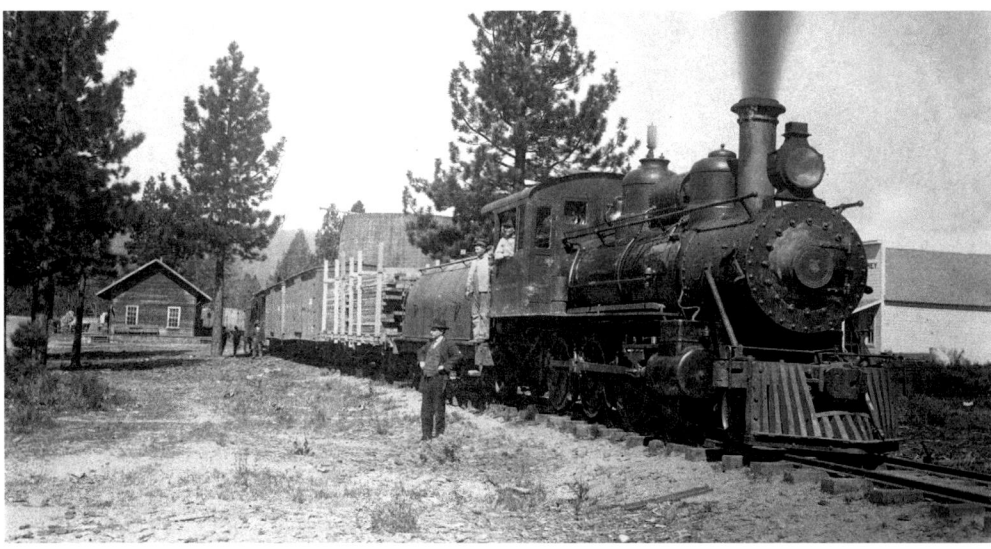

SV No. 5 preparing to depart Clio with lumber loads. *Jeff Moore collection*

Valleys Railway, then Sierra & Mohawk Railway, and finally Sierra Valley & Mohawk. The railroad completed its line to Clairville in 1896, Clio in 1903, and Graeagle in 1916.

Sawmills at various points along the line provided the bulk of the company's revenues, supplemented with passenger and mail traffic. The N-C-O controlled the railroad directly in one way or another after 1901. Competition arrived with the Boca & Loyalton built up from the south, followed by the Western Pacific mainline closely paralleling SV's entire length. Traffic plummeted, and in 1918 the N-C-O sold the southern part of its system—Reno to Hackstaff, along with the entire SV line—to the Western Pacific, who converted part of the line into a branch into Reno and abandoned the rest, including the entire old SV. Lumbering activity continued on for several more decades, served by WP spurs built off its mainline.

YOSEMITE VALLEY

A group of San Francisco and Oakland businessmen incorporated the Yosemite Valley Railroad (YV) on December 18, 1902. Construction started east from a connection with both the Southern Pacific and Atchison, Topeka & Santa Fe railroads at Merced in 1905, with El Portal at the western gates of Yosemite National Park reached in May 1907.

YV's principle role in life was to deliver tourists to Yosemite. The railroad also handled whatever freight the area generated. In 1912, the Yosemite Lumber Company built a substantial sawmill and box factory at Merced Falls, fed by a series of logging railroads built off the YV near El Portal. The logging railroads used steep inclines to get out of the narrow Merced River canyon. The YV handled a steady stream of logs down to Merced Falls and then lumber and box shook out to the mainline connections. The mill closed in 1927, reopened under the Sugar Pine Lumber Company flag in 1928, closed again in 1930, reopened in 1935, and finally closed for good in 1942. By this point vehicles and all-weather highways cut into the tourist business, and the received permission to abandon the line in 1945.

PRINCIPLE REFERENCES

—. *A Riders Guide to The Skunk Line, Willits to Ft. Bragg.* Robert Wallen Publications, 1986.
—. Camino, Placerville & Lake Tahoe R.R. *The Western Railroader* #218: pp. 3-5.
—. California Western Railroad & Navigation Co. *The Western Railroader* #130: Pgs 3-5.
—. California Western's "Super Skunk" Steam Train. *The Western Railroader* #307, August 1965.
—, Rails to Amador, Amador Central Railroad. *The Western Railroader* #403, Nov-Dec 1973.
—. The Feather River Railway. *The Western Railroader* #180, October 1954: Pgs 1-5.
—, The Story of a Short Short-Line, The Amador Central RR. *The Western Railroader* #104, Issued May 16,1948.
Baldo, Chris and Theron Brown. California Western Railroad and Navigation Company—A Centennial Tribute. *Highline* (Roots of Motive Power Newsletter), Volume 29, No. 2, August 2011: pp. 4-29.
Beebe, Lucius. *Mixed Train Daily, A Book of Short-Line Railroads.* Howell–North, Berkeley, California, 1947.
Beier, Glenn. *Steam Echoes: The Railroad Photograph of Glenn Beier.* TimberTimes, Hillsboro, Oregon, 2004.
Benson, Ted. Amador Album. *Railfan & Railroad*, April 2004: pp. 26-37.
Benson, Ted. The Amador Central Railroad. *Pacific News* #92, June 1969: pp. 3-9.
Benson, Ted. Centennial of the Sierra. *Trains* December 1997: pp. 50-59.
Benson, Ted. The Quincy Railroad. *Pacific News* #86, December 1968: pp. 3-8.
Benson, Ted. *Mother Lode Shortline.* Chatham Publishing Company, Burlingame, CA, 1970.
Benson, Ted. *One Track Mind, Photographic Essays on Western Railroading.* The Boston Mills Press, Erin, Ontario, Canada, 1999.
Borden, Stanley T. Arcata & Mad River: 100 Years of Railroading in the Redwood Empire. *Western Railroader* #176. Originally published 1954, then republished 1965 as a special issue.
Borden, Stanley. The California Western Railroad. *The Western Railroader* #212, published 1957.
Borden, Stanley T. Yreka Western RR. *The Western Railroader* #249, September 1969: pp. 1-16.
Bowden, Jack, and Tom Dill. *The Modoc, Southern Pacific's Back Door to Oregon.* Oso Publishing, Hamilton, MT, 2002.
Boyd, Jim. *Baldwin Diesels In Color* Volumes 1, 2, and 3. Morning Sun Books, Inc., Scotch Plains, New Jersey, 2002.
Brown, Greg. Tough Times in Timber Country. *Pacific RailNews* November 1990: pp. 24-34.
Burwash, Martin. Hauling the Big Burn. *CTC Board* May 2003: pp. 48-55.

Cantrall, Larry. Skunk Railroad, The California Western. *Railfan & Railroad* May 1999: pp. 30-37.

Carranco, Lynwood, and Henry L. Sorenson. *Steam in the Redwoods*. The Caxton Printers, Ltd., Caldwell, Idaho, 1988.

Crump, Spencer. *The California Western "Skunk" Railroad*. Zeta Publishers Company, Corona del Mar, California, 1991.

Cupper, Dan. Amador Central: A Final Farewell. *Diesel Era*, Volume 8, No. 3: pp. 38-41.

Fox, Wesley. *Northwestern Pacific Railroad and its Successors*. Fox Publications, Arvada, Colorado, 1995.

French, Gerald. *When Steam Was King*. Eureka Publishing, Petaluma, CA.

Hanft, Robert M. *Pine Across the Mountain—California's McCloud River Railroad*. Trans-Anglo Books, Glendale, CA, 1971 (revised & updated 1990).

Hanft, Robert M. *Red River, Paul Bunyan's Own Lumber Company and Its Railroads*. California State University-Chico, Chico, CA, 1980.

Hansen, Don A. Almanor Railroad. *Pacific News* #38: pp. 3-6.

Hansen, Don A. Feather River Railway. *Pacific News* #60, October 1966: pp. 3-7.

Johnson, Shirly. The Short Line Connection. *Southern Pacific Bulletin* Jan/Feb 1991: pp. 10-15.

Lewis, Edward. *American Shortline Railway Guide*. The Baggage Car, Morrisville, VT, 1978 (2nd edition); Kalmbach, Waukesha, WI, 1986 (3rd edition), 1991 (4th edition), and 1996 (5th edition).

Lothes, Scott. Modoc Reprieve: Pipeline Project Helps Bring New Life To A Remote Railroad. *Railroads Illustrated* #381, February 2011: pp. 32-45.

Lustig, David C. The Amador Central. *Railfan & Railroad,* January 1987: pp. 62-67.

Moore, Jeff. *Rails Around McCloud.* Arcadia Publishing, Charleston, SC, 2008.

Moore, Jeff. *The Great Northern's Hambone Branch.* Great Northern Railway Historical Society Reference Sheet No. 384, GNRHS, St. Paul, MN, 2013.

Mueller, Tom. Baldwins of Martell. *CTC Board*, February 1980, Issue #56L pp. 8-10.

Myrick, David F. Quincy Railroad Company. *The Western Railroader* #213, August 1957: pp. 3-9.

Myrick, David F. *Railroads of Nevada and Eastern California Volume III: More On the Northern Roads.* University of Nevada Press, Reno and Las Vegas, NV, 2007.

Polkinghorn, R. Steve. *Pino Grande, Logging Railroads of the Michigan-California Lumber Co.* R/Robb Ltd., Union City, CA, 1984.

Replinger, Peter J. and John T. Labbe. *Logging to the Salt Chuck*. North West Short Line, Seattle, Washington, 1990.

Rose, Al, *et al.* The Most Recognizable Railroad in the World. *Locomotive & Railway Preservation* Jan-Feb 1989: pp. 14-33.

Sims, Ronald D. *General Electric 70-ton Diesel Locomotives.* Shade Tree Books, Bellflower, CA, 2013.

Starman, Matt, and Tim Stricker. *Yreka Western Railroad*. Arcadia Publishing, Charleston, South Carolina, 2011.

Stephens, Kent. Pulling Up the Feather River Railway. *Pacific News* #67, May 1967: Pgs 3-7.

Stephens, Kent. The Feather River Railway in 1965. *The Western Railroader* #306, July 1965: pp. 5-12.

Stephens, Kent. Feather River Railway, A casualty of Oroville Dam. *Western Pacific Headlight* #14: pp. 18-21.

Stephens, Kent. Michigan-California Lumber Co. *The Western Railroader* #359, January 1970: pp. 3-15.

Stephens, Kent. *The Yreka Western Railroad.* Northstate Publishing, Chico, CA, 1992.

Stindt, Fred A. *Northwestern Pacific Railroad, Volume 2.* Self published, Kelseyville, CA, 1988 (2nd printing).

Strapac, Joseph A. *California's Locomotives, ALCO and GE Shortline and Industrial Diesels.* Shade Tree Books, Bellflower, CA, 2012.

Tahja, Katy M. *Rails Across the Noyo.* Tahjanjoki Press, Comptche, CA, 2008.

Tahja, Katy M. *Logging Railroads of Humboldt and Mendocino Counties.* Arcadia Publishing, Charleston, South Carolina, 2013.

Wagner, Jack R. *Short Line Junction—A Collection of California and Nevada Railroads.* Valley Publishers, Fresno, CA, 1956 (revised edition 1971).

Wilson, Burr. Eureka Southern. *CTC Board* September 1985: pp. 24-37.

Zwagerman, Sean. Amador Central. *Pacific Rail News,* February 1994: pp. 32-37.

Zwagerman, Sean. Northwestern Pacific's Undying Spirit. *RailNews* December 1997; pp. 5 -56.

Some locomotive roster information derived from the Shortline Rosters (trainweb.org/rosters) and Northern California Shortline Rosters (trainweb.org/foothill/ncslros.html) websites.

News items and clippings from a variety of sources, including *Pacific News/Pacific RailNews, CTC Board, The Western Railroader,* and others.

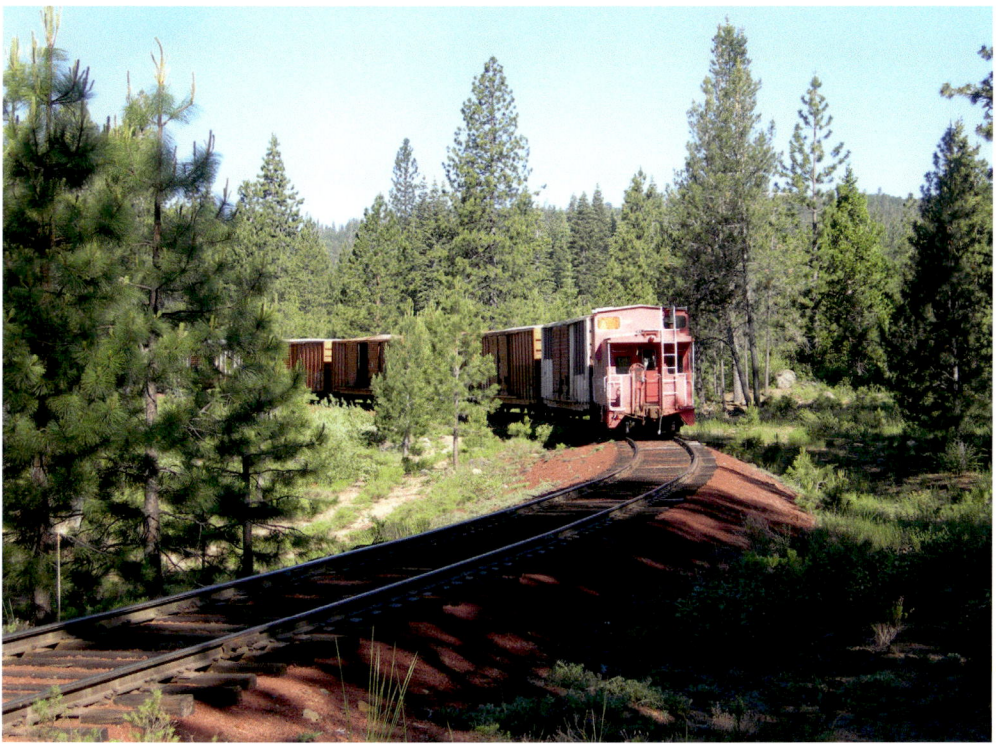

McCloud Railway caboose No. 102 in June 2006. *Jeff Moore*

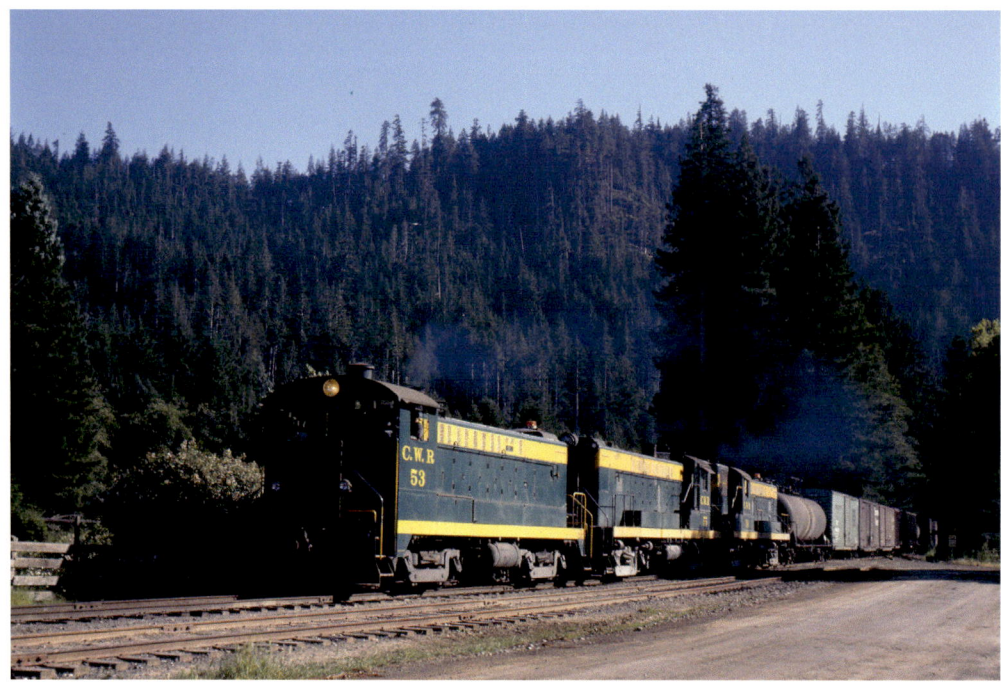

California Western Nos. 53, 55, and 56 leading a train through the redwoods. *Charles Heimerdinger Jr.*

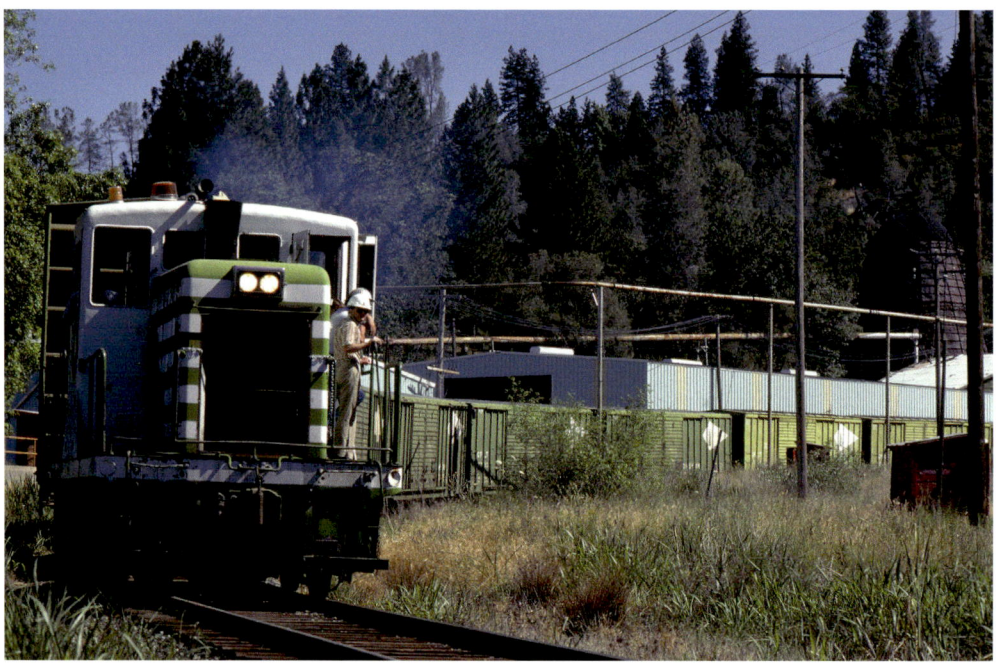

Camino, Placerville & Lake Tahoe No. 102 leads a train of empty boxcars through the closed sawmill at Smith Flat on 6/17/1986. *Dave Stanley*